Venedikt Erofeev's
Moscow-Petushki

Critical Perspectives

Karen L. Ryan-Hayes, editor

PETER LANG
New York • Washington, D.C./Baltimore
Bern • Frankfurt am Main • Berlin • Vienna • Paris

891.73
E7 lm-xr

Library of Congress Cataloging-in-Publication Data

Venedikt Erofeev's Moscow-Petushki:
critical perspectives/ Karen L. Ryan-Hayes, editor.
p. cm. — (Middlebury studies in Russian language and literature; vol. 14)
Some text in Russian.
Includes bibliographical references.
1. Erofeev, Venedikt, 1933–1990. Moskva-Petushki. I. Title. II. Series.
PG3479.7.R59M637   891.73'44—dc20   96-34896
ISBN 0-8204-3666-6
ISSN 0888-8752

Die Deutsche Bibliothek-CIP-Einheitsaufnahme

Venedikt Erofeev's Moscow-Petushki: critical perspectives/
Karen L. Ryan-Hayes, ed. –New York; Washington, D.C./Baltimore; Bern;
Frankfurt am Main; Berlin; Vienna; Paris: Lang.
(Middlebury studies in Russian language and literature; Vol. 14)
ISBN 0-8204-3666-6
NE: Ryan-Hayes, Karen L.[Hrsg.]

Cover art by Catherine Fet.
Cover design by Nona Reuter.

AFT—9692

Venedikt Erofeev's
Moscow-Petushki

Middlebury Studies in Russian Language and Literature

Thomas R. Beyer, Jr.
General Editor

Vol. 14

PETER LANG
New York • Washington, D.C./Baltimore
Bern • Frankfurt am Main • Berlin • Vienna • Paris

Acknowledgements

I am much indebted to the individual contributors to this volume for their efforts, both intellectual and logistical. It is thanks to their collegial support and encouragement that this collection has been realized. I am particularly grateful to Laura Beraha for her advice and help with bibliographic and editorical matters. Without the technical support of Ann Zook, the secretary of the Slavic Department at the University of Virginia, the manuscript would never have emerged from my word processor. Finally, a generous grant from the offices of the Dean of Arts and Sciences and the Vice-Provost for Research at the University of Virginia made the publication of this book possible.

A Note on Translation and Transliteration of Russian

Russian titles and terms which appear in this collection are transliterated according to the modified Library of Congress Transliteration System (System II in J. Thomas Shaw's *The Transliteration of Modern Russian for English-Language Publications*). Titles of books, stories, poems, journals and the like are given initially in each article in Russian with English translation provided in brackets; thereafter, the English titles are used. For the sake of consistency, *Moskva — Petushki* is rendered as *Moscow—Petushki* throughout. In cases where Russian names or terms have become anglicized through common usage, these anglicized forms are used (e.g. Dostoevsky, Tolstoy).

Quotations from all of Erofeev's texts are given first in Russian, followed by English translation. In the case of Erofeev's *Moscow—Petushki*, all quotations from the original are taken from the 1989 Prometei edition; all translations are adapted from H. William Tjalsma's translation of *Moscow—Petushki*, entitled *Moscow to the End of the Line*. Because individual authors exercised varying degrees of faithfulness to Tjalsma's translation, English renditions of an identical passage from *Moscow—Petushki* may vary significantly from article to article. The only exception to my treatment of the Prometei text as definitive is obscenities which were abbreviated in this edition; these have been restored in the version of the text included in the collection *Ostav'te moiu dushu v pokoe* [*Leave My Soul in Peace*] and are included in passages quoted in this volume. Page numbers are cited in parentheses after quotations, with "R" indicating the Russian text and "E" the English translation. Other

Russian-language sources are quoted only in English translation. Translations of these quotes, are, unless otherwise noted, the authors' own.

Contents

Introduction

Karen Ryan-Hayes

Venedikt Erofeev may well be known to future generations as the author of a single text, the brilliantly euphoric and achingly sad *Moscow—Petushki*. This is not unjust, nor is it cause for regret; the genius of Erofeev's *poema*—his own generic appellation—is its uniqueness, its defiance of comparison, its unrepeatability. *Moscow—Petushki* has been described variously as picaresque, as parodic and as postmodern. It has been presented as a nihilistic journey into the void and a profound statement of religious faith. It has been celebrated as a Rabelaisian masterpiece and decried as the incoherent ramblings of an alcoholic. In fact, Erofeev's text is broad and tensile enough to bear all these interpretations.

The author's death in 1990 coincided with radical changes in Russian literary culture. Erofeev lived to see his work published in the Soviet Union in the late eighties and became the subject of critical acclaim in the last years of his life. His posthumous reputation has grown apace and it is not an exaggeration to speak of a "cult of Erofeev." Fragments of his manuscripts, diaries and letters have been published in literary and theatrical journals. Reminiscences and eulogies by his friends and relatives have proliferated in the last few years. An interesting parallel phenomenon has been a reassessment of Erofeev's life and work. Readers and critics are of late daring to disparage *Moscow—Petushki*, and this suggests that the time is ripe to attempt new readings, to engage the text in light of recent developments (social, political and literary), to approach Erofeev's accomplishment with the perspectives afforded by time and history. That is the project of this volume, which combines the diverse scholarly efforts of American, Russian and Canadian specialists.

Biography

Although Erofeev was a rather mysterious, enigmatic figure during his lifetime—indeed, he seems to have cultivated this image —the events of his life can be reconstructed on the basis of his own and others' accounts. One of three children, Venedikt Erofeev was born in 1938 in Zapoliar'e, a town in the Murmansk region. He grew up and attended school through the tenth grade in Kirovsk, a city located on the Kol'skii Peninsula in the far north. After completing his primary schooling with a gold medal for academic excellence, he was accepted into the Philological Department of Moscow State University in 1955, no small feat for a young man who had never been south of the Arctic Circle.

Nina Frolova recalls that her brother was quietly rebellious and resisted pressure to conform to social norms even as a child. He stubbornly refused to become an Octobrist, shocking his first-grade teacher; he joined neither the Pioneers nor the Komsomol, organizations that were virtually obligatory for Soviet children in the forties and fifties. While it is difficult to determine cause and effect, his father's arrest in 1946 must have shaped Erofeev's perspective significantly. He was arrested under the infamous Article 58, dissemination of anti-Soviet propaganda; Frolova suggests that her father's penchant for relating anecdotes may have led to a denunciation. Because Erofeev's mother was unable to care single-handedly for all of her children in the lean post-War years, he and his brother were placed in a children's home in Kirovsk until their father was released from prison in 1954.[1]

Erofeev's start at Moscow State University had been auspicious, but he was expelled after only three semesters. There is some dispute as to the reason for his expulsion. Svetlana Gaiser-Shnitman suggests that his participation in an unauthorized student play aroused the wrath of university authorities; Vladimir Murav'ev recalls that he refused to attend mandatory military preparation classes.[2] It is quite possible that these were contributing factors, but Erofeev's behavior during this period was in any case sufficiently unconventional and erratic to warrant expulsion from the authorities' point of view. After leaving MGU, Erofeev enrolled in several educational institutions in succession, for maintaining his student status allowed him to remain in Moscow. At the Vladimir Pedagogical Institute, Erofeev became acquainted with a group of moderately dissident young writers and artists who came to constitute his closest circle of friends. However, his official affiliation with the Vladimir institute was short-lived; he was expelled either for composing satirical poems (according to Ol'ga Sedakova) or for possessing a Bible (his own version).[3]

In the course of the sixties and seventies, Erofeev held a rather bizarre assortment of odd, mostly menial jobs. He worked as a glassware inspector, stoker, watchman, fitter and laborer on highway and construction projects. From 1964 to 1969 he was employed laying telephone cable, which involved travelling to various regions of the Soviet Union. From 1969 to 1974—the period during which he composed *Moscow—Petushki*—he worked as a telephone line repairman in the Moscow region. After 1974, Erofeev was engaged in biological research projects (including one investigating mosquitos) and geophysical research expeditions.

According to the reminiscences of friends and relatives, Erofeev was an attractive, charming, but shy man. His appeal to women was apparently considerable, and he had numerous love affairs. He met his first wife, Valentina Zimakova, during his stay at the Vladimir Pedagogical Institute, where she was a student. She bore him a son in 1966, and though he and Zimakova soon separated, his attachment to the child continued. During the late sixties and early seventies, he often travelled to Myshlino, a settlement near Petushki where Zimakova was living, in order to visit his son. Indeed, much of his "literary" work in the seventies was devoted to his son's education (see below). Galina Erofeeva, the author's second wife, provided him with a relatively secure, comfortable home during his last years; ironically, her apartment was located in a building formerly reserved for employees of the MVD.[4] She was active in preserving and publishing Erofeev's manuscripts and notebooks until her suicide in 1993.

In the mid-eighties, Erofeev fell ill and was diagnosed with cancer of the throat. He underwent an operation that left him able to speak only with the aid of a mechanical device which he pressed to his throat. Although he was invited to Paris to undergo treatment for the disease, he was unable to secure permission from the Soviet authorities to travel abroad, ostensibly because of an unexplained gap in his work record.[5] Following a second operation, Erofeev's condition deteriorated and he died May 11, 1990 at the age of fifty-two. It is symptomatic of the ambivalent atmosphere of that period that obituaries for Erofeev appeared in publications as diverse as *Russkaia mysl'* [*Russian Thought*] (an emigré newspaper published in Paris) and *Literaturnaia gazeta* [*The Literary Gazette*] (the official organ of the Soviet Writers' Union).

While one would like to distinguish definitively between Venedikt Erofeev, the author and Venichka Erofeev, the narrator of *Moscow—Petushki*, confusion of the two personae is perhaps inevitable. Like his literary alter ego, Erofeev was by all accounts eccentric and introverted. Despite the sketchiness of his formal education, he was extraordinarily well read; history and literature particularly captivated Erofeev. He committed a great deal of Russian poetry to memory (especially the Symbolist and Acmeist poets), read Latin and German and experienced classical music in a highly personal, emotional way. His "archives" consist of numerous notebooks and boxes of cards inscribed—all in his meticulous, cramped handwriting—with ideas and citations which apparently struck him as insightful or interesting in the course of his voracious reading. When questioned about the literary influences on his own writing, Erofeev named Saltykov-Shchedrin, Gogol, the early Dostoevsky, Sterne, Sasha Chernyi and Vasilii Kniazev.[6]

Religious faith was a significant component of Erofeev's world view, but in this respect too his approach was individualistic. He read the Bible from an early age and in 1987, a few years before his death, was baptized a Catholic under the influence of his friend Vladimir Murav'ev. According to his widow, Erofeev viewed

Russian Orthodoxy as a potential totalitarian force in Russian culture and rejected what he regarded as its rigid dogmatism.[7] Alcoholism also played an important role throughout Erofeev's life, but on the basis of biographical accounts, it would be inaccurate to assert that he "suffered from" alcholism in a conventional sense. His friends tend to regard his drinking as facilitating his talent and they stress that his reticent demeanor did not change under the influence of alcohol. Igor' Avdiev postulates drinking as a calling and a vocation for Erofeev; it was, he writes, an integral part of the writer's personality.[8] Indeed, Erofeev's alcoholism has been the subject of considerable mythologization, and Murav'ev's suggestion that heavy drinking may have contributed to his premature death[9] has been largely ignored, while the more popular version of Erofeev's life as a continuous creative bacchanalia has been given greater currency.

For most of his adult life, Erofeev had no fixed place of residence. His numerous jobs in the sixties and seventies entailed constant travel, so that he did not have a residence permit for Moscow until his last years. Although he managed to slip continuously through the cracks of the Soviet bureaucracy, Erofeev cannot be called a dissident. The reality that surrounded him may have been a source of pain and grief, but it also contributed to his peculiar satiric genius. Soviet *byt* nourished Erofeev's intellectual playfulness, his finely tuned sense of the absurd to the extent that the relationship between the writer and his milieu was symbiotic.

Moscow—Petushki

In Erofeev's *poema*, the narrator—variously called Erofeev, Venia and Venichka—recounts his attempt to travel from Moscow to Petushki on the Moskovskaia-Gor'kovskaia suburban train line. In Edenic Petushki dwell Venichka's little boy and his lover, the "whitish one" who has previously raised him from the depths of despair, from death itself. As the tale begins, Venichka wakes from a drunken stupor in a strange entranceway. Painfully, he makes his way to Kursk Station (supplying himself first with antidotes for his hangover) and departs for Petushki. On the train, he discourses on many topics—alchemic cocktail recipes, the tyranny of work, gender relationships, Russian literature and philosophy—in dialogues with his travelling companions and in monologues addressed to the reader. As Venichka becomes more and more inebriated, the narrative becomes more and more hallucinogenic and nightmarish. Long digressions about a farcical revolution and the narrator's peregrinations abroad veer wildly into the realm of the fantastic. Eventually, Venichka discovers that he has missed his stop at Petushki / has fallen asleep / has been wandering in the countryside / has never left Moscow: all of these are possible explanations for his disorientation. After verbal and physical altercations with a Sphinx, Satan, Mithridates and others, the narrator finds himself wandering near the Kremlin, a place he has never seen despite years of living in Moscow. Pursued by four anonymous attackers, Venichka attempts to flee but is caught and stabbed to death with an awl, at which point his narrative ends.

By Erofeev's own account, *Moscow—Petushki* was written between January 18 and March 7, 1970 while he was employed laying telephone cable and living in a train car that served as a travelling dormitory.[10] Avdiev recalls Erofeev's composing the tale to entertain his friends; they would, he believed, recognize themselves in the various characters and events.[11] Shortly after it was completed, the manuscript of *Moscow—Petushki* disappeared briefly, but soon surfaced in the Vladimir region. In her reminiscences, Lidiia Liubchikova recounts an unsuccessful attempt by Erofeev and Vadim Tikhonov (to whom the text is dedicated) to sell the manuscript when they needed money to buy alcohol.[12] In any case, the text quickly took on a life of its own, circulating quite widely in *samizdat* within the Soviet Union. By the early seventies, *Moscow—Petushki* had made its way to the West, where it was published in *tamizdat*. It first appeared in 1973 in a short-lived Israeli emigré journal called *AMI*; it was published in Paris in a French translation the same year. In 1977, an offset copy of the original Russian text was printed by YMCA-Press in Paris. Two English translations of *Moscow—Petushki* have been published: *Moscow to the End of the Line* in 1980 and *Moscow Circles* in 1981. It has since been translated into many other languages, including German, Polish and Italian. Within the first years of *glasnost'* (1988–89), *Moscow—Petushki* was published in the Soviet Union. However, the text, in a substantially cut version, was first presented to the reading public as an anti-alcohol tract in the journal *Trezvost' i kul'tura* [*Sobriety and Culture*]. A nearly complete version was included in an anthology issued by the independent publishing concern Vest' in 1989; what Murav'ev calls the "first authentic text" of the work[13] was published by Prometei the same year. It was not until 1995, however, that an unexpurgated edition of the Russian original—restoring the previously cut expletives and obscenties—appeared; a collection of Erofeev's works (complete and fragmentary) called *Ostav'te moiu dushu v pokoe* [*Leave My Soul in Peace*] includes the full text of *Moscow—Petushki*.

Criticism

Erofeev and his chef-d'oeuvre have become increasingly popular subjects of critical research and writing. However, the only monograph devoted to *Moscow—Petushki* which has appeared to date is Gaiser-Shnitman's *Venedikt Erofeev. "Moskva — Petushki" ili "The rest is silence"* [*Venedikt Erofeev. "Moscow—Petushki" or "The rest is silence"*]. Basing her analysis on Venichka's monologues (or soliloquies), Gaiser-Shnitman demonstrates that citations, references and intertextual allusions— all of which comprise the literary quality of *tsitatnost'*—saturate the text. Indeed, she argues, *tsitatnost'* is a major thematic and structural component of Erofeev's work. Her close reading examines the derivation of many of the verbal echoes in *Moscow—Petushki*, including Biblical, literary/philosophical, historical/political and folkloric sources. Venichka, she concludes, perishes because of spiritual malnourishment. In a world defined by clichés and formulae, there is no possibility of creative, individualistic association with God, with the Word. While this barrenness dooms Venichka, the *poema* itself transcends linguistic stagnation and represents freedom of the imagination. Gaiser-Shnitman's monograph is an invaluable resource for tracing the multitudinous specific allusions in

Moscow—Petushki. She convincingly places Erofeev's work in the Russian/Soviet tradition of "forbidden laughter" that depends heavily on intimate knowledge of cultural nuances.

Chapters are devoted to Erofeev's *poema* in two larger volumes of criticism. Cynthia Simmons, in her book *Their Fathers' Voice. Vassily Aksyonov, Venedikt Erofeev, Eduard Limonov, and Sasha Sokolov*, approaches *Moscow—Petushki* as an example of "aberrant discourse" in general and of alcoholic narrative in particular. She examines Venichka's complex relationship with his own dissolution and interprets his narrative as an extended confrontation between the sacred and the profane. Adopting Mircea Eliade's formulations of these oppositional concepts, Simmons casts Venichka in the role of an artist-seer who effects his own liberation from profane existence and attempts to enter sacred space by drinking. Erofeev's often jarring juxtapositions of linguistic registers, she suggests, represent the struggle between the sacred and the profane on the textual level. Simmons' discussion of doubles in Erofeev's work is innovative; she does not rely solely on the literary models with which Russian literature is replete, but delves into the psychological implications of doubling. Venichka's fellow travellers—weirdly paired as Stupid-Stupid and Smart-Smart, the Mitrich imbeciles and the Decembrist and the mustachioed girl—are personifications of opposing social or psychic impulses. These forces are associated by Simmons with the literal and figurative poles of Moscow and Petushki and their dissonance, their incompatibility arises out of the modern disintegration of the self. Simmons' conclusions that the text denies postmodern desolation, that Petushki offers an "exit," and that one may infer a call to sober social reform in Venichka's discourse all merit further discussion.

A lengthy chapter of the book *Contemporary Russian Satire. A Genre Study* (by the present author) offers an alternative analysis of *Moscow—Petushki*. This work postulates as the parodic basis of Erofeev's work the picaresque novel and it examines how he deftly adapts its structure and thematic conventions in order to satirize the spiritual void of Soviet culture. Erofeev engages in a parodic transposition of picaresque generic traditions. Venichka's trip to

Petushki—to Eden, innocence and purity—is a mock quest, for the nasty, brutal world of the commuter train turns out to be inescapable. Venichka completes a circular journey (refuting the linear model) and is murdered (reversing the near-canonical open-endedness of the picaro's *vita*). Moreover, regarding *Moscow—Petushki* as a pastiche of borrowed ideas and styles allows us to speculate that for Erofeev, in a culture where individualism is suspect (the Soviet Union of the seventies), no unique creation is possible. Philosophically and artistically, the text stands as a brilliant satiric indictment of the *zastoi* period.

A plethora of journal articles treating *Moscow—Petushki* have appeared in a variety of languages; the bibliography included in this volume attempts to be as exhaustive as possible in citing contributions to the critical literature on Erofeev and his work. Two particularly seminal articles merit brief discussion here. Irina Paperno and Boris Gasparov's "'Vstan' i idi'" ["'Arise and Go'"], published in 1981 in *Slavica Hierosolymitana*, provides a very insightful reading of Erofeev's text. The authors trace the motif of resurrection in the *poema*, focusing on Biblical allusions and parallels between Venichka and Christ. The reversed order of Venichka's crucifixion/resurrection and the incongruity of the contexts in which the motif is developed suggest, according to the authors, a vicious, hopeless circle. Their analysis of Dostoevskian themes in *Moscow—Petushki* is also valuable; Erofeev borrows much, they suggest, from Dostoevsky in his treatment of drunkenness and grief, and may indeed have modelled the time and space orientations in his work upon those operative in *Prestuplenie i nakazanie* [*Crime and Punishment*]. Paperno and Gasparov examine the derivation of numerous philosophical and literary allusions in Erofeev's text, including the works of Shakespeare, Goethe, Pasternak, Kuprin, Chekhov and Bunin. They identify several echoes of Bulgakov's *Master i Margarita* [*Master and Margarita*] in *Moscow—Petushki*, which apprently enraged the author. Murav'ev recalls his insisting that he could not even bear to read Bulgakov and that Paperno and Gasparov's parallels were spurious.[14]

Apropos of the scant citations in Paperno and Gasparov's article, Gaiser-Shnitman conjectures that it was written and circulated as a *samizdat* work.[15] An article that has conversely benefitted from the full light of *glasnost'* is Mikhail Epshtein's "Posle karnavala, ili vechnyi Venichka" ["After Carnival, or the Eternal Venichka"]. Erofeev, according to Epshtein, has been mythologized as the image of his hero Venichka has become conflated with that of the lyrical poet-author. His death at a relatively young age and his very limited oeuvre have contributed to this process of mythologization. Epshtein points out the rather stark contradictions that coexist in Erofeev's literary biography (talent and creative silence, intelligence and intoxication to the point of oblivion, refinement and vulgarity) and suggests that the holy fool, or *iurodivyi*, offers a useful model for understanding the myth. Unlike Esenin and Vysotskii, with whose myths his own has many points of contact, Erofeev preferred understatement to hyperbole. His style, suggests Epshtein, may be characterized as "anti-irony," for it reverses the meaning of irony and restores seriousness; what is achieved is a new degree of complexity, of polyvalency. Delicacy and restraint, which Epshtein posits as integral features of Erofeev's internal world, are now superimposed on the extreme physicality previously associated with the carnivalesque. It is not the life-affirming energy of the carnival vision that Erofeev celebrates, however, but the entropy of its obverse side. This world view constitutes a new form of sentimentality which Epshtein regards as an alternative mode for the twenty-first century: introspection, quiet meditation and refined meloncholy may come to replace noisy carnival. In Epshtein's reading, Erofeev's eccentric work becomes programmatic and illumines the possibility of a kind of post-postmodernism.

Erofeev's Other Writings

Several other works by Erofeev are extant, and these have been published in the collection *Leave My Soul in Peace* (aptly subtitled *pochti vse* or "almost everything"). Other texts, mentioned in his own or his friends' reminiscences, have been lost (if they indeed existed). Erofeev's first literary effort, a "lyrical diary" entitled *Zapiski psikhopata* [*Notes of a Psychopath*], was composed while he was a student at Moscow State University and has never been published.[16] Several critics make reference to a novel about student life written in the early sixties, possibly called *Zapiski veselogo nevrastenika* [*Notes of a Happy Neurasthenic*].[17] *Blagaia vest'* [*Good News*], ostensibly a novel from the same period, vanished somewhere in the Tula region after being read by a small group of the author's friends; a fragment was preserved and has been published in *Leave My Soul in Peace*. In the late sixties, Erofeev wrote several anthologies of poetry for his son to provide examples of various verse constructions.[18] Aside from some early attempts at writing poetry under the influence of Severianin (also unpublished), these anthologies were Erofeev's only experiments with verse. A third novel, tentatively entitled *Dmitrii Shostakovich*, was written in 1972, but the manuscript was left either on a train or in a phone booth. (The hero of this work was not, as one might expect, the composer Shostakovich, but a glassware inspector by the same name.[19]) *Vasilii Rozanov glazami ektsentrika* [*Vasilii Rozanov Through the Eyes of an Eccentric*], a surrealistic philosophic and literary essay, was written by Erofeev in 1973 and published in 1978.[20] In the mid-seventies, Erofeev again turned to writing for his son and composed textbooks on geography, history, philosophy, literature and other subjects. He also undertook literary studies of the Norwegian authors Hamsun and Ibsen; these have never been published. In 1988, he completed a work called *Moia malen'kaia leniniana* [*My Little Leniniana*], in which he collected and strategically arranged quotations from Lenin's essays, speeches and letters and interpolated his own wry comments; the piece was originally published in the emigré journal *Kontinent* [*Continent*] and is included in *Leave My Soul in Peace*.

Toward the end of his life, Erofeev took up writing plays, though he rarely attended the theater himself.[21] Of the trilogy he was working on in the eighties, only *Val'purgieva noch', ili Shagi komandora* [*Valpurgis Night, or the Steps of the Commander*] was completed. This play was published in the West in 1985; four years later, it was published in the Soviet Union and staged at the Malaia Bronnaia Theater in Moscow. Erofeev envisioned *Valpurgis Night*, which takes place in a psychiatric ward and has as its hero a Jewish alcoholic, as the second work in the trilogy. The first, *Dissidenty, ili Fanni Kaplan* [*Dissidents, or Fanni Kaplan*], was left unfinished at Erofeev's death. This play was to be, according to Erofeev, "the gayest and most disastrous for all its characters."[22] Fragments of this play have been published in *Moskovskii nabliudatel'* [*The Moscow Observer*] and in the collection *Leave My Soul in Peace*. The play projected as the third in Erofeev's trilogy is not extant.

New Perspectives

The present volume brings together the work of eight scholars on Venedikt Erofeev and his *poema*, *Moscow—Petushki*. The essays included here represent a broad spectrum of interpretation informed by a diverse range of critical theory. Laura Beraha, in her article "Out of and Into the Void: Picaresque Absences on the Move," considers Erofeev's text in light of the generic conventions of the picaresque. She demonstrates that structurally and thematically, Venichka's tale continually works toward an emptying, a hollowing out. What is left, Beraha argues, is absence, a metaphysical void. *Moscow—Petushki* thus constitutes a reversal of the picaresque dynamic as described by Bakhtin; responding as it does to a plethora of texts and genres and ending in silence, Erofeev's work signifies the *de*volution of the novel. Many critics have noted the generic multiplicity and instability of *Moscow—Petushki*; Beraha's essay contributes significantly to our understanding of this question.

Valentina Baslyk's essay "Venichka's Divided Self: The Sacred and the Monstrous" takes as its starting point the text's status as aberrant discourse and constructs an interpretation of Venichka as a schizophrenic narrator. In the tradition of dual or multiple narrative voices now established by Limonov, Sokolov, Aksenov and Bokov, Erofeev creates a narrative persona who is alternately gentle and violent. The struggle between self and other, Baslyk suggests, is a manifestation of the dichotomy between the Sacred and the Monstrous (defined as irascible, rude, vulgar and aggressive). Her essay acknowledges Simmons' establishment of a sacred/profane differential in Erofeev's work, but considers textual discourse in light of psychological behavior. A related issue treated extensively by Baslyk is character doubling. She posits the grotesque pairs who converse with Venichka on his trip as projections of his monstrous self, thus advancing the critical debate on the ontological and symbolic significance of Erofeev's doubles.

Mark Lipovetsky has written extensively on Erofeev and his article included in the present volume, entitled "S potustoronnei tochki zreniia: postmodernistskaia versiia dialogizma," ["A Viewpoint From the Other Side: A Postmodern Version of Dialogism"], examines the *poema* as a seminal text of Russian postmodernism. Stylistic ambivalence, the combination of incongruous levels of language and meaning, is a key device in Erofeev's prose; Venichka himself embodies this ambivalence and this connects him with the tradition of *iurodstvo*, or the holy fool. Erofeev's parodying and travestying religious imagery, his lowering it to the level of an alcoholic's *byt*, Lipovetsky argues, revives the strain of *iurodstvo* represented by Kharms' writing. In Lipovetsky's reading, chaos is a metaphysical category in the text, but it is associated by Erofeev with the people (*narod*) and with stereotypes of Soviet culture. Venichka's attempt to engage in dialogue with chaos fails insofar as it results in his death (which is irreversible and not subject to resurrection). Yet the "death of the author" takes on special meaning here, for death is ironically the only stable category from which chaos may be encountered. *Moscow—Petushki*, Lipovetsky asserts, is the aesthetic product of that encounter.

"Erofeev's Grief: Inconsolable and Otherwise," an essay contributed by the present author, considers the sources of this prominent motif in *Moscow—Petushki*. Erofeev's explicit references to Kramskoi's painting *Neuteshnoe gore* [*Inconsolable Grief*] encourage us to read his text as a narrative analogue of Kramskoi's visual depiction of grief. The painting's use of scale, empty space, characterization through expression and gesture and other elements suggest significant resonance between Kramskoi's and Erofeev's conceptions of grief. A second important source that provides a key to understanding Erofeev's treatment of grief is the anonymous seventeenth-century tale *Povest' o Gore-Zlochastii* [*The Tale of Grief-Misfortune*]. On the basis of comparison with this early model (which is justified by numerous thematic and stylistic allusions), we see more clearly the contrast between the world views of the authors. For Venichka/Erofeev, there is no hope of escape or withdrawal from the brutal reality of life, since in his postmodern vision of Brezhnev's *zastoi*, there is no faith which can rescue us from pursuant Grief.

Konstantin Kustanovich's article, "Venichka Erofeev's Grief and Solitude: Existentialist Motifs in the *Poema*," examines the topos of grief in *Moscow—Petushki* from a somewhat different angle. Noting the unusual combination of the tragic and comic in the text, Kustanovich finds literary precedents in the prose of Bulgakov and Gogol. However, what he defines as "anti-irony" (a term coined by Murav'ev and borrowed by Epshtein) is best understood in light of existentialism. Briefly surveying the thought of Berdiaev, Heidegger, Kierkegaard, Sartre and Nietzsche, Kustanovich demonstrates that Venichka's condition—grief, fear, muteness, alienation—is an amalgam of existentialist themes. Erofeev's alter ego can thus be regarded as an authentic Being among inauthentic Beings and it becomes irrelevant whether the "other" is Soviet power (a common misconception, in Kustanovich's view) or Western capitalism.

Marie Martin's contribution, "The Story of Russian," engages Erofeev's text on the level of lexicon. By analyzing specific examples from the work (many of them often cited but inadequately understood), she shows how Erofeev accomplishes parody of literary and political clichés. Martin argues that Erofeev's technique compels the reader to resituate the clichéd phrase or image in its original context, to carry out what she calls "demythologization" (the converse of Roland Barthes' "mythologization"). This device is particularly effective in deflating and exposing the grandiloquent, monumental language of Socialist Realism and Soviet propaganda, for Erofeev consistently shows us that the signifiers lack signifieds, that the verbal formulae are empty shells devoid of meaning.

Through parody, *Moscow—Petushki* achieves nothing less, Martin argues, than the revivification of the "great, powerful, truthful, free Russian language."

"Erofeev and Evtushenko," an essay by Guy Houk, considers the poet Evgenii Evtushenko's image as a recurring subtext in *Moscow—Petushki*. While the "tractor driver Evtiushkin" has been widely decoded as a satiric conflation of the names of Evtushenko and Pushkin, there are other less obvious instances of allusion that Houk explores here. In excoriating Evtushenko for perceived cowardice and hypocrisy, Erofeev apparently targets both his public and poetic personae. *Bratskaia GES* [*The Bratsk Hydroelectric Station*], Evtushenko's controversial epic poem celebrating a famous Soviet construction project, is seminal in this regard, for Erofeev parodically echoes the text of the poem itself and also comments on Evtushenko's mendacity in writing and publishing this work. Given Erofeev's keen awareness of the power of literary myth in the case of Evtushenko, Houk asserts, it is reasonable to reexamine his own attempts at myth-making through the agency of *Moscow—Petushki*. This article constitutes a provocative response to Epshtein's and Lipovetsky's work, for Houk attributes the urge to mythologization not to Erofeev's friends and readers, but to the author himself.

The final essay included here, by Eduard Vlasov, is entitled "Zagranitsa glazami ekstsentrika. K analizu 'zagranichnykh' glav" ["Abroad Through the Eyes of an Eccentric. Toward an Analysis of the 'Abroad' Chapters"]. Vlasov focuses attention on the chapters of *Moscow—Petushki* in which Venichka recounts his travels abroad and demonstrates the significance of both "horizontal" (or diachronic) and "vertical" (or synchronic) links with other texts. Expanding on the preliminary studies of Gaiser-Shnitman and Paperno and Gasparov, Vlasov shows that at least three (and perhaps more) works by Il'ia Erenburg are rich sources of details and motifs in Erofeev's *poema*. He points out numerous echoes from Erenburg's fictional *Trinadtsat' trubok* [*Thirteen Pipes*] and *Khulio Khurenito* [*Julio Jurenito*], and his memoirs, *Liudi, gody, zhizn'* [*People, Years, Life*]. Noting the disparity between Erenburg's public persona as conformist and Erofeev's as dissident, Vlasov locates a point of contact in the work of Francois Villon. Erofeev and Villon were doubles in their work and their lives, Vlasov argues, while Erenburg played the safe role of "privy councillor" by translating Villon's poetry. Having established this synchronic triangle, he goes on to broaden the associative field of *Moscow—Petushki* and finds a profound connection between Erofeev and Mandel'shtam, specifically in their multileveled use of citations and allusions. Most importantly, Villon, Mandel'shtam and Erofeev all succeed in constructing a higher sphere—a space "abroad"—in their art.

Endnotes

1. Frolova et al., "Neskol'ko monologov," 74–76.
2. Gaiser-Shnitman, *Venedikt Erofeev*, 23; Frolova et al., "Neskol'ko monologov," 90. Guy Houk's article "Erofeev and Evtushenko," included in this volume, sheds additional light on this issue.
3. Frolova et al., "Neskol'ko monologov," 101; Erofeev, "Ot Moskvy do samykh Petushkov," 5.
4. Ignatova, "Venedikt," *Panorama*, 22.
5. Erofeev, "'Umru, no nikogda ne poimu...'," 13.
6. Venedikt Erofeev, "Sasha Chernyi i dr.," 316–17; Erofeev, "'Umru, no nikogda ne poimu...'," 13; Frolova et al., "Neskol'ko monologov," 113.
7. Galina Erofeeva, interview by author, Moscow, May 1992.
8. Frolova et al., "Neskol'ko monologov," 90, 100, 109; Erofeev, "Ot Moskvy do samykh Petushkov," 5.
9. Frolova et al., "Neskol'ko monologov," 94.
10. Other sources place the composition of the text in the late sixties. See Kasack, *Dictionary of Russian Literature*, 471; Monas, review of *Moscow to the End of the Line*, 509; Dunham, introduction to *Moscow to the End of the Line*, 8.
11. Frolova et al., "Neskol'ko monologov," 115; see also Gaiser-Shnitman, *Venedikt Erofeev*, 22.
12. Frolova et al., "Neskol'ko monologov," 86.
13. Ibid., 91.
14. Ibid., 93.
15. Gaiser-Shnitman, *Venedikt Erofeev*, 27.
16. Frolova et al., "Neskol'ko monologov," 91.
17. Kasack, *Dictionary of Russian Literature*, 471; Gaiser-Shnitman, *Venedikt Erofeev*, 20.
18. Gaiser-Shnitman, *Venedikt Erofeev*, 21.

19. Frolova et al., "Neskol'ko monologov," 95; Gaiser-Shnitman, *Venedikt Erofeev*, 23.
20. This essay has been translated into English and included in an anthology of contemporary Russian prose called *The Penguin Book of New Russian Writing. Russia's Fleurs du Mal.*
21. Frolova et al., "Neskol'ko monologov," 85.
22. Mikhaleva, foreword to *Fanni Kaplan*, 58.

Out of and Into the Void: Picaresque Absence and Annihilation

Laura Beraha

Excess and Emptying Through Genre

Moscow—Petushki travels through as many genres as its hero does stops. From *poema* [narrative poem] in the subtitle, it passes to *tragicheskie listy* [tragic pages] in the dedication. Well into his tale, the narrator reflects on its passage from philosophical essays, memoirs and poems in prose à la Ivan Turgenev, to detective novel; it is here that he wonders—*Chert znaet* [the devil only knows]—in what genre the journey will end (R59/E73). Menippean satire, *putevye zapiski* [travelogue], *misteriia* [miracle-play], *zhitie* [saint's life] *predanie* [legend], confession, fantastic novel, and *iroi-komicheskaia poema* [burlesque] are some of the generic tags scholars have applied to the work.[1] Others include meta-utopia, Dionysian tragedy, travestied epic, apocalyptic fiction and alcoholic narrative.[2] More suggestive affiliations emerge from descriptions along the lines of *nepreryvnoe tsitirovanie* [incessant citation], cento and phantasmagoria; from Siniavskii-Terts' "anecdote" and the coining *poliv* or "outpouring."[3]

In this broad range of genre associations, the term *picaresque* is a late-comer, despite the many surface features that seem to beg the definition: a peripatetic, marginal hero; a pointedly loose, episodic structure overloaded with interpolated tales and short on psychological development; a first-person quasi-autobiographical form and what could be taken to pass for a panoramic view of a society in chaos.⁴ There is even, in the genre's prototype, *Lazarillo de Tormes* (1553), a comparable transubstantiation or parodic exchange between a drunkard's intake and the wine of the Eucharist. By no means, however, is this the tale of a rogue's struggle for subsistence or scramble for success. As Ryan-Hayes demonstrates, picaresque parallels—structural, thematic and stylistic—are effectively parodied, transgressed and transcended in Erofeev's master work. This parodic context supplies, as it were, a support mechanism for the eerie and at times even corrosive ambiguity of *Moscow—Petushki*. What subsumes, what in fact generates and simultaneously negates all the picaresque traits that stud the surface of Erofeev's text, is an inherently paradoxical picaresque dynamic. It is this relentless, self-annihilating momentum that is invoked to embrace Erofeev's potpourri of genres, and then turned back on itself to expose and exploit the absences latent in the rogue, his world and his entire narrative project.

The picaresque, a mongrel breed, has responded to and interacted with the heroic epic, the chivalrous romance, the Augustine confession, even the saint's life.⁵ It has proven most prolific as precursor, paradigm, catalyst of heteroglossia and participant in an ongoing inter- and intra-generic dialogue. The rogue form played a recognized role in launching both the West European and the Russian novel, and has lent its protean imprint to a flux of subgenres ever since, from *Bildungsroman* to novel of manners, from Gothic to historical romance.⁶ This constant slippage in to, out of and in sheer defiance of form has something of a postmodern flavor, with the picaresque as a prototype of generic cross-breeding, compromise and disintegration; a site of resistance to the "totalization" of form; or even a model of genre-in-process, subject to the continual and fruitful rupture of "novelization." If *Moscow—Petushki* is now hailed as the *pra-tekst russkogo postmodernizma* [the prototext of Russian postmodernism], it is perhaps on a neo- or post-picaresque license.⁷

The picaresque connection in *Moscow—Petushki*, however, goes beyond genre mixing. A form that aspires to be any and all things to any and all times is outer-focused, stretched to its own porous limits, shunted so far from its own constantly shifting center as to empty that center out. The picaro is the rogue-hero of a thousand—not faces, but masks; this external excess disguises, betrays and perpetuates an internal lack. The picaro has no stable identity or fixed destination; his story is pure sequence without consequence or closure; he both reflects and infects a world of chaos. In *Moscow—Petushki*, the picaresque reveals itself as a gutted core and scattered fringe activity. Its itinerary is mapped through a wasteland between the two compelling extremes of Erofeev's title; a hollowed-out hero hangs in picaresque balance between saintly and soused, clairvoyant and deluded, lowly outcast and prince or president. From a gap between monologue and dialogue Venichka spins a series of paired and polar doubles. On every level absence generates and is circumscribed by mutually exclusive ends. Inevitably, the voided middle collapses in on itself, Moscow collides with Petushki and crushes the traveler into silence.

A hollow itinerant, Chichikov, moves through the trivial, and hence barren (or barren of meaning) landscape of Gogol's *Mertvye dushi* [*Dead Souls*], a work often associated with the picaresque, and widely acknowledged as a precedent for *Moscow—Petushki*.⁸ Erofeev's other predecessors—Radishchev in *Puteshestvie iz Peterburga v Moskvu* [*Journey from Petersburg to Moscow*] and Sterne in *Sentimental Journey*—replace the picaro's self-serving indifference with self-reflective dismay, but they too react to and travel through a world without proper purpose, and so relate to the rogue genre on the basis of the road motif, the all but universal chronotope of narrative fiction.⁹

Erofeev combines this picaresque momentum with a postmodern focus on absence. If it is the road that provides the channel for the picaro's interaction with the questing knight and the saint's pursuit of the divine, then it is between the Soviet Sir Galahad of Nikolai Ostrovskii and a St. Anthony tortured by the demon drink that Venichka measures his lack of valor, his *malodushie* or "chicken-heartedness," and his lack of faith. The road chronotope is activated not so much to subvert its familiar allegorical potential of a "journey through life," since Venichka travels to, through and even, perhaps, after death;[10] nor to recharge the sentimentalist's search for the sensitive self (since Erofeev refines physical momentum or energy into what, in Epshtein's challenging interpretation, becomes a rehabilitation of quiet and reflective entropy); nor even to undo Radishchev's more rationalistic notion of progress[11] translated from the spiritual to the civic realm. These features, both Enlightened and sentimental, remain, but they remain as gaps designed not to be filled but rather to register, precisely and disturbingly, as vertical gaps in a narrative whose surface structure is resolutely linear.

There is no ignoring the intrusiveness of the chapter headings: they not only break the narrative mid-sentence, as Sterne's did, they force upon the reader an awkward "verisimilitude" (consider "Kilometer 61—Kilometer 65," chapter 26) that might surpass even the anti-aesthetic of cursing and reference to the lower body functions. What is more, by shifting from Radishchev's travel notes *at* waystations to travel ravings *between* stops,[12] Erofeev "blinkers" his narrative, traps it into a kind of tunnel vision closed on all four sides. He strips the landscape of all but place names; the place names thus become signposts without reference, hollow traces of squeezed-out signifieds. Set between Radishchev's *Journey from Petersburg to Moscow* and Pushkin's reversal, "Puteshestvie iz Moskvy v Peterburg" ["Journey from Moscow to Petersburg"] Erofeev's "journey" is effaced from the title[13] and from the novel's action: nothing moves, for this is a journey in nothing but non-existent name. As the Sphinx tells Venichka in his third riddle, no one gets from point A to point C, not only because neither exist, but because in between there is nothing but a meaningless series of points B. Distinctions implode into identity, and the distances in between are measured by spitting, yet another emptying out (R103/E 137–38).

Even before this collapse, from the outset, in fact, Venichka pursues an elusive destination. Petushki is a multiple overlay of denials: of size and significance, via its diminutive suffix (*petushki* < *petukhi* [cockerels < cocks]); of divine identity, as an echo of *Pete*r's denial of Christ before the third cock crowed; of the drive towards human or social perfection, when it is not even considered for the role of capital in the drunkards' *utopian* ("no-place") republic.

Negations crowd the paeans to Petushki:

> Петушки — это место, где *не* умолкают птицы, *ни* днем, *ни* ночью, где *ни* зимой, *ни* летом не отцветает жасмин. Первородный грех...там *никого не* тяготит. Там даже у тех, кто *не* просыхает по неделям, взгляд *без*донен и ясен...
>
> [Petushki is the place where the birds *never* cease singing, *not* by day or by night, where winter and summer the jasmine *never* cease blooming...There, even those who *don't* dry out for weeks, have a bottom*less,* clear look in their eyes.] (R37/E43; as a refrain, with similar negations, R44/E52, R89/E116–17, R102/E135) (Emphasis added)

Given this excess of denial, it seems only fitting the non-stop birds of Petushki should be slaughtered and its never-fading jasmine trampled; that the absence of Original Sin be perverted into the absence of taboo (or removal of a distinction) when, blocked by the Sphinx, Venichka wonders if this post-lapsarian Eden has succumbed to the temptation of incest. Petushki is just as negated as the Kremlin, three times denied at the beginning of Venichka's trip, with skewed symmetry twice more (R17/E14, R35/E39) before he is finally brought within its murderous grasp. The entire earthly domain is circumscribed between these two ever-receding voids and marked there by an empty boast: "Во всей земле...во всей земле, от самой Москвы и до самых Петушков — нет ничего такого, что было бы для меня слишком многим" [In the whole world...in the whole world all the way from Moscow to Petushki there has never been anything like "too much" for me] (R41/E48).

As for the genre itself, the picaresque is evoked and erased in *Moscow—Petushki*. Erenburg's *Trinadtsat' trubok* [*Thirteen Pipes*] (1923), the only analogue alluded to, is in effect "smoked out": first twelve, then thirteen pipes are consumed between revisions of an abortive article, whose own titles signal languages that fail to materialize in the texts they head (R82/E106). The picaresque proper is marked by a high incidence of inserted novellas, proliferating digressions told at random interludes to heighten the genre's intrinsic want of purpose, order and cohesion. In Erofeev's handling, the pattern folds in on itself when into the embedded and irrelevant tales of his chance companions Erofeev's embedding narrator inveigles his own. In this, the segment of *Moscow—Petushki* closest to the rogue tale,[14] he tells of his sweaty-socked trek through Europe and America (R78–84/E100–109). Its geographic sweep—the *razmakh* [boldness] that startled the character Black Mustache (R83/107)—rivals that of Guzmán de Alfarache and countless footloose rogues after him.

Erofeev's adaptation drains the motif, surrounding it with images of absence and futility. Venichka's transcontinental monologue, his most sustained narrative effort to this point in the tale, evokes what Kuritsyn has called a "disturbing sense of emptiness" and "non-existence," in that it stands as an uneasy substitute for the true topic of a drunkards' colloquium—the fate of Russia—and deals with what for most Soviet citizens in the 1970s, the time of writing and of Brezhnev's closed borders, was an utterly inconceivable itinerary.[15] In Venichka's account Fifth Avenue and Harlem are empty of black people; Mt. Vesuvius, Pompei and Herculaneum have been swallowed by the earth and in any case bounce him back and forth like some human, and quite picaresque, shuttle-cock. Other voids include the ineffective Maginot Line; the ephemeral halls of a Sorbonne that expels him; Paris as a ratrace from bordello to VD clinic and back; a Quixotic LaMancha; a mythical Albion that eclipses England; even hypothetical stopovers, one at the home of a recently deceased Palmiro Togliatti (R80/E103). Such toponymic excess wipes out distinctions, for this is the *abstraktnaia prostranstvennaia ekstensivnost'* [abstract expanse of space] of Bakhtin's adventure chronotope that ignores even the most fundamental demarcation between "us" and "others."[16] In Venichka's terms: "по одну сторону границы говорят на русском и больше пьют, а по другую — меньше пьют и говорят на нерусском..." [on one side of the border people speak Russian and drink more and on the other side they speak non-Russian and drink less] (R83/E107).

Boundaries are porous in *Moscow—Petushki*, like the line from less to more drink, since alcohol blots out the divide between heart and reason (R37/E43). In fact, this marginal hero spends most of his time hovering in liminal spaces: in the much-discussed "unfamiliar/unidentified front hallway"; on the platform between two railcars that witnesses his gagging resurrection with the first dose of the day; in variously a "mansard, mezzanine, wing, entresol and attic" from his list of Paris residences (R82/E105); in the cattleyard between the villages of Tartino and Eliseikovo from which he launches the drunkards' revolt. Even the Orekhovo-Zuevo dormitory marks, for Venichka, an uncomfortable compromise between public and private space, a compromise he carries with him outside onto city streets in the form of his preferred footwear—bedroom slippers (R110/E147). Since thresholds, as Bakhtin pointed out so many times, are charged with the atmosphere of crisis and the straining towards decisive change, one threshold after another signals one change after another, a movement which eventually leads, via the logic of *plus ça change,* to the perverse stability of constant flux that is the hallmark of the picaresque.

Emptying Through Time, Space and Word

When it forgoes the Gil Blas or Horatio Alger success story, when it founders on the Dantean path to redemption sought in *Simplicissimus* or the projected three-volume version of *Dead Souls,* the picaresque activates its own codes of futility. The perpetual ups and downs of a rogue's career—in *El Buscón,* in *Guzmán,* in the Ostap Bender novels—can, if extended far enough, take on a Sisyphus rhythm,[17] a pattern recognized in Venichka's perpetual round of resurrection and crucifixion, from the hair-of-the-dog to the morning-after. Infinite extension is inherent in the picaresque through the implicit open-endedness of first adventures conveyed in the everlasting present of the narrating "I."[18] In certain works, in *El Buscón, Guzmán* and Ellison's *Invisible Man,* for example, the never-ending travels of the happy-go-lucky rogue take him back to his not-so lucky starting point.[19] Whether the end of Venichka's tale marks the end of his life or he is doomed to repeat this journey forever, *Moscow—Petushki* signals the vicious circle in its very title, with its ambiguous reading as entrapment between and/or the equation of two points. When the vicious circle collapses, it takes on the aspect of a tightening noose; thus Erofeev transposes the nails of crucifixion from the outspread arms of Christ to the throat, choking the very essence of Venichka as a *samovozrastaiushchii Logos* [self-generating *Logos*] (R81/E104).

The picaresque prototype, *Lazarillo de Tormes*, was the first such self-generating *logos*,[20] a discourse spun from nothing but a bare tissue of narrative non-entities: an anonymous author, an absent addressee in the person of the mysterious *Vuestra Merced*, both wrapped in an abdicating irony that turns a blind eye to a dead-end career in a dead-end world of a low-born nobody. It modeled an attempt to constitute a self stripped of all rights and all pretension, reduced to nothing more than the power of a word undercut by the sheer tenacity of its determination to keep on stripping down. It is in this context that Bakhtin described picaresque discourse as *opustoshaia* [emptying out], clearing the expressive ground of "oppressive pathos" for true novelistic dialogue.[21] Standing at the other end of the novel's history, Erofeev's work conveys a sense of the futility of this effort. If "in the beginning was the Word," the end can contain, dialectically, nothing but silence, in Erofeev's unforgettable ending—irredeemable silence, so that in between stands not a self-generating, but a self-extinguishing *logos*.

Like Lazarillo's, Venichka's addressees are absent, not only the God that forsakes him and the angels that betray him, but the faceless plural *vy* [you] persistently focused on the most trivial, least retrievable details: what exactly did Venichka drink or buy, where, in what order and for what price (R16/E13, R23/E23); just what transpired during his first sexual encounter with his Beloved (R45/E52); and so on. No less persistent is the attention drawn to holes in the narrative: the single-copy first edition now sold out; the all-but non-existent chapter "Serp i Molot—Karacharovo" ["Hammer and Sickle—Karacharovo"], a casualty of self-censorship before the fact; the moment of silence called for the indescribable (un-narratable) business of foraging drink (R22/E22). The repeated announcement that the train will not stop at Esino opens a gap in the itinerary glossed by Venichka as inevitability, the inevitability of momentum: just as the Esino passengers must find other, substitute boarding points, an author, "privy councilor Goethe," must create other, vicarious drinkers and surrogate suicides in his characters (R67/E84–85). A prominent motif is silence as the refused reply: notably, from the angels to Venichka's complaint that it is difficult to walk (R19/E17); from Venichka to God's wondering why he is silent (R116/E155); from God to Venichka's asking why he has been abandoned (R121/E162). Silence surrounds the well-known treatise on hiccups, their sudden onset and equally inexplicable, quiet end; the "arbitrary power," unnamable and inescapable, they stand for (R54/E65); the holes they punch in meaning, in making and communicating sense.

The most challenging gap addressed in *Moscow—Petushki* is that between the narrating and narrated personae. Where all first-person narratives must contend with the illusion and the elusiveness of closing that gap, the picaresque used its momentum—a flurry of changing places, circumstances and voices—to distract the reader from it. Still, the picaro-narrator never pretended to be otherwise than retrospective. He might have deferred closure—the end of his story could only coincide with the end of his life—and so hold out at least the promise of "further adventures," but he would always call a narrative "time-out," as it were, a pause in the narrating continuum to accumulate the experience for the next narrated installment. Hence, on the simplest possible level, the hiatuses between those installments: from 1599 to 1604 for parts I and II of *Guzmán*, for example; from 1715 to 1724 and then to 1735 in the case of Lesage's *Gil Blas*; in more recent Russian practice, Voinovich's *Chonkin* remains apparently incomplete after installments of 1969, 1975 and 1979, as does Iskander's *Sandro iz Chegema* [*Sandro of Chegem*], building through versions of 1973, 1977, 1979, 1981 and 1989.

More important, of course, is the retrospective gap encoded in the picaresque text itself as an alternation between the chronotopes of the road and the inn to mark rhythmic breaks between the acquiring of experience and its relay-recounting, as in the *Quixote* or *Pickwick*, for example. On a broader scope, the genre stretches between the road, its dynamic *fabula* chronotope and the retreat, its more static *siuzhet* locus, incarnated usually as confinement: on a galley ship, from which place the paradigmatic *Guzmán* inspired such figures as Cervantes' galley slave Ginés de Pasamonte; or in a prison, as Moll Flanders, Chichikov, Humbert Humbert (and to a certain extent, Chonkin and Palisandr Dal'berg) demonstrate; in a monastery or hermitage, as represented by *Simplicissimus*, *Povest' o Gore-Zlochastii* [*The Tale of Grief-Misfortune*), *Savva Grudtsyn*, Novikov's "Pokhozhdeniia Ivana gostinago syna" ["Adventures of Ivan the Merchant's Son"], and the like.

It is memory that forges the link between the road as traveled and the retreat from which it is recalled and recreated. Like all middlegrounds, in Erofeev's work this one too is obliterated. Alcohol provides the obvious motivation: the "Spirit of Geneva" cocktail combines ingredients that erase first a mother's face and then her name; the "Tear of the Komsomol Girl" dissolves the *zdravyi um i tverduiu pamiat'* [sound mind and firm recall] (R57/E69) that in Russian legal parlance guarantee a last will and testament, the settled citizen's attempt to fix some record of his or her life's journey. Venichka's remembrances of things past involve abandonment: as tears shed or unshed on his twentieth and thirtieth birthdays (R48/E57–58); because of a smile when the angels leave him to his own devices (R43/E51). The theme takes on a spatial dimension and momentum under the rubric of "delirium" (*bespamiatstvo* < *pamiat'*, "memory"), which obscures the "unfamiliar/unidentified front hallway" that marks the beginning and end of this day's journey. Delirium carves holes in his itinerary: "я и сам *путем* не знаю" [I myself don't *rightly* know] he declares when unable to retrace the steps taken, the drinks consumed and the order of presents bought the day before (R16/E13) (emphasis added). His *oslabevshaia pamiat'* [failing memory] has him almost lie to God before yielding to the "mighty flow of dreams and idle drowsiness" (R89/E116) that ushers in the lengthy recollection of a failed utopia. That "adventure" (the Russian *avantiura* connoting shady enterprises often associated with the rogue) is not only "fruitless as the fig-tree" blasted by Christ (Matt. 21:19), it opens the largest and most dangerous breach in Venichka's recalling of the trip to Petushki, for it is here that the tale breaks down, and the teller, apparently, loses his way.

There are no resting-points on Venichka's route. His narrating voice is perpetually on the move, to its last word: "и с тех пор я не приходил в сознание, и никогда не *приду*" [and since then I have not regained consciousness and I *never will*] (R122/E164) (emphasis added). Though negated, *pridu* is a verb of *motion*, and it is highlighted by its end-position. The chilling finality of this pronouncement from beyond even consciousness draws its paradoxical force from the collapse of a middleground: Erofeev implodes the gap between the temporal positions of the narrating and narrated personae, and he does so by turning picaresque momentum against itself. In this context the ungainly chapter titles do not impede the narrative flow; they mark its uninterrupted passage, like station signs glimpsed from a railcar window or rather, given Venichka's inebriated self-focus, the memory of a route he is now traveling for the thirteenth time. The passed-by station/chapter titles also mark the passing of narrated and narrating time: from boarding at 8:16 am, to arrival expected at precisely eleven o'clock, for a projected lapse of "ровно два часа пятнадцать минут" [exactly two hours and fifteen minutes] (R100/E132). One minute less (two hours and fourteen minutes) is the time recalled by Erofeev during an interview of 1989,[22] where he claims a fortuitous match with the time it takes to read *Moscow—Petushki*, presumably aloud, adding an extra-textual dimension to the convergence of narrated and narrating voice, and basing this convergence on the non-stop linear momentum of the picaresque.

Traveling time does not pass in *Moscow—Petushki*; it is consumed, whether measured in terms of drink (one gram per kilometer for a total of 125 grams) or historical anecdote recounted to the train conductor (one "alcove" or "intimate" incident per trip). Time that runs out is much more dynamic than time that simply passes; there is an extra sense of urgency in the process of emptying-out as compared to the state of emptiness that attends, for example, the "pure hiatus" of Bakhtin's adventure chronotope. There time goes by without effect, without changing or even aging the hero.[23] It is zero-impact adventure time that operates in the "travel novel" (*roman strantstvovanii*), under which category Bakhtin discusses the picaresque novel in his *Bildungsroman* essay ("Roman vospitaniia").[24]

By contrast, the chronotope study treats the picaresque as a variant of the "adventure novel of everyday life" (*avantiurno-bytovoi roman*) which takes a detour from empty adventure time to plunge its hero into the wash, into the nether-world of daily existence. In its strictest model, in *The Golden Ass*, the plunge produces a metamorphosis; in *The Satyricon* and the European picaresque, the two chronotopes of adventure and everyday life are more closely intertwined and the metamorphosis, says Bakhtin, "less clearly defined."[25] The chronotope study does not elaborate directly on this second sort of metamorphosis; its discussion focuses more on the picaro's spying on the private lives of others from a position of detachment. That detachment, though, is manifested in the picaro's constant changing of "everyday masks" (*bytovye lichiny*) which anticipates metamorphosis in an external, repeatable form.[26] Whether Venichka undergoes the significant change modeled by *The Golden Ass* or the interchangeable mask-metamorphoses of *The Satyricon* and the European picaresque, depends on how we interpret the ending of his tale: as a death beyond resurrection or as one lap on a never-ending cycle of death-in-life. In either case, a sense of doom prevails, and it is this sense, combining both urgency and futility, that empties out time in the very process of its unfolding in *Moscow—Petushki*.

The potential for such emptying-out is embedded in the picaresque dynamic. Speaking of what he calls the genre's "cancellation of time," Ralph Freedman observes:

> although he [the picaro] exists in time, i.e. in the temporal flow of the novel and the events in which he is engaged, he performs actions without structure or end beyond themselves. Hence the

very time he uses for his purpose becomes ultimately meaningless.[27]

Aligning this insight with the trajectory presented in the chronotope essay suggests that purposeless acts performed within everyday time serve to cancel that time from within. Since metamorphosis can only register in terms of before and after, a gutting-out of the time in between serves to gut out transformation in process. Metamorphosis of this sort is not stillborn, or nipped in the bud but rather left to, challenged to proceed and be foiled at its every turn. As a pre-modern form, the picaresque can thus be said to carry out its "negative job of work" (*negativnaia rabota*)[28] by a constant prodding to break out of the no-impact zone and highlighting through counterexample the need to create a truly organic reflection of time-based and time-tested becoming. In the neo-picaresque, as a postmodern return to past, already used and used-up forms, the emphasis can only be on the process of negation, not on becoming but on un-doing. Time is no longer suspended but passes, inexorably, to its own abnegation.

Several motifs in *Moscow—Petushki* promote such a neo-picaresque cancellation of time in process. Time is a black hole, as evident in the anti-eulogy to "самое бессильное и позорное время в жизни моего народа — время от рассвета до открытия магазинов!" [that most helpless and shameful of times in the life of my people, the time from dawn until the liquor stores open up!] (R18/E15; echoed R32/E36, R115/E153). The present is drained of meaning by the promise of a "brighter tomorrow," worn thread-bare in official Soviet rhetoric, and utterly undone by exposing the shifting grounds of all deictic reference:

Наше завтра светлее, чем наше вчера и наше сегодня. Но кто поручится, что наше послезавтра не будет хуже нашего позавчера?
[Our tomorrow is brighter than our yesterday and our today. But who'll see to it that our day after tomorrow won't be worse than our day before yesterday?] (R39/E45)

If it is narration that confers meaning, then Venichka's inviting Semenych to leap with him out of stories about the "dark past" and into tales of the "golden age" (R87/E113) condemns the not-to-be-narrated present in between. Satan taunts him with living entirely in the past, refusing to think of the future (R101/E133)—another sidestepping of time in an on-going present. Time lacks meaningful direction; it makes no difference which way the clock hands are moved, forward or back, so long as some decree on time is passed by President Venichka (R93/E122), so long as some meddling and muddling occurs. Time loses calculable duration, if suffering can be said to last "Не то пять минут, не то семь минут, не то целую вечность" [five minutes, seven minutes, a whole eternity] (R26/E27); if the Princess of Inconsolable Grief can scorn the mundane for "на день или на три" [a day or three] (R40/E47); if Venichka dozed off for a pseudo-precise "минут 12 или тридцать пять" [twelve or thirty-five minutes] (R111/E148). Time is ultimately pointless: "зачем тебе время" [what do you need time for], Venichka asks himself on the empty station square of a Petushki now fused with Moscow; there is no "living soul" to ask the time of day now that his heavenly (or out-of-time) paradise is no more, now that morning, evening and night have blurred into a round of "groaning," "weeping" and the "gnashing of teeth" (R116/E155–56).

Losses, (Criss-) Crosses and Cavings-In

In this disorder, or rather anti-order of canceled measure and distinction, carnival reversals are themselves reversed: crowning comes after uncrowning,[29] crucifixion after assumption (R36/E40–41), for, as Venichka observes:

Все на свете должно происходить медленно и неправильно, чтобы не сумел загордиться человек, чтобы человек был грустен и растерян.

[Everything should take place slowly and incorrectly so that man doesn't get a chance to start feeling proud, so that man is sad and perplexed.] (R17/E14)

The dictum follows the logic of the picaresque, its mistaken world of chaos and futility, its hero's tongue-in-cheek self-deflation, with one exception: the insistence on a slow pace runs counter to the rogue genre's frenetic confusion. Venichka's plunge into everyday time embroils him in the hustle-bustle of the here-and-now, which he sees in Biblical (and empty) terms of vanity: "захотел ты суеты — вот и получай свою суету" [you wanted vanity—so here it is] (R18/E16). His mistake was in thinking he could hold his ground against it.

The effort to cancel space traces an entire network of circles and crossings-out in *Moscow—Petushki*. From its well-known opening words:

Все говорят: Кремль, Кремль. Ото всех я слышал про него, а сам ни разу не видел. Сколько раз уже (тысячу раз), напившись или с похмелюги, проходил по Москве с севера на юг, с запада на восток,...и ни разу не видел Кремля.
[Everyone says, "The Kremlin, the Kremlin." I hear about it from everybody, but I've never seen it myself. How many times (thousands) I've walked, drunk or hung over, across Moscow from north to south, east to west,...and never did I see the Kremlin.] (R16/E13)

Vse [everyone], *oto vsekh* [from everybody] and *tysiachu raz* [a thousand times] imply a universal scope. The Kremlin is placed at the center of the universe; and to confirm it, Venichka spends the night before his attempted departure describing circles around the spot. Over it is superimposed the image of the cross, from north to south, west to east.[30] Crossed and encircled, the Kremlin resembles Gogol's *zakoldovannoe mesto* [bewitched spot], an elusive, godforsaken ground. At the end of the day, the same point is made by the same circling motion:

А если Он никогда земли моей не покидал, если всю ее *исходил* босой и в рабском виде, — Он это место *обогнул* и *прошел* стороной.
[And if He never left the earth, if He passed through it barefoot and dressed as a slave, He *passed* this place *by* (lit. circumvented it) and *went off* somewhere (lit. skirted it).] (R119/E160) (Emphasis added)

Venichka wards off the Kremlin by using the Catholic benediction, which proceeds from left shoulder to right (west to east), whereas the Orthodox blessing (east to west on these coordinates) is seen in the non-response to the drunkards' revolution:

[П]очему такое молчание в мире?...почему никто не подает нам руки ни с Востока, ни с Запада? Куда смотрит король Улаф? Почему нас не давят с юга регулярные части?
[Why such silence in the world?...why has no one extended his hand—not from the east, not from the west. What's become of King Olaf? Why don't regular units crush us from the south?] (R95/E125)

Joining in the cruel laughter at his grandfather's expense, the younger Mitrich shakes from bottom to top so as not to spatter himself from left to right (R75/E95). That the latter gesture might represent a Satanic inversion of the Orthodox benediction is suggested by the character's fiendishly contorted anatomy: his neck does not grow into his torso, but out of it; he breathes backwards—first out, then in; he speaks, or rather squeals, through his left nostril; it is not his eyes, but his armpits that blink (R60–62/E74–77); he drinks by pressing the glass not to his mouth, but to his left nipple, and not with his hand, but his right thigh (R68/E85).

"Режьте меня вдоль и поперек" [Cut me up left and right] Venichka proposes in defense of his stirring method for the cocktail "Tear of the Komsomol Girl" (R57/E71). The violence actually inflicted on him turns criss-crossing into a murderous beating. One of the Erinyes hits him on the left cheek (R112/E150); the Pontic King Mithridates stabs him first on the left, then on the right, then left and right again (R114/E152). Left-right confusions, and the reeling momentum their constant alternation sets up, lie at the very heart of the mystery that returns Venichka to his starting point and leads him beyond, to his death. Horror sets in when he cannot recall whether he saw the lights of Pokrov on the left or right, which side of the car his now vanished suitcase lay on, which of his absconding companions sat where. The inherent schizophrenia of his inner debates is now externalized, as he leans his head from left to right (R107/E143). At the beginning and end of his tale, on the approach to the Kremlin, he takes comfort in the thought that turning left or right is immaterial: the diabolical spot will automatically repel him towards Kursk Station, and from there to Petushki. Symmetry, the ostensible identity of left and right, provides false succor; by concentrating on the interchangeability of external oppositions, it undermines the middleground that keeps them apart. All it can offer is a *golaia zerkal'nost'* [bare symmetry] as Black Mustache says of the too-neat, perhaps amoral, but *strogo geometrichna* [strictly geometrical] balance of light and gloom in his lemma of the tippler's daily existence (R69/E87). When the middleground caves in, either/or becomes both/and—to lethal effect, in the case of Venichka and the distinction between Moscow and Petushki.[31]

The *plut,* the morally ambiguous rogue who chooses *both* good and bad, does so at his peril, as is seen in the word's etymological links to *plutat',* "to go astray," emphasizing the crucial choice of *either* the right way *or* the wrong. The wrong way, Venichka declares, was forced upon Russia by Peter the Great and one misnamed Kibal'chich,[32] whereas he will lead his compatriots back down the right path to their true vocation (R52/E63). Venichka needs distinctions, especially mutually exclusive distinctions in space; he longs for a "corner," a refuge with no room for deeds of valor (R21/E20–21). Antitheses, like the initial mutually exclusive difference between the Kremlin and Kursk Station, must repel each other like opposite ends of a magnet. Hence Venichka's uneasy disgust in noticing that the waitress at the Kursk Station restaurant has no seams on her stockings, whereas "шов бы меня смирил, может быть, разгрузил бы душу и совесть" [a seam would have made me feel at peace, perhaps even unburdened my soul and my conscience] (R21/E20).

The first and most insidious step in the erosion of distinctions comes from within: they tend to succumb to their own quibbling rhetoric, from that between puke and vomit (R24/E24) to the more arcane gradation of "превратно,...*строго наоборот*,...совершенно по-свински, то есть *антиномично*" [wrongly,...*strictly the other way around*,...like a complete bastard, i.e. *antinomially*] (R31/E34). The whole of Hegelian dialectics is reduced to:

> "Нет различий, кроме различия в степени между различными степенями и отсутствием различия". То-есть, если перевести это на хороший язык: "Кто же сейчас не пьет?"
> ["There are no distinctions, except distinctions in degree, between various degrees and the absence of distinction." That is, if you translate it into good language: "Who doesn't drink these days?"]
> (R110/E147)

Early in his tale, Venichka struggles to describe his indescribable state as *gorchaishee mesivo* [the bitterest of mishmashes] of "fear," "sorrow" and "muteness" (R40/E46), where the absence of distinction is itself a compound of absences: fear, the lack of confidence; sorrow as *skorb'* implying the mourning of some loss; and muteness (*nemota*), the inability to speak. When later he quotes: "Есть бытие, но именем каким его назвать? — ни сон оно, ни бденье" [There's a state, but there's no name for it, not sleep nor wake is it] (R111/E148), from Baratynskii's poem "Posledniaia smert'" ["The Last Death," dated 1827], either/or has sunk into a nebulous neither/nor. It is from this state that Venichka drifts into the half-hallucinatory, completely helpless state that will carry him to his doom.

Caved-in middlegrounds leave gaping centers in their wake. In the tourist heart of Paris, perched on the Eiffel Tower, General de Gaulle is seen scanning the four corners of the horizon (another criss-crossed circle), but the general scans in vain for there is nothing to be seen but whorehouses (R81/E104). A vacuum becomes a vortex, evoked in the tale by the train station of Omutishche (from *omut*, "whirlpool"), where for want of a bottle, Venichka begins his downward spiral into sobriety. This is the spot where in the absence of all other passengers a suddenly vicious Peter unleashes the Erinyes as foretold by the proverb "в тихом омуте черти водятся" (lit. "in a quiet eddy demons abound"; English equivalent: "still waters run deep"). Those who heed Venichka's advice to alternate strictly the extremes of "white [i.e. pure] vodka" and "red [cheap port-] wines" will become "flaming" centers; girls will leap over them instead of the usual bonfires lit for the pagan fertility rituals of Ivan Kupala Eve (R51–52/E62).

The reference evokes Gogol's Dikan'ka tale and by association another empty, godless center—the "bewitched spot" of Venichka's invisible Kremlin, discussed above. It fits in as well with the work's relentless linear momentum, via the theme of gathering, eventually impassable gloom: since the feast of St. John the Baptist comes almost directly after the summer solstice, on this, almost the shortest night of the year (23–24 June), it is possible to complete the jump, to land safely on the other side. Venichka, on the other hand, cannot clear the devil's ground of the Kremlin for, it seems, that leap was made closer to the winter solstice, if his anticipating (in vain) the Christmas Star of Bethlehem (R117/E157) is any indication of time.

Venichka himself is shot through with absences. "[K]акие во мне бездны!" [what chasms open up in me!] he exclaims (R25/E25). It is the "absence of a deed" (going to the bathroom) that, in the eyes of his four roommates, confirms his arrogance. He compares his soul to the belly of the Trojan horse, empty enough to accommodate many things (R62/E76), then confesses to Louis Aragon that he has despaired of everything (an absence of hope), has no doubt of anything (an absence of an absence of faith); to Elsa Triolet he complains he is dying of a lack of impressions (R81/E105). Sir Silage Corn dubs him a *chuchelo* [straw man], a *pugalo* [scarecrow] (R84/E109). "Отчего я и дурак, и демон, и пустомеля разом?" [Why am I a fool, a demon and a bag of wind all at the same time?] (R41/E47), Venichka asks himself. The three-pronged self-accusation combines the diabolic (or negation of the divine), the innocence of simplicity (a negation of worldly wiles), and the motif of absence, through the component of *pustoi* [empty] in *pustomelia* [idle talker, windbag]. *Pustomelia* may also take absence into the narrative sphere: the words of a windbag are devoid of significance.

To some extent, the vacant middle finds a precedent in the picaresque, whose hero is predicated on a gap, on the rupturing of a legalistic ("rhetorical") "unity of person and conduct" (or doer and deed), on a "sharp break between the individual and his/her external position" in society.[33] Attacking or vindicating the picaro's lack of interiority has become all but a ritual in commentary on the genre. An early prototype, Quevedo's *Buscón* (1626) stands accused of a virtual absence of inner life, "apart from his digestive processes"; he is said to display an "inconsistency of character, which verges on the absurd."[34] The picaro plays out his voided middle in a dynamic inconsistency of character, in non-stop role-playing as "servant of many masters." This picaresque theme is under-represented in *Moscow—Petushki*, where Venichka's curriculum vitae notes only brief stints as brigade foreman and drunkards' president, and one derogatory reference to his writer's vocation (R45/E53).[35] By contrast, the Venichka legend that extends beyond the text emphasizes a career both checkered and geographically mobile: box loader in a Kolomna grocery store, bricklayer and construction assistant in Cheremushki and Moscow, boiler-stoker in Vladimir, militiaman in Orekhovo-Zuevo, bottle-collector in Moscow, drill-operator on geological expeditions in Ukraine, and cable-layer from Tambov to Smolensk, Gomel' to Polotsk.[36] Sustaining the myth, both Erofeev and his widow recall one of the more macabre and picaresque episodes in this anti-vita: where the picaro scrounges in a dog-eat-dog world, Erofeev apparently passed some time as a fly-feeder, or rather fly-food, offering his bare arm to *okrylenn[yi] krovososushch[ii] gnus* [winged blood-sucking vermin].[37]

Emptying the Person

Within the text itself, picaresque role-playing is evoked at one remove, not by acting but by alluding to literary precedents, as figures of fiction less "real" and less "present," as characters from classic works of the past. Absence and negation, in other words, pervade this theme too. In Shakespeare's *Othello*, Venichka takes on all parts to mime a scene of murder and suicide (R27/E29); he envisages himself as Pasternak's Hamlet, pierced by public scrutiny.[38] At the third Plenary Session of the drunkards' republic, he identifies himself with Pontius Pilate, more precisely, with the latter's dramatic hand-washing gesture, where absence is conveyed as abdication. By his roommates he is charged with posing as Cain and Manfred (R28–30/E31–32)—in the Russian canon, Byronic avatars of the "superfluous man," who suffers for want of application.

Similarly, Erofeev places the picaro's parodic opposition to the heroic in contexts of emptiness. Thus Venichka denies any resemblance between himself and a drunken Nietzschean superman on the grounds that he couldn't possibly have bought presents for his loved ones in a thirty-second *pause* between drinks (R19/E18). He deflates—in both senses of degrading and emptying out—Gorky's "Song of the Stormy Petrel" by comparing to it an alcoholic's *consumption* chart (R35/E39–40). From the picaresque tradition he selects the genre's trademark homelessness, and then adds to it an emotional sense of loss when counting himself in the ranks of the *bezdomnykh i toskuiushchikh shatenov* [homeless and grieving brunets] (R18/E15). He assumes the picaro's all but obligatory orphanhood (R22/E21, R80/E104), claiming as his abandoned homeland a Siberia marked by a distinct lack of food—in the classic picaresque, the chief driving force behind roguery.[39]

This picaresque deficiency, the hero's lack of a fixed identity, becomes in *Moscow—Petushki* a summary statement on the whole of Venichka's character when the British House of Lords collectively observes: "этот пыльный мудак впишется в любой интерьер!" [this dusty bastard would fit in in any interior!] (R84/E109). Chameleon-like dependency on external definition multiplies into a series of confusions as Venichka is taken by disembarking passengers for a schoolboy, an officer, and a woman pilgrim (R97–98/E129), addressed by Semenych as Scheherazade (R85/E111), then accosted

40

by Peter the valet as *babulen'ka* [granny] and *staraia sterva* [old bitch] (R121/E149). The androgynous imagery accruing to Venichka here and elsewhere in the tale carries picaresque instability into an attack on gender identity, arguably the most fundamental marker of selfhood. It internalizes the picaresque penchant for cross-dressing, for the genre as a whole is trans-sexual, embracing a long line of *pícaras* or female rogues, from *Celestina* (ca. 1497) anticipating the picaresque, to Ubeda's *Justina* (1605), *Moll Flanders* (1722), Chulkov's *Prigozhaia povarikha* (*Comely Cook*, 1770), and possibly Viktor Erofeev's *Russkaia krasavitsa* (*Russian Beauty*, 1990). Sokolov's *Palisandriia* (in English translation as *Astrophobia*, 1985) supplies a rare example of gender-bending actually manifest in the protagonist when its hero/heroine transforms into a hermaphrodite for hire.

In *Moscow—Petushki*, however, Venichka is not the only character to exhibit this tendency. The Decembrist is urged to produce a love story where he, like Turgenev's heroine, will be struck across the face with a riding crop (R73/E93); Grandfather Mitrich weeps like a woman when his drinking companions explode into laughter (R74/E95); while Tikhonov materializes in the jasmine bushes where Venichka had been expecting his Beloved (R89/E117). The fact that androgyny is imputed to and shared by the company Venichka finds himself in, rather than isolated as his sole prerogative, points to yet another facet of picaresque instability. In the rogue genre key traits are often parceled out through a system of multiple doubling or splintering, as shown, for example, in the parallels between Lazarillo and his roguish masters; Il'f and Petrov's Ostap Bender, the Antelope-Gnu team and Aleksandr Koreiko; Iskander's Uncle Sandro, Tengiz, Abesalomon Nartovich, Vakhtang Bochua, and Marat; Sokolov's Palisandr, Brikabrakov, Kerbabaev, and the three Striutskiis. Like role-playing, career-changing and geographic mobility, splintering compensates for and projects outward the picaro's empty center; it erodes a personality porous to begin with, and highlights the hero's dependency on and complicity with the society he must fend for himself in.

Forced by the splintering system to confront a host of counterparts, the classic picaro must either outwit a series of other, individual knaves, or sham conformity with entire brotherhoods of con artists.[40] Erofeev's approach is to lay bare the emptiness the strategy emerged from and sought to disguise. What survives of the picaresque brotherhood of rogues in *Moscow—Petushki* is the drinking ritual of *Brüderschaft*, but even this is canceled when Venichka recalls an old acquaintance, now deceased, who turned the concept inside out: to his mind, *pit' na brudershaft* [to drink *Brüderschaft*] amounted to imbibing stolen eau de cologne on the sly at the Petushki Station toilet (R62/E77). The absence of drinking buddies in this example highlights the absence of real ties, the stability of genuine friendship among Venichka's traveling companions, the lack of fellow feeling in this group, in the category of *sobutylniki* [drinking partners] as a whole, where alliances evaporate with the onset of sobriety, and throughout Venichka's odyssey of solitude.[41]

More than on any supply of spirits, though, companionship in Venichka's world, as in that of the picaresque, depends on chance, an empty logic beyond control, interpretation and meaningful impact. This in Bakhtin's description is a kaleidoscope of purely abstract, almost mathematically calibrated random "road encounters."[42] In a similar vein, Bakhtin casts the hero of the travel novel (the category, as noted above, includes the picaresque) as "a moving point in space," and the world this figure moved through as one of "static social variety," conceived of and depicted as a "spatial juxtaposition of differences and contrasts."[43] The terms of analysis here are both implicitly negative—hollow points, random collisions with hollow counterpoints, all gaps destined to be filled in by later and richer chronotopes—and historically optimistic, given Bakhtin's focus on the slow but productive process of filling in and fleshing out their potential. It is by contrast with an already completed fleshing out and filling in, with a potential already achieved and arguably unsurpassable in the many hundreds of works Venichka constantly (anxiously?) alludes to, that the gaps are re-opened and all the more keenly felt. His counterpoints are not hollow but rather hollowed *out*; his chance encounters stripped of meaning even before the moment of impact, by simple conjecture. Thus, while he insists on respecting the "dark reaches" (*potemki*) of the souls of others, he does not discount the possibility that they might turn out to be empty, or contain nothing but trash (R74/E95).

Splintering in Erofeev's neo-picaresque adaptation underscores double and multiple gaps, so that the void that was the picaro now operates in a total vacuum. Each of Venichka's doubles embodies some aspect of absence. The all but indistinguishable Mitriches reflect his fear of collapsed divisions; Stupid-Stupid and Smart-Smart flank the anomaly of his declassed intellectual; the angels and Satan trap him in the no-man's land between the sacred and the satanic. The only promise the perfidious angels keep is to abandon Venichka at the moment of his first smile. The Princess, identified as Venichka's "copy" (R107/E143), inspires on her first appearance a short list of exotic losses: a phial of Sèvres porcelain, a peignoir of "inconceivable price" (R40/E47). The Woman in the Beret, who takes after the *pícara* or female rogue in her Joan-of-Arc quest for adventure, fails in her search for her self, as pointed out by her deaf-and-dumb grandmother (R77/E99). The Sphinx, a mass of missing parts, manages to beat him and thus mirrors a possible masochistic, even suicidal streak in Venichka;[44] it also deflates all that he holds dear: his urine-based modesty (transferred to Aleksei Stakhanov), his Beloved (violated by the American Seventh Fleet), his progress to Petushki. Pushkin, whom Venichka seems to mourn and perhaps emulate as a model of poetic perfection ignored in an all too prosaic world, is doubled with the parodic and missing-in-action Evtiushkin, and appears as a double absence himself: he is dead, and no one knows what he died of (R55/E67, R70/E89). The anecdotal Pushkin invoked by the Woman in the Beret when she wonders who will raise her non-existent children is likewise founded on absence: Pushkin is not around to do the job, yet Evtiushkin refuses to take on the responsibility himself (R77/E98–99).

Venichka's son and his Beloved as goals of his journey are necessarily absent. The former is threatened by the motif of dying children;[45] struck with a fever he becomes in his worried father's eyes a *nichtozhestvo* [a little nothing] (R42/E49). To his bewitching queen Venichka applies the epithet *neslykhannaia* [unheard of], and describes in tones of awe her breathing out everything that was sacred in her. She is perfection, he adds, and perfection has no limit (R45–46/E53–54). Her swaying hips generate a trembling and a tumbling into Eden and oblivion; her *sokrovennye izgiby* [innermost curves] cannot be counted (R47/E56). She is the "prototype" of a Golden Age that never was (R89/E116). Perhaps the Beloved's most unsettling mark of absence is to be found in her eyes: cloud-white in their hollow inaccessibility, they hold neither shame nor conscience (R38/E43) and form an ominous contrast with the *zamutnennost'* [murkiness] detected in Venichka's eyes (R68/E86), which lack (of light and clarity) is ascribed, via yet another of the drunkard's self-canceling, circular arguments, to sorrow caused either by a "broad" or by drink, a necessity when dealing with all such creatures, good or bad (R71–72/E91). Venichka sees the eyes of his fellow Russians bulge with the absence of tension; the oxymoron is stressed in their "*[п]олное* отсутствие всякого смысла" [*complete* lack (a set and fairly bureaucratic phraseologism) of any sense whatsoever] (R27/E28, emphasis added). Finally, this submotif of empty but bulging eyes culminates in the orbs of Venichka's four executioners, compared to sewage churning under the round holes of the Petushki Station toilet (R118/E158).

Doubling, then, has overextended itself to produce a perilously large and lethally empty host of others. In the light of psychopathology, doubling is an attempt to stave off the other by surrounding oneself with more tractable surrogates. From the picaresque perspective, it is the coping strategy of a self forced to make do as its own anchor in a world without center. In *Moscow—Petushki*, both the attempt and the compromise fail. Venichka, as painfully chaste as Alesha Karamazov, claims to have "expanded the sphere of intimacy" and suffered the consequences (R28/E30), but it is not so much intimacy, as the very process of expansion that betrays him. "Я отдаю себя вам без остатка" [I'll give of myself to the last drop], Venichka boasts to an empty railway car, and immediately undercuts the pathos with a pun that emphasizes consumption: "Потому что остаток только что допил, ха-ха!" [because I just drank up the last drop, ha-ha!] (R107/E143). The nightmarish swell of hostile doubles is the result of an emptying-out; the effort to produce it drains Venichka, so that ultimately here too, the center, Venichka's own center, collapses in on itself.

Images of voiding pervade the novel. Nausea rises in Venichka like lava in Mt. Vesuvius, like May-Day fireworks (R26/E27–28); all of Russia is so deep in its own alcoholic spew that no clarion call for reform could ever wake or sober it up (R66/E83); the Lord Chamberlain slips in vomit; Semenych regularly disgorges the spirits he receives in lieu of train fare. Spitting is ubiquitous and, proverbially, expressive of contempt; from countless examples: Sir Silage Corn's for Venichka's smelly feet (R83/E108); Venichka's for every rung of the Soviet "ladder" of success (R36/E41), for the presidency of the drunkards' republic (R94/E124), for all stars other than the absent Star of Bethlehem (R117/E157). It is protested against by Venichka's roommates, who suspect he considers them "spit" beneath his feet (R30/E32); universally applied by a younger generation to whom nothing is sacred (R51/E62); meekly withstood by the *odukhotvorennyi* [enspiritized] imbiber of "Bitches' Brew" (R58/E71).

The picaresque canon regularly subjects its protagonists to physiological humiliation, but, it seems, only the *Buscón* can match *Moscow—Petushki* for the sheer volume of spittle expended: in a horrific scene, Pablos is the target of a "barrage and shower" of phlegm; he is turned into "an old man's spittoon" and protests, "Please don't, I'm not Christ on the Cross, you know," whereupon he finds himself immersed in still more body wastes. There is one significant difference: Quevedo's victim, a young lad, treats the incident as an initiation ritual, resolving the next day to "do as the Romans do...and even worse than them, if [he] could."[46] Venichka on this, his last journey to Petushki, can find no such release, no initiation or advance, however perverse, on to some new stage; this is a picaresque career short-circuited by the simple expedient of superimposing beginnings on ends, and canceling out even the illusion of progress in between.

Urination, mentioned with Rabelaisan frequency in the work, is stripped of its joyous surplus, its celebration of release from the cerebral. These are not drinkers exploding from abundance, as do the rivals of Iskander's Uncle Sandro, or wallowing in excess, like Chonkin and his neighbor Gladyshev.[47] Instead, Venichka exempts himself from the carnival celebration of community;[48] what is more, he does not so much mark himself off from the rest of humanity by his own continence, as raise the incontinence of others to an occasion for reflection, for stepping aside to contemplate the vulnerability of the world at large, be it the so-called "weaker sex," including the assassins among them (R46/E55), Chairman Lohengrin cornered in his office, or even the wall he urinated on (R74–75/E95–96).[49] Grandfather Mitrich is awash in tears and other body fluids, from his rheumy eyes, like two drowned men, streaming into his boots (R60/E74–75) to his runny nose, which latter feature he shares with Mithridates (R113/E151–52).

Breath, with its readily recognizable links to the *spiri*tual, is also subject to expulsion: as cited above, Venichka's Beloved breathes out all that is sacred in her; Grandson Mitrich exhales before inhaling (R60/E74); one can die the easiest death after releasing, from the depths of one's heart, forty of the deepest breaths, and with them, the soul (R115/E154). The expression Venichka uses here is *isputit' dushu* [to release the soul], in lieu of the more standard *isputit' dukh* [to give up the ghost], as did Premier Boria, out of melancholy and a "чрезмерной склонности к обобщениям" [extreme proclivity for generalization] (R95/E126). Breathing *in*, on the other hand, is to be approached with caution and restraint: Paris is so full of gonorrhea that it is difficult to breathe (R81/E104–105); to keep yourself "on the go," to participate, in other words, in the daily challenge of *talifa kumi* [rise and walk], you must breathe *redko, redko* [oh so seldom] and carefully, "чтобы ноги за коленки не задевали" [so that your legs don't bump into your knees] (R18/E15).

46

The climax of this theme is highlighted by its setting at Orekhovo-Zuevo, the one and only break in Venichka's train ride, the immediate prelude to his loss of consciousness and direction. The passage in question reads:

> Старшего ревизора Семеныча...вынесло на перрон и ударило головой о перила...[Он] рухнул под ноги выходящей публике, и все штрафы за безбилетный проезд хлынули у него из чрева, растекаясь по перрону...выходящая в Орехове лавина публики запуталась во мне и вбирала меня, чтобы накопить меня в себе, как паршивую слюну, — и выплюнуть на ореховский перрон. Но плевок все не получался, потому что входящая в вагон публика затыкала рот выходящей. Я мотался, как говно в проруби.
>
> [Senior Inspector Semenych was propelled out onto the platform, bumping his head on the railing. He then collapsed under the feet of the people getting off the train, and all the fines he had collected spewed out of his gullet and flowed away over the platform...the human avalanche which was getting off at Orekhovo overwhelmed me and sucked at me so as to gather me into itself like a nasty wad to be spit out on the Orekhovo platform. But without quite spitting, because the people getting on the train plugged up the mouth of the ones getting off. I was spun about like shit in an ice-hole.]
> (R88–89/E115–16)

The scene captures in miniature the many different vectors of the picaresque itinerary in *Moscow—Petushki*: its carnival emphasis on the physiological directed towards expulsion; its churning impetus of motion at once circular, to and fro, frustrated and in-between. Churning might even allude to the picaro's ambiguous allegiance with both oppressors and oppressed, for it aligns Venichka with the swirling sewage he will find in the eyes of his executioners. It echoes the spin of Edenic oblivion he finds in the gyrating embrace of his Beloved. It partakes of the childlike innocence the picaresque encodes and corrupts through its primal burden of orphanhood: in the merry threats of the round-dance he sings of to his son (R43/E50), in the bleakly innocuous pleasures of the carousel both Mitriches are headed for (R61/E75–76, R85/E111).

This picture of chaos trapped for one brief but crowded moment could be taken as well to symbolize the intergeneric hubbub of the picaresque as it is recreated and packed into *Moscow—Petushki*. The record of Venichka's journey has held in colloidal suspension adventure, carnival, confession, quest and ordeal, together with many other genres that grew out of, back into, and on parallel track with the picaresque. Like the hundreds of quotations, parallels and borrowed imagery in the work, these genre allusions build towards excess and collapse into silence. In part, they have collapsed under their own weight, through a chaos of reciprocal cancellations, a messy counter-dialectic that moves from one too many antitheses not to synthesis, but to absolute negation. Venichka's many identities —mistaken, assumed, parodied and parceled out—build toward the same excess and a similar self-depletion. The result is a simulacrum, a false copy of the non-existent original or hollow husk that was the picaro, swept along by the residual momentum of a genre once powered by the absences of purpose, order, certainty and effect. It is this picaresque dynamic that, doubled back itself, empties out time, space, language and destiny to suspend them in the many-layered void of *Moscow—Petushki*.

Endnotes

1. See respectively Zhivolupova, "Palomnichestvo v Petushki," 79–86 and Gaiser-Shnitman, *Venedikt Erofeev*, 263–64; Gaiser-Shnitman, *Venedikt Erofeev*, 258; Dravich, "Bilet ot Petushkov," 8; Kavadeev, "Sokrovennyi Venedikt," 85; Paperno and Gasparov, "'Vstan' i idi'," 387, 389; Zhivolupova, "Palomnichestvo v Petushki," 87; Vail' and Genis, "Strasti po Erofeevu," *Ekho*, 110; Lakshin, "Bezzakonnyi meteor," 225.

2. See respectively Clowes, *Russian Experimental Fiction*, 46, 139; Smirnova, "Mifologema stradaiushchego boga," 96; Al'tshuller, "*Moskva — Petushki* Venedikta Erofeeva," 77–78; Bethea, *The Shape of Apocalypse*, 275; Simmons, *Their Father's Voice*, 58.

3. See respectively Gaiser-Shnitman, *Venedikt Erofeev*, 40; Sedakova, "Neskazannaia rech'," 264; Kuznetsov, "*Vest'* i drugie," 14; Terts, "Anekdot v anekdote," 91; Vail' and Genis, "Strasti po Erofeevu," *Ekho*, 100.

4. Before Ryan-Hayes' 1995 study of its satiric aspects (see *Contemporary Russian Satire*, 58–100), the picaresque connection in *Moscow—Petushki* was largely neglected. Two reviewers applied the term directly: Glusman, "Under the Soviet Volcano," 15 and Updike, "How the Other Half Lives," 127. Porter (*Russia's Alternative Prose*, 84) implied but did not develop the connection when he compared Erofeev's protagonist to the Good Soldier Shvejk. Novikov ("Tri stakana tertsovki," 56) faulted the work on grounds often used to criticize the picaresque, for what he saw as a lack of psychological development and a purely mechanistic linkage of episodes.

5. With the heroic epic, the picaresque shares roots in the quest motif of myth and folk epic. The rogue genre is seen by many to have arisen in parodic opposition to the adventure tales of knights in shining armor. See in particular Robert Alter, *Rogue's Progress: Studies in the Picaresque Novel* (Cambridge: Harvard University Press, 1968), 72; L. Pinskii, "Ispanskii roman i barokko," *Voprosy literatury*, no. 7 (1962): 141; Helen H. Reed, *The Reader in the Picaresque Novel* (London: Tamesis, 1984), 21, 54. On the picaresque connection to the confession see Edward H. Friedman, *The Anti-Heroine's Voice: Narrative Discourse and the Transformation of the Picaresque* (Columbia: University of Missouri Press, 1987), xii–xiii, 70–71; Helen H. Reed, *The Reader in the Picaresque Novel*, 56; Paul Julian Smith, *Writing in the Margins: Spanish Literature of the Golden Age* (Oxford: Clarendon Press, 1988), 109. Hagiographic affiliations are discussed in Edmond Cros, *Protée et le gueux: Recherches sur les origines et la nature du récit picaresque dans Guzmán de Alfarache* (Paris: Didier, 1967), 62, 167 and Peter N. Dunn, *Spanish Picaresque Fiction: A New Literary History* (Ithaca: Cornell University Press, 1993), 41.

6. The picaresque is said to herald the European modern or "new" novel in Alter, *Rogue's Progress*, 32; F. W. Chandler, *Romances of Roguery* (London: Macmillan, 1899), 2; Helen H. Reed, *The Reader in the Picaresque Novel*, 18–19, 56; Walter L. Reed, *An Exemplary History of the Novel: The Quixotic versus the Picaresque* (Chicago: University of Chicago Press, 1981), 12–13, 24; William Riggan, *Pícaros, Madmen, Naïfs and Clowns: The Unreliable First Person Narrator* (Norman: University of Oklahoma Press, 1981), 27; V. Kozhinov, *Proiskhozhdenie romana: Teoretiko-istoricheskii ocherk* (Moskva: Sovetskii pisatel', 1963), 136–88. On Russian soil, the same contribution is recognized in Ronald D. LeBlanc, "Literary Strategy in Narezhnyj's *Rossijskij Zhilblaz*," *Russian Language Journal* 40, no. 135 (1986): 55; Iu. M. Lotman, "Puti razvitiia russkoi prosvetitel'skoi prozy XVIII veka," in *Problemy russkogo*

prosveshcheniia v literature XVIII veka (Leningrad: AN SSSR, 1961), 78; Marcia A. Morris, "Russian Variations on the Picaresque: The Narrative Short-Form," *Canadian Slavonic Papers* 34, no. 2 (March–June 1992): 57–58; V. V. Sipovskii, *Ocherki iz istorii russkogo romana*, vol. 1, no. 1 *XVIII vek* (Sankt-Peterburg: Trud, 1909), 345, 618. On the paradigmatic picaresque see Ralph Freedman, "The Possibility of a Theory of the Novel," in *The Disciplines of Criticism: Essays in Literary Theory, Interpretation and History*, ed. Peter Demetz, Thomas Greene and Lowry Nelson Jr. (New Haven: Yale University Press, 1968), 75–77; Ronald Paulson, *The Fictions of Satire* (Baltimore: Johns Hopkins Press, 1967), 70. The picaro's role as an agent of heteroglossia is examined in M. M. Bakhtin, "Slovo v romane," in *Voprosy literatury i estetiki: Issledovaniia raznykh let*, comp. S. L. Leibovich (Moskva: Khudozhestvennaia literatura, 1975), 213, 217–20.

7. The accolade, attributed to Andrei Zorin, is cited and discussed in Lipovetskii, "Apofeoz chastits," 214. "Neopicaresque" is among the "progressively crazy and disruptive forms" that literature is said to "reinvent" in its move towards "antiliterature" in Ihab Hassan, *The Postmodern Turn: Essays in Postmodern Theory and Culture* (Ohio State University Press, 1987), 17.

8. The most extensive treatment of the Gogolian connection is Smirnova, "Venedikt Erofeev glazami gogoloveda." On Gogol's debt to the picaresque see Iurii Mann, "*Mertvye dushi* Gogolia i traditsii zapadnoevropeiskogo romana," in *Slavianskie literatury: VIII Mezhdunarodnyi s"ezd slavistov, Doklady sovetskikh delegatov*, ed. M. P. Alekseev et al. (Moskva: Nauka, 1978), 235–54; I. V. Egorov, "*Mertvye dushi* i zhanr plutovskogo romana," *Izvestiia Akademii Nauk SSSR*, Seriia literatury i iazyka 37, no. 1 (1978): 322–37; T. E. Little, "Dead Souls," in *Knaves and Swindlers: Essays in the Picaresque Novel in Europe*, ed. C. J. Whitbourne (London: Oxford University Press, 1974), 112–38; Olga Markof-Belaeff, "*Dead Souls* and the Picaresque Tradition: A Study in the Definition of Genre," Ph. D. diss., University of California, Berkeley, 1982; and Karl Ludwig Selig, "Concerning Gogol's *Dead Souls* and *Lazarillo de Tormes*," *Symposium* 8 (1954): 138–40.

9. M. M. Bakhtin, "Formy vremeni i khronotopa v romane: Ocherki po istoricheskoi poetike," in *Voprosy literatury i estetiki: Issledovaniia raznykh let*, comp. S. L. Leibovich (Moskva: Khudozhestvennaia literatura, 1975), 248.

10. See Kuritsyn, "My poedem s toboiu na 'a' i na 'iu'."

11. See Clowes, *Russian Experimental Fiction*, 47.

50

12. Paperno and Gasparov, "'Vstan' i idi'," 387; Simmons, *Their Father's Voice*, 59.

13. That the trace can still be felt is evident from the misnomer "Puteshestvie iz Moskvy v Petushki," pointed out by Zorin ("Prigorodnyi poezd," 257) and used by Pomerants ("Sny zemli," 153).

14. Paperno and Gasparov, "'Vstan' i idi'," 387.

15. Kuritsyn, "My poedem s toboiu na 'a' i na 'iu'," 302.

16. Bakhtin, "Formy vremeni i khronotopa," 249, 251.

17. Ulrich Wicks, *Picaresque Narrative, Picaresque Fictions: A Theory and Research Guide* (New York: Greenwood Press, 1989), 55–56, 324–26. The genre's repetitive "labor of Sisyphus motif," Ryan-Hayes maintains, works towards the "frustration of forward moment" she discovers through a dual reading of Venichka's train ride and entrapment in the front hallway (*Contemporary Russian Satire*, 82). Frustration certainly affects the overall trajectory of *Moscow—Petushki*, particularly in the dove-tailing of its beginning and end. Between them, the pattern Ryan-Hayes points to works not only against, but also through and on the strength of that same parodoxical momentum.

18. Ginés de Pasamonte, for example, declares that his picaresque autobiography cannot be finished until his life is over (*Don Quixote* Part I, chapter 22). Cervantes' parody of this picaresque conceit has been seen to have far-reaching implications for the genre as a whole. See particularly Claudio Guillén, "Toward a Definition of the Picaresque," in *Literature as System: Essays Toward the Theory of Literary History* (Princeton: Princeton University Press, 1971), 157; and Wicks, *Picaresque Narrative, Picaresque Fictions*, 8–10.

19. Richard Bjornson discusses the circularity of the picaresque in his *Picaresque Hero in European Fiction* (Madison: University of Wisconsin Press, 1977), 64, 116–17, 186–87, 241. See also Wicks, *Picaresque Narrative, Picaresque Fictions*, 48, 213, 321–22. Dunn contrasts the up-beat, spiral movement of romance to the dead-end circle of the picaresque "anti-romance" (*Spanish Picaresque Fiction*, 68, 147, 221). In the circular structure and closure of *Moscow—Petushki*, Ryan-Hayes discerns a transcendence and parodic enhancement of picaresque linearity (*Contemporary Russian Satire*, 81–83).

20. See particularly Harry Sieber, *Language and Society in "La Vida de Lazarillo de Tormes"* (Baltimore: Johns Hopkins University Press, 1978).

21. Bakhtin, "Slovo v romane," 220.

22. Erofeev, "Nechto vrode besedy," 34.

23. Bakhtin, "Formy vremeni i khronotopa," 240.

24. *Estetika slovesnogo tvorchestva*, ed. S. G. Bocharov (Moskva: Iskusstvo, 1979), 189.

25. Bakhtin, "Formy vremeni i khronotopa," 272, 279.

26. Ibid., 272.

27. Freedman, "The Possibility of a Theory of the Novel," 75.

28. This function is attributed to the genre by Bakhtin in "Slovo v romane," 219.

29. In the passage in question, Venichka recalls first his expulsion from and only then his appointment to the post of brigade foreman (R31/E34). Among the many discussions devoted to the carnivalesque aspects of *Moscow—Petushki*, those in Gaiser-Shnitman (*Venedikt Erofeev*, 82), Ryan-Hayes (*Contemporary Russian Satire*, 83–84), Verkhovtseva-Drubchek, "*Moskva — Petushki* kak *parodia sacra*," 90, and Zhivolupova ("Palomnichestvo v Petushki," 29) deal specifically with the double reversal of both switching-places (substituting high for low) and re-ordering the switch itself (first lowering, then raising).

30. Baslyk, "Venedikt Erofeev's *Moskva — Petushki*," 29.

31. Clowes (*Russian Experimental Fiction*, 43, 48–49) notes the disintegration in Erofeev's work of the "dystopian wall," which guarantees Petushki's role as a separate, "satiric double for Moscow and Soviet society." Once corroded by the double action of meta-utopia (in terms of the present argument, a kind of playing both ends against the middle), the distinction collapses and with it, the "hope for escape" to some other side. Oleg Dark, on the other hand, insists that throughout his oeuvre Erofeev, like Solzhenitsyn, pursues a "struggle between good and evil, strictly differentiated and no less strictly 'adjudicated'" ("Mir mozhet byt' liuboi," 235).

32. Porter, *Russia's Alternative Prose*, 81.

33. Bakhtin, "Slovo v romane," 219.

34. Francisco Rico, *The Spanish Picaresque Novel and Point of View*, trans. Charles Davis with Harry Sieber (Cambridge: Cambridge University Press, 1984), 78.

35. See also Ryan-Hayes on the transposition of this canonical picaresque motif to the satirical and metaphysical realms, the latter represented by Venichka's battle against "spiritual subservience" (*Contemporary Russian Satire*, 70).

36. Aikhenval'd, "Strasti po Venediktu Erofeevu," 75; Gaiser-Shnitman, *Venedikt Erofeev*, 20–21.

37. Erofeeva, "I priroda cheshet v zatylke," 63; Erofeev, "Nechto vrode besedy," 34.

38. The analogy is noted by Paperno and Gasparov ("'Vstan' i idi'," 393), who discern in the motif of unblinking eyes and streetlights (R26/E38, R59/E72) an allusion to the line "На меня наставлен сумрак ночи / Тысячью биноклей на оси" [The darkness of the night is aimed at me / Along the sights of a thousand opera-glasses].

39. Orphanhood and "half-outsidership" are held by Guillén to be the first and most important of eight definitive features of the picaresque novel "in the strict sense." The fifth is a "general stress on the material level of existence or subsistence," which includes hunger ("Toward a Definition of the Picaresque," 75–80, 83). Ryan-Hayes treats Venichka's re-creation of picaresque orphanhood in terms of a lack of a "coherent past," his "uncertain class background" and the "more profound metaphysical" status of a "spiritual outcast" (*Contemporary Russian Satire*, 68–69). Picaresque hunger, she notes, is replaced in *Moscow—Petushki* by alcoholic thirst (70).

40. Cervantes' "Rinconete and Cortadillo" illuminates the strategem through parody. This is discussed in Wicks, *Picaresque Narrative, Picaresque Fictions*, 47–48, 293–94 and Ruth S. El Safar, *Novel to Romance: A Study in Cervantes's "Novelas ejemplares"* (Baltimore: Johns Hopkins University Press, 1974), 35–36. On Venichka's picaresque confrontations and neo-picaresque quest for companionship, see Ryan-Hayes, *Contemporary Russian Satire*, 76–77, 85–86.

41. Kuritsyn, "My poedem s toboiu na 'a' i na 'iu'," 301, 303.

42. Bakhtin, "Formy vremeni i khronotopa," 247–48, 392.

43. Bakhtin, "Roman vospitaniia," 188–90.

44. Gaiser-Shnitman, *Venedikt Erofeev*, 218.

45. Gaiser-Shnitman, *Venedikt Erofeev*, 121–23; Paperno and Gasparov, "'Vstan' i idi'," 399–400.

46. Cited from "The Swindler" in the edition *Two Spanish Picaresque Novels*, trans. Michael Alpert (London: Penguin, 1969), 107–108, 112. The link to initiation is made by Yuri K. Shcheglov, "Some Themes and Archetypes in Babel's *Red Cavalry*," *Slavic Review* 52 (Fall 1994): 664–65.

47. Fazil' Iskander, *Sandro iz Chegema* (Moskva: Moskovskii rabochii, 1989) 2: 373; V. N. Voinovich, *Zhizn' i neobychainye prikliucheniia soldata Ivana Chonkina* (Paris: YMCA-Press, 1976), 237.

48. Epshtein, "Posle karnavala," *Zolotoi vek*, 89–90; Zhivolupova, "Palomnichestvo v Petushki," 87–88.

49. Sedakova recalls: "The greatest tenderness is owed, in his opinion, and I quote, 'to someone who has wet his pants in front of everyone'" ("Gadkikh utiat liubil," 62).

Venichka's Divided Self: The Sacred and the Monstrous

Valentina Baslyk

From the late 1950s to the late 1970s the nonconformist *samizdat* writers generated a body of literature which challenged the ethos underlying the Socialist Realist's world view that reality is stable and knowable. Instead of entrusting their fictions to Olympian narrators who had mastered the laws of history,[1] thereby underscoring the stability and rational impetus of the world, the nonconformist *samizdat* writers chose a mode which suggested the opposite. Their narrators did not subscribe to the official view that "present-day reality" reflected a better world, one that combined what Katerina Clark describes as the uncombinable: verisimilitude and mythicization.[2] Nor did they ascribe to the *derevenshchiki's* guarded optimism that although Russia was on the verge of moral bankruptcy, its saintly Matrenas and Darias could teach others the right way to live.[3] Instead they handed over the reins of their fictions to narrators for whom the "real world" was so hostile and intolerable that the only way they could survive was to fragment reality in the image of their aberrant, often divided psyches.

Compare the narrators in what are arguably three seminal works of the 1970s: Eduard Limonov's *Eto ia — Edichka* [*It's Me, Eddie*], Sasha Sokolov's *Shkola dlia durakov* [*A School for Fools*], and Venedikt Erofeev's *Moscow—Petushki*. All three works feature troubled hero-narrators who dramatically subvert the positive hero of Socialist Realism: one is sexually promiscuous, the other clinically deranged, and the third an alcoholic who displays the symptoms of some profound spiritual, if not pathological malaise. Furthermore, all three narrators blur the distinctions between reality and fiction. The two confessional works whose protagonists bear diminutives of their authors' first names—Edichka and Venichka—meld their narratorial and authorial voices so radically that at times it is impossible to distinguish between them. Sokolov's schizophrenic youth and Erofeev's alcoholic create a mental landscape in which the unreal embraces the delusional and the fantastic to a point that it is difficult to discern where one ends and the other begins. Although these and other *samizdat* works attenuate the boundaries between fiction and/or fantasy and reality, the rift between the aberrant I-narrator and the other—whether it be his alter ego or society at large—prevails. While Sokolov's intricate play on author/narrator/character conflations represents a *tour de force*, it is bound by the romantic-ironic tradition it so skillfully manipulates. By contrast, in no work is the fundamental struggle between self and other more manifest or more irreconcilable than in *Moscow—Petushki*.⁴

Division Without: Self Against Society

The dissonance between self and other, as many critics have observed, is one of the central concerns of modern literature.⁵ Generally depicted as the plight of the individual in a hostile environment, this theme was brilliantly embodied by Dostoevsky in *Chelovek iz podpolia* [*Notes from Underground*]. Like his nineteenth-century forebear, the Underground Man, Venichka rejects the materialistic, deterministic world; but unlike him, Venichka does not take refuge in perversity. Nor does he harbor either malice or spite towards his fellow human beings, despite his vigorous anti-Soviet stance. He does, however, depict his fellow Russians as hostile and abusive; to be more specific, he describes them as rude, apathetic, and violent, all of which fills him with dread and repulsion (R21/E20). Yet this aggressively rude behavior is curiously offset by the impression of passivity, lethargy and indifference that emerges particulary in the well-known apostrophe to the "eyes of the people" (R27/E28). By mocking "his people's" spiritual power, Venichka also challenges the long-held and widely promoted cultural belief that Russians have a special destiny, as inheritors of the proverbial Third Rome.

Although Venichka is misanthropic, Cynthia Simmons is surely right when she observes that he "captures our sympathy far too often for him to be classified as a Dostoevskian villain who nonetheless speaks the truth."[6] The truth is that our dipsomaniac is alienated from his fellow human beings not only because of ideological differences. The more important source of Venichka's isolation lies in his own psyche: Venichka readily acknowledges that he is mentally ill.

Потому что я болен душой, но не подаю и вида. Потому что с тех пор, как помню себя, я только и делаю, что симулирую душевное здоровье, каждый миг, и на это расходую все (все без остатка) и умственные, и физические, и какие угодно силы. Вот оттого и скушен. Все, о чем вы говорите, все, что повседневно вас занимает, — мне бесконечно посторонне. Да. А о том, что *меня* занимает, — об этом никогда и никому не скажу ни слова. Может, из боязни прослыть стебанутым, может еще отчего, но все-таки — *ни слова*. [Because I am sick in my soul, though I don't look it. Because, since that time, as I remember my condition, I do nothing but simulate mental health, expending everything, without a scrap left over, all powers, mental, physical, whatever. This is what makes me boring. Everything that you speak of, everything that occupies your time, is forever alien to me. While that which occupies me, I'll not say a word about. Maybe from fear I'll be taken for crazy, maybe from something else, but—all the same—not a word.] (R39–40/E46)

This self-diagnosis precludes all but the most superficial communication with other human beings; and this is what isolates Venichka physically, emotionally, and intellectually from the world at large. In other words, characterized by an acute sense of despair, he lives in a metaphysical void.

Articulate throughout the *poema*, Venichka breaks down when he tries to explain the essence of his despair. The best he can do is confess that he lives in fear and sadness, in a state of perpetual loss akin to the sudden death of a loved one because he has seen the truth close up:

Я не утверждаю, что мне — теперь — истина уже известна или что я вплотную к ней подошел. Вовсе нет. Но я уже на такое расстояние к ней подошел, с которого ее удобнее всего рассмотреть.

И я смотрю и вижу, и поэтому скорбен. И я не верю, чтобы кто-нибудь еще из вас таскал в себе это горчайшее месиво — из чего это месиво, сказать затруднительно, да вы все равно не поймете — но больше всего в нем "скорби" и "страха". Назовем хоть так. Вот: "скорби" и "страха" больше всего, и еще немоты. И каждый день, с утра, "мое прекрасное сердце" источает этот настой и купается в нем до вечера. У других, я знаю, у других это случается, если кто-нибудь вдруг умрет, если самое необходимое существо на свете вдруг умрет. Но у меня-то ведь это вечно! — хоть это-то поймите.

[I'm not saying that now the truth is known to me, or that I've approached it close up. Not at all. But I've gotten close enough to it so that it's convenient to look it over.

And I look, and I see, and for that reason, I'm sorrowful. And I don't believe that any one of you has dragged around within himself this bitter, bitter swill. I'm in a quandary over saying what this swill is composed of, and, all the same, you would never understand, but mostly there's "sorrow" and "fear" in it. "Sorrow" and "fear" most of all and, then, muteness. And every day, the first thing in the morning, my "beautiful heart" exudes this infusion and bathes in it till night. I know this happens with others if somebody dies suddenly, if the most important being on earth dies suddenly. But with me this is an eternal condition. At least understand this.] (R40/E46–47)

Why does he describe his despair in debased terms as "bitter swill" (*mesivo*) and "this infusion" (*etot nastoi*), no doubt of an alcoholic nature, emanating from his heart? In keeping with the "lowering tendency" so hilariously evident throughout the *poema*[7] is he trying to make light of the situation? If "lowering" is the key issue here, it is lowering of a profoundly philosophical bent. Venichka's isolation and despair recall the Platonic myth of the soul aching to escape the confines of human existence and thus return to its former pure life.

Venichka's desperate sense of solitude reverberated several years later in the estranged voices of two of his fictional contemporaries: Limonov's Edichka: "я сверходинокий человек" [I'm super lonely][8] and Nikolai Bokov's protagonist in *NIKTO, Disangelie ot Marii Dementnoi* [*No One, the Digospel According to Maria the Demented*], Philipp Petatorov: "Я один. Я слаб, все бесполезно. Я уже ничего не могу. Все разошлись" [I'm alone. I'm weak, there's no point. There's nothing I can do anymore. Everyone's gone].[9]

Possessing neither Venichka's psychological complexity nor his philosophical orientation, Edichka's story nonetheless evokes our dispsomaniac's in that it focuses on the estrangement between self and society. After relocating from Moscow to New York, Edichka not only loses his status as a poet, but more importantly, his beloved wife as well. Devastated by her betrayal, he embarks on a series of sexual escapades hoping to retrieve the love he lost, but to no avail. Although he fails in his quest for love, he does recover his self-esteem, unlike Nikolai Bokov's Philipp Petatorov.

No One also explores the rift between self and society. Philipp Arkadievich Petatorov, former university professor (*docent*) and scholar, now unemployed Russian *intelligent* and modern-day nihilist, is reduced to living the life of a skid row bum. The narrative's camera eye follows Petatorov in his peregrinations through a sombre, bleak Moscow, and through the nightmarish, alcoholized landscape of his mind. Through flashback and interior monologue, we learn, in the first chapter, that Petatorov's mental and spiritual decline began four years ago when a faculty meeting revealed to him the depths of deception to which academia had sunk. This realization precipitated a crisis in the form of a mental breakdown from which he never recovered; it cost him career and family, and undermined all faith in himself, Russia and God. The narrative comes to an abrupt end with his violent, but accidental death in the basement of a condemned building. In a grisly scene, evocative of Christ's crucifixion, the protagonist generates a smile. So radical is Petatorov's alienation that in his final moments he faces death by laughing at it, and at the absurdity of life as well.

While all three protagonists are alienated from *society*, only Venichka despairs that he is not of this *world*, that he longs to be liberated from the confines of earthly existence altogether. In this respect, his spiritual isolation echoes that of the extraterrestrial, Andrei Kazimirovich, in Andrei Siniavskii's "Pkhents." After years of masquerading as a human being, the alien succumbs to despair and returns to die in the Siberian forest where his spaceship has crashed. Whereas his estrangement from humanity can be explained on one level by his alien origin, Venichka's cannot. But on another, the extraterrestrial's story has been interpreted allegorically as the desire of a superior being "to seek transcendence at any price."[10] Like Andrei Kazimirovich and the other protagonists in Siniavskii's *Fantasticheskie povesti* [*The Fantastic Tales*],[11] Venichka longs to escape earthly existence; his yearning is more metaphysical and more poignantly unsubstantiated, however, for he intuits the existence of a higher realm, one he can achieve only with the help of drink.

To sum up, in Venichka's case, the problem of self and other manifests itself in a more extreme form than in any other of the works discussed so far. Venichka is a schizophrenically divided narrator who continuously addresses the other: sometimes as an irritable self, more often than not as an imaginary audience, and occasionally as God and His angels. Venichka's drink-sodden mind also conjures up strange characters whose ontological status is even more uncertain. But the problem of his schizophrenia is compounded by his alcoholism, for the drunker he becomes, the more anxious and frenetic the discourse, the more grisly and violent the imagery. Played in so many variations throughout the *poema*, the self/other confrontation acquires yet another configuration in the work on the level of character through the Sacred/Monstrous polarity. This is an extensive and complex facet of Venichka's self, best seen in the conflict between violent agression and its gentle victim.

Division Within: Sacred vs. Monstrous

The Sacred/Monstrous dichotomy manifests itself in the I-narrator as his gentle and violent selves. The positively marked self, the principal narrative voice, is witty, lonely, faint-hearted, but above all gentle. The negatively marked self is aggressive, hostile, and delights in insulting the I-narrator with such coarse appellations as *durak,* or "fool." The relationship between the two is akin to that of a compassionate, benevolent self, or parent, tending to a demanding, yet frightened alter ego, or child. This aspect of their relationship becomes apparent in the first segment when the I-narrator, suffering from a hangover, interrupts his discourse to comfort his alter ego, who is also experiencing acute discomfort. The gentle narrator addresses his irritable double with the endearing diminutive, Ven*ichka,* and as he will do from this moment on, speaks to him silently. His thoughts on this and future occasions are enclosed in quotation marks:

> "Ничего, ничего, — *сказал я сам себе,* — ничего. Вон — аптека, видишь? А вон — этот пидор в коричневой куртке скребет тротуар. Это ты тоже видишь. Ну вот и успокойся. Все идет как следует. Если хочешь идти налево, Веничка, иди налево, я тебя не принуждаю ни к · чему. Если хочешь идти направо — иди направо."
>
> ["It's nothing," *I said to myself.* "Nothing. There's a pharmacy, see? And over there, that creep in the brown jacket scraping the sidewalk. You see that too? So calm down. Everything is going along as it should. If you want to turn left, Venichka, turn left, I'm not forcing you to do anything. If you want to turn right, turn right."] (R17/E15) (Emphasis added)

Erofeev further emphasizes the dialogic aspect of the narrator's discourse by violating verb governance: instead of observing standard usage to convey the idea of saying something to himself—*skazat' pro sebia*—he resorts to the unusual *skazal ia sam sebe.*

The other self, whose direct speech is marked not by quotation marks but by dashes, does not respond to the I-narrator on this occasion. Yet when the I-narrator suggests that he is going to Kursk

Station not to find drink but to look for company, the other self seizes the opportunity to lash out at him. Venichka's aggressive self, lusting not for company but for drink, rudely dismisses his alter ego's need for human contact:

> — Да, брось ты, — отмахнулся я сам от себя, — разве суета мне твоя нужна? люди разве твои нужны? До того ли мне теперь? Ведь вот Искупитель даже, и даже Маме своей родной, и то говорил: "Что мне до тебя?" А уж тем более мне — что мне до этих суетящихся и постылых?
>
> ["Oh, forget it." I gave myself the brush-off. "Do I really need your crowd? Are your people really necessary? Take the Redeemer even, who to his own Mother said, 'What art thou to me?' And, indeed, what do these vain and repellent creatures have to do with me?"] (R18/E16)

This negative self does more than engage in verbal hostility, however; he also displays violent tendencies as he grabs himself by the throat, and then tries to strangle himself while forcing down "a hair of the dog." This violent, caustic self may be the one who dominates the narrative when the I-narrator exhausts his supply of drink and begins hallucinating towards the end of the *poema*.

These two selves may correspond to the heart/reason polarity which manifests itself the day Venichka is fired from his job as foreman. Nursing its pride, Venichka's "beautiful heart" encourages the I-narrator to go and get drunk, despite opposition from reason. They thrash it out in grand tragic style, a là Pierre Corneille. Accordingly, the lines of battle are drawn, or so it seems, between heart and reason, duty and sentiment, and ultimately between Venichka's aggressive and gentle selves:

> Да, да, в тот день мое сердце целых полчаса боролось с рассудком. Как в трагедиях Пьера Корнеля, поэта-лауреата: долг борется с сердечным влечением. Только у меня наоборот: сердечное влечение боролось с рассудком и долгом. Сердце мне говорило: "Тебя обидели, тебя сравняли с говном. Поди, Веничка, и напейся. Встань и поди напейся как сука". Так говорило мое прекрасное сердце. А мой рассудок? А он брюзжал и упорствовал: "Ты не встанешь, Ерофеев,

ты никуда не пойдешь и ни капли не выпьешь". А сердце на это: "Ну ладно, Веничка, ладно. Много пить не надо, не надо напиваться как сука: а выпей четыреста грамм и завязывай". "Никаких грамм! — отчеканивал рассудок. — Если уж без этого нельзя, поди и выпей три кружки пива, и о граммах своих, Ерофеев, и помнить забудь". А сердце заныло: "Ну хоть двести грамм. Ну...

Реутово — Никольское

ну, хоть сто пятьдесят..." И тогда рассудок: "Ну хорошо, Веня, — сказал — хорошо, выпей сто пятьдесят, только никуда не ходи, сиди дома..."

[Yes, yes, on that day my beautiful heart struggled for a whole half hour with reason. As in the tragedies of the poet laureate Pierre Corneille, duty struggles with the heart's desire. But with me it was the reverse—the heart struggled with reason and duty. The heart said to me, "They've insulted you, they've dragged you through shit. Go on and get drunk, Venichka, go on and get drunk as a skunk." This is what my beautiful heart said. But my reason? It grumbled and insisted, "You won't get up, Erofeev, you won't go anywhere and you won't drink a drop." While my heart responded, "Well, OK, Venichka, OK. You don't have to drink a lot. You don't have to get drunk as a skunk —drink 400 grams and let it go at that." "No grams at all," reason enunciated. "If you can't get along without anything, go on and drink three mugs of beer, Erofeev, and forget about the hard stuff." But my heart whimpered, "Maybe just 200 grams. Maybe...

REUTOVO—NIKOLSKOE

..maybe just 150." And reason then: "Well, all right, Venya," it said, "all right, drink 150, only don't go out anywhere, stay home."] (R37/E42–43)

The first, under the guise of reason, forbids Venichka to drink, reversing the stance it had taken earlier; then it too agrees, as the cliché has it, to drown his sorrows in drink. (That Venichka will succumb to drink is, of course, a foregone conclusion, which adds to the humor of the situation.) Thus, while heart and reason seem to be neatly divided into his gentle and aggressive selves, that reason should yield to heart in the matter of drink suggests that one cannot compartmentalize the I-narrator's schizophrenic personality into two fixed polarities. The Sacred/Monstrous dichotomy does not always embrace the two sides of his personality described earlier because they are at odds with each other only some of the time. Like so many other distinctions in Venichka's drink-befuddled world, this too is unstable, even achingly precarious.

Venichka's schizophrenia is similar to that exhibited by Sokolov's I-narrator in *A School for Fools*, who also converses with his double. Both Sokolov's and Erofeev's schizophrenic narrators possess a dominant narrating voice which competes with a querulous alter ego. Furthermore, the language and styles of these competing voices are so similar that it is seemingly impossible to separate them. Still, for Venichka schizophrenia per se is not an issue. The I-narrator is not threatened by the other self, and therefore does not try to submerge it as does the I-narrator of *A School for Fools*.[12] *Moscow—Petushki*'s I-narrator prides himself on being "faint-hearted" and appears uninterested in subduing his aggressive self; in fact, he does everything in his power to placate and appease it lest it turn hostile. This attitude towards his truculent half recalls his bemoaning the excessive enthusiasm of his people; once again discretion, or in Venichka's parlance, "chicken-heartedness," is the better part of valor. The I-narrator seems unaware of the fact that there is anything unusual about hearing voices, or talking to God. Just as the issue of alienation in Erofeev's handling becomes far broader and far more poignant than the testimony of his contemporaries, here too Venichka's concerns, it seems, are more metaphysical than psychopathological in nature.

Both *Moscow—Petushki* and *A School for Fools* share another trait dependent on their schizophrenic narrators—character doublings, which in both cases has been explained by the narrator's desire to create a reality that reflects his divided self.[13] In Sokolov's novel, all the principal characters bear dual names, if not identities—Pavel Petrovich/Savl Petrovich, Trakhtenberg/Tinbergen, Nikolaev Semen/Semen Nikolaev. The nature of their interactions is also dual, fluctuating between the real and the imagined. In the same spirit, Erofeev's narrator conveniently "creates" doubles on the train with whom to engage in drunken dialogue, and they just as conveniently disappear at the onset of his nightmares. Furthermore, the system of character-doublings in *Moscow—Petushki* is not as obscure as that in *A School for Fools* because the narrator belabors the obvious point that his fellow passengers are indeed doubles. Such overt signalling relieves the reader of the burden he or she bears in interpreting *A School for Fools,* where the doubling is primarily psychological in nature and therefore more difficult to ascertain. Erofeev's conspicuous doubling is evident, for example, in the obvious designation *dvoe* applied to the first pair of twinned characters he encounters on board the suburban train:

Я взглянул направо: там все до сих пор сидят эти двое, тупой-тупой и умный-умный. Тупой в телегрейке уже давно закосел и спит. А умный в коверкотовом пальто сидит напротив тупого и будит его.
[I glance to the right—the same pair is still sitting there, Stupid-Stupid and Smart-Smart. The stupid one in the quilt jacket has long since gotten tipsy and fallen asleep. The smart one in the worsted overcoat is sitting opposite him, trying to wake him up.] (R59/E73)

As if to drive home the point, *dvoe* [the two of them] is then reinforced by echolalia in the double-barrelled epithets *tupoi-tupoi* [Stupid-Stupid] and *umnyi-umnyi* [Smart-Smart].[14] The second pair is introduced first collectively via, once again, *dvoe* and, then, generically as *on* [he] and *ona* [she], and like the first couple, is not identified by name:

Очень странные люди эти двое: он и она. Они сидят по разным сторонам вагона, у противоположных окон, и явно незнакомы друг с другом. Но при всем том — до странности похожи: он в жакетке, и она — в жакетке; он в коричневом берете и при усах, и она — при усах и в коричневом берете...
[Very strange, this man and woman. They are sitting on different sides of the car at opposite windows and obviously are not acquainted. But for all that, they look amazingly similar—he is wearing a jacket and

64

she is wearing a jacket; he has a brown beret and a black moustache, she has a brown beret and a black moustache.] (R60/E74)

Two more devices highlight the stark nature of the doubling maneuver here: the anonymity of the pair and the coyly "strange" (*do strannosti*) coincidence of dress and facial features.

The final couple consists of a feeble-minded grandfather and an equally feeble-minded grandson. Note once again the tell-tale use of the marker *dvoe*, the banal (because automatic) association of "grandfather" and "grandson," and the teasingly trivial distinction in height instantly cancelled out by the coincidence of mental deficiency:

> И впереди то же самое — странных только двое, дедушка и внучек. Внучек на две головы длиннее дедушки и от рождения слабоумен. Дедушка — на две головы короче, но слабоумен тоже...Оба глядят мне прямо в глаза и облизываются...
>
> [Ahead, another strange pair: a grandfather and his grandson. The grandson is two heads taller than his grandfather and feebleminded probably from birth. The grandfather is two heads shorter but feebleminded, too. Both look me straight in the eye and lick their lips.] (R60/E74)

By fixating on such heavily underscored variations of the number two, the narrator is clearly drawing the reader's attention to the fact that these characters are indeed doubles of each other, if not physical manifestations of his Monstrous self.

Each of these doubles is depicted as either physically and/or mentally aberrant, recalling the impression that Venichka himself leaves with the reader. In his drunken stupor, he constructs a world of doubles which mirrors that part of his fragmented personality prone to violence against the self. The grotesque appearance of the idiot grandson reveals a deformity of the throat, echoing the earlier image of Venichka's self-strangulation of Othello and Desdemona, and foreshadowing, of course, the piercing blow of the awl at the novel's end:

> Нет, внучек — совершенный кретин. У него и шея-то не как у всех, у него шея не врастает в торс, а как-то вырастает из него, вздымаясь к затылку вместе с ключицами.
>
> [No, the grandson is a complete cretin. Even his neck is abnormal; it doesn't grow into his torso, it grows out of it, rising toward the back of his head together with the collarbones.] (R60/E74)[15]

The grandfather's face embodies death and reflects Venichka's subconscious fear that his own is imminent. Every detail of the grandfather's appearance is transformed by a simile to suggest an aspect of death, whether it be something as abstract as fear or as concrete as drowned corpses with rheumy eyes, as the bullet-riddled head of the victim of a firing squad, as a mangled nose resembling a suicide hanging from a noose:

> А дедушка — тот смотрит еще напряженнее, смотрит, как в дуло орудия. И такими синими, такими разбухшими глазами, что из обоих этих глаз, как из двух утопленников, влага течет ему прямо на сапоги. И весь он как приговоренный к высшей мере, и на лысой голове его мертво. И вся физиономия — в оспинах, как расстрелянная в упор. А посередке расстрелянной физии — распухший и посиневший нос, висит и качается, как старый удавленник...
>
> [But the grandfather—he looked at me even more intensely, as if into the muzzle of a gun. And with such blue swollen eyes that from both of these eyes moisture flowed—as from two drowned men—straight into his boots. And he was like a man condemned to be shot, with a deathly pallor on his bald head. And his whole physiognomy was pockmarked as if he had been shot point-blank. In the middle of his shot face dangled a swollen, bluish nose that swayed like a victim of hanging.] (R60–61/E74–75)

Each of the twinned characters partakes, however obliquely, in the ominous atmosphere of impending or implied violence. *On* [he] and *ona* [she], as seen above, bear the Kafkaesque imprint of almost identical appearances. Like Venichka's alter ego, *on*, also known as *cherno-usy* [black moustache], advocates drinking to cure society's ills, regardless of the consequences. *Ona* as the victim—the woman who was assaulted by her poet-boyfriend to the point of losing several teeth—symbolizes Venichka's fear of being attacked. Even Smart-Smart is prone to violence as he almost skins Stupid-Stupid alive, after attempting to wake him up from his drunken stupor:

И как-то по-живодерски будит: берет его за пуговицу и до отказа подтаскивает к себе, как бы натягивая тетиву, — а потом отпускает: и тупой-тупой в телегрейке летит на прежнее место, вонзаясь в спинку лавочки, как в сердце тупая стрела Амура...

[He is going about it as if he were trying to skin the stupid one alive: he takes him by a button and jerks him as far as he can toward himself, as if drawing a bowstring, and then lets him go. And Stupid-Stupid flies back and buries himself into the back of the bench like Cupid's dull arrow into the heart.] (R59–60/E73)

Outlandish as this scene may be, an act of aggression constitutes its essence. And the imagery of an arrow piercing the heart prefigures Venichka's violent death—an awl will pierce his throat. The narrator is clearly creating a world of aberrant and violent doubles, who, while repulsive, are nonetheless perversely funny. Because these doubles appear when Venichka is drunk, the reader cannot be sure if they have not been induced by a surfeit of alcohol. In fact, some critics suggest that these "pairings" are a figment of Venichka's drunken imagination.[16]

Another way in which the narrator blurs the distinction between his doubled self and his doubled characters is to deprive the latter of names. By addressing them synecdochically, he divests them of a real identity, and by varying their synecdochic markers, he makes it difficult to determine who is speaking. For example, the narrator first refers to the idiot as *tupoi-tupoi* but then he alters the designation to *tupoi v telegreike* [the stupid one in a quilt jacket]. In a similar manner, his twin's designation changes from *umnyi-umnyi* to *umnyi v koverkotovom pal'to* [the smart one in a quilt jacket]. Then he inexplicably becomes a *dekabrist* [Decembrist]. To add to the confusion, the second pair, *on* and *ona*, are also identified by the jackets they are wearing. Each member of the third pair does not even merit an individual designation as the narrator sometimes refers to them as a single entity: *slaboumen, dedushka, vnuchek* [feebleminded, grandfather, grandson] and *Mitrich staryi, Mitrich molodoi* [old Mitrich, young Mitrich]. Although the feeble-minded grandfather and his idiot grandson are actually designated by a patronymic, their shared name erases their individuality, mocking the distinctions between Venichka and his fellow passengers or between Venichka and the various facets of his troubled self. Because of his deeply fragmented personality, Venickhka, it appears, can neither personalize nor bestow upon his Monstrous doubles any kind of stability.

Not only does Venichka engage in dialogue with himself, he also addresses the reader, often making it difficult to ascertain just whom he is addressing as the following section illustrates:

Давайте лучше так — давайте почтим минутой молчания два этих смертных часа. Помни, Веничка, об этих часах. В самые восторженные, в самые искрометные дни своей жизни — помни о них. В минуты блаженств и упоений — не забывай о них. Это не должно повториться. Я обращаюсь ко всем родным и близким, ко всем людям доброй воли, я обращаюсь ко всем, чье сердце открыто для поэзии и сострадания:

"Оставьте ваши занятия. Остановитесь вместе со мной, и почтим минутой молчания то, что невыразимо. Если есть у вас под рукой какой-нибудь завалящий гудок — нажмите на этот гудок".

Так. Я тоже останавливаюсь.

[Instead, let's do this: let's honor those two deadly hours with a minute of silence. Remember those two hours, Venichka. In the most ecstatic, in the most sparkling days of your life, remember them. They should not be repeated. I turn to all who are kindred, to all people of good will, I turn to all whose hearts are open to poetry and fellow feelings:

"Leave what you're doing. Stop together with me and honor with a minute of silence that which is inexpressible. If you've got any kind of an old noisemaker, whistle, or horn handy, let's hear it."

So, I also stop.] (R22–23/E22)

The passage begins with the plural inclusive imperative, suggesting that the I-narrator is addressing his reader, but then in the second and third sentences he clearly turns to his alter ego—Venichka—as he addresses him by name. In the fourth and last sentence of this paragraph, however, he clearly enlarges his audience by turning to humanity at large, at least to those who fall under the three categories he lists: near ones and dear ones, all people of good will, and the open-hearted. Thus, in the confines of the first quoted paragraph, the I-narrator appears to be addressing three different interlocutors, which intimates that he suffers from an inability to focus for even the shortest period of time on a single audience.[17]

A linguistic feature underscoring the fragmented nature of his consciousness obtains in the narrator's liberal use of negations. The *poema* is rife with negated parts of speech, which are often repeated in the space of a single paragraph.

Хорошая люстра. Но уж слишком тяжелая. Если она сейчас сорвется и упадет кому-нибудь на голову, — будет страшно больно... Да *нет*, наверное, даже и *не* больно: пока она срывается и летит, ты сидишь и *ничего не* подозревая пьешь, например, херес. А как она до тебя долетела — тебя уже *нет* в живых. Тяжелая это мысль:... ты сидишь, а не тебя сверху — люстра. Очень тяжелая мысль...

[It was a good chandelier. But really too heavy. If it should break away and fall on someone's head, it'd be terribly painful. Well, *no*, probably *not* even painful. While it's tearing away and falling, you're sitting, *not* suspecting a thing—drinking sherry, for instance. But as soon as it hits you, you're *not* alive. A weighty thought, that... you're sitting there and a chandelier falls from above. A very weighty thought.] (R21/E19) (Emphasis added)

On the one hand, the negations highlight the dialectical, the questing nature of our protagonist's discourse, but on the other, they accentuate his cynical, perhaps nihilistic, philosophical stance. Some things, he seems to be implying, are simply beyond human cognition. Erofeev's highly idiosyncratic use of narrative voice accords with the contemporary context of Russian nonconformist prose in the 1970s, for it transposes instability to the level of narration.

The themes of alienation, fragmentation, and disintegration, so prevalent in the years of stagnation, as we saw above, are writ large in Bokov's nihilistic *No One* and Aksenov's chaotic *Ozhog* [*The Burn*].

Although each chapter of *No One* focuses on the disintegrating psyche of its protagonist, Petatorov, his mental instability is most readily evident in the first and most cohesive chapter, if only because it (the chapter in question) focuses primarily on Petatorov himself. The reader quickly discerns through a flashback that Petatorov was almost institutionalized after his mental breakdown several years ago. But the most incriminating evidence of his mental instability is the staccato rhythms of shifts in the point of view, in a series of abrupt switches from external (third-person, omniscient) to internal (quasi-direct discourse in the third-, or first-, and sometimes second-person). The skittering focus of a schizophrenic is seen in such passages as:

Подкладку пальто Петаторов весной отпорол, и квартирная хозяйка сшила ему новые брюки. Сукно на рукавах источилось, местами до полного отсутствия. Засаленный пиджак под пальто не грел вовсе.

Я, кажется, очень опустился. Летом встретил на Арбате знакомого и отвернулся, терпеть их всех не могу, и услышал, как сказали в спину сострадальчески: «Как он опустился!»

Неужели я выглядел хоть когда-нибудь иначе!..

Им всем главное в жизни «выглядеть». «Как он опустился!» Хе! А вы поднялись, что ли! Соколики! Коршуны! В поднебесье парите!

[In the spring, Petatorov had ripped out the lining of the coat, and his landlady made him a pair of pants. The sleeves had worn thin, in places the fabric had disappeared altogether. The soiled jacket under his coat didn't keep him warm at all.

I, it seems, have let myself go. Last summer I had met an acquaintance on the Arbat and turned away from him, can't stand any of them, and heard them saying behind my back, "He's really let himself go!"

Have I ever looked any different ?

Looking good is very important to them. "He's really let himself go!" Ha! And did you ever climb the ladder of success! Falcons! Vultures! You're soaring in the heavens!][18]

Like a camera, the narrative zooms in and out of the narrator and/or protagonist's mind, exposing a fragile, disintegrating psyche. Petatorov, whose name is derived from *petarda* ("petard" or "firecracker"), appears to be a walking time bomb, ready to discharge at any moment. The sudden shifting from an external to an internal point of view also has a structural function: it disrupts narrative syntax, retards the forward momentum of the narrative by disorienting the reader, and arrests temporal progression by changing tenses from the narrated past (third-person) to the experiencing present (first-person).

As the narrative progresses and Petatorov's hold on reality diminishes, the chapters become more and more disconnected. Segments, scenes, and episodes within chapters become more perfunctory or are ignored altogether. The number of loosely juxtaposed episodes increases from chapter to chapter. The jagged movement from scene to scene is underscored by the visual elements of the work. This graphic aspect is fully exploited by the incremental use of disjunct elements such as sentences with no punctuation (reminiscent of the style used in telegrams), phrases alternating between Latin and English, lines of incomprehensible Chinese-like hieroglyphs in lieu of obscenities, short poems, excerpts from the

Bible, lengthy sentences in large type, and onomatopoeic allusions to gunfire, moaning and howling. These jarring visible devices expand the novella's spatial perspective and thereby help to create a vivid portrait of a demented, disintegrating psyche, against a background of morally crippled and spiritually dead Russians.

Aksenov's *The Burn*, which depicts the plight of the Russian intelligentsia during the stagnation of the Brezhnev years, is driven by a similarly fractured perception of the world. Points of view shift abruptly from third- to first-person, with frequent authorial interpolations. But perhaps the most confusing aspect of the novel is the multiple embodiments of the main character. Recall, for example, the principal protagonist, Tolia von Steinbok's five incarnations, all sharing the patronymic Apollinarievich: the writer Pantelei Apollinarievich Pantelei, the researcher and heart surgeon, Gennadii Apollinarievich Malkolmov, the research physicist Aristarkh Apollinarievich Kunitser, the saxophonist Samson Apollinarievich Sabler, and the sculptor Radii Apollinarievich Khvastishchev. Not only does the reader have to keep track of who is speaking (any one of these characters may assume, without warning, the role of the I-narrator), but he or she also has to deal with several other incarnations, not to mention a plethora of minor characters. Chaos, at least upon a first reading, reigns supreme.[19]

By comparison with the fragmented and multiple perspectives of *No One* and *The Burn*, Erofeev's work appears tame indeed, for one may argue that it revolves exclusively around the consciousness of a single I-narrator; *Moscow—Petushki* replaces panoramic breadth with a more circumscribed space. As the *poema* unfolds, it moves slowly inward, penetrating deeper and deeper into Venichka's complex and fragmented consciousness. In *Moscow—Petushki* the reader is continuously putting fragments of Venichka's portrait together as he or she grapples with a bifurcated structure and discourse laden with ambiguity.

Division Above All: God and His Angels

If the physical world as represented by Venichka's abusive fellow Russians and his aberrant doubles falls under the rubric of the

Monstrous, God and His angels should ideally embody the Sacred.

An alcoholic for whom drink is a means of transcending a painful empirical reality, Venichka, more specifically his gentle self, fights the addiction that should deliver him to paradise. "Не в радость обратятся тебе эти тринадцать глотков" [These thirteen swallows will bring you no joy] (R38/E44). But to no avail, for Venichka ultimately defers to a divinity who endorses his addiction to alcohol or who at least embodies the spiritual aspirations it fuels. In this respect Venichka's relationship with his Heavenly Father resembles the parent/child paradigm, which, as we saw above, characterizes the relationship between his two selves. The aggressive self, who may also be the voice of reason, is fully cognizant of the ill effects of spirits, and while he tries to dissuade his alter ego from indulging this passion, he always capitulates to his other. God, as Venichka's spiritual father, goes one step further: He actually encourages and justifies Venichka's drinking. The Heavenly Father generates but one utterance in the *poema,* and it comes at a crucial moment just before Venichka has his first drink. Reluctant to take the first swallow, Venichka turns to the Lord in an accusatory tone and asks Him if this is what he needs; he replies: "— А для чего нужны стигматы святой Терезе? Они ведь ей тоже не нужны. Но они ей желанны" [So what did St. Teresa need her stigmata for? It, too, was unnecessary, yet she desired it] (R26/E27).

By comparing Venichka's drinking to St. Teresa's stigmata, God is suggesting, on the one hand, that drink is a scourge Venichka has to endure just as St. Teresa endured her stigmata because suffering is the price one must pay to be a martyr for Christ. In other words, he is underscoring the concept of *imitatio Christi*: mimicking the suffering of Christ brings the sufferer closer to the Divine. On the other hand, God is implying that Venichka drinks, that is, suffers, by choice because it is something he desires. The implication here is that God, while validating Venichka's monstrous habit, declines to take responsibility for it.[20] A God who in ungodly fashion teases the supplicant is a strange divinity indeed. Furthermore, this God speaks not from a burning bush of the Old Testament, but from a slightly ominous halo of blue lightning. As Gaiser-Shnitman points out, this reference might possibly be to the blue flame of pure alcohol (incidentally, a common test in a country deluged by counterfeit moonshine).[21] This ambiguous divinity, if not specifically identified with "the demon drink," certainly leads Venichka here into temptation.

The angels also reflect the Sacred/Monstous dichotomy but in a radical and subversive manner. They clearly serve as an extension of Venichka's compassionate and gentle self, at least in the initial stages of his journey. The angels first evince their kindness shortly after Venichka's hostile self has "given himself the brush-off" (*otmakhnulsia ia sam ot sebia*) (R18/E16). Just as God will later rationalize Venichka's drinking at a strategic moment, the angels appear at the right place and at the right time to give him the information he desperately needs early in the morning: where to procure that vital first drink of the day (R19/E17).

"Тяжело мне..."

"*Да мы знает, что тяжело*, пропели ангелы. — *А ты походи, походи, легче будет, а через полчаса магазин откроется: водка там с девяти, правда, а красненького сразу дадут...*

"Красенького?"

"*Красенького*," — нараспев повторили ангелы Господни.

["It's tough for me."

"*Yes, we know that it's tough*," the angels sang out. "*But get moving, you'll feel better, and the stores will be open in half an hour—no vodka until nine, it's true, but they'll have a little red wine the first thing.*"

"Red wine?"

"*A little red wine*," the angels of God chorused.] (R18–19/E16)

By supplying this information the angels perform the ultimate act of kindness. In dire need of compassion, no less than drink, Venichka certainly appreciates their gentle demeanor, for he underscores it by doubling the adverbs of manner: *I oni tak tikho-tikho propeli* [They sang ever so softly-softly] and *A potom tak laskovo-laskovo* [And then ever so gently-gently]. And then to highlight their goodness, he proffers his opinion: *Kakie oni milye!..* [They're so nice!] (R19/E17). (As seen from the excerpt above the discourse of the angels is enclosed in quotation marks and printed in italics.) The narrator, therefore, has endowed the angels with the very traits he exhibits himself as he tends to his alter ego's demand for alcohol.

While the angels symbolize the Sacred in Venichka, they would not be an extension of his divided self if they did not also embody the Monstrous—the violence he perpetrates against himself. Although he abhors rudeness and aggression in others, Venichka is nonetheless guilty of violent conduct towards the self. Not only does he attempt to strangle himself, but he also abuses his body with drink. Even the trysts with his Beloved in his alternate reality are marked by "тот же хмель и то же душегубство" [intoxication and slaughter] (R47/E56).

That angels should be present at the end of his fateful journey is comforting, for throughout Venichka's journey they have been associated with his beloved, but sickly three-year-old.[22] In fact, it is because of their concern for the welfare of Venichka's three-year-old in the second segment that the reader learns of the child's existence: "Это ангелы мне напомнили о гостинцах, потому что те, для кого они куплены, сами напоминают ангелов" [It was the angels who reminded me about the goodies, because I bought them for the ones who are themselves like angels] (R19/E17). But that in the closing episodes of this work they should laugh demonically as he flees his persecutors is at best astonishing because one does not expect God's messengers, courted as unequivocal symbols of gentleness and compassion, suddenly to switch allegiances and align themselves with the forces of evil:

И ангелы — засмеялись. Вы знаете, как смеются ангелы? И они обещали встретить меня, и не встретили, и вот теперь засмеялись, — вы знаете, как они смеются? Это позорные твари, теперь я знаю — вам сказать, как они сейчас засмеялись? Когда-то, очень давно, в Лобне, у вокзала, зарезало поездом человека, и непостижимо зарезало: всю его нижнюю половину измололо в мелкие дребезги и расшвыряло по полотну, а верхняя половина, от пояса, осталась как

бы живою, и стояла у рельсов, как стоят на постаментах бюсты разной сволочи. Поезд ушел, а он, эта половина, так и остался стоять, и на лице у него была какая-то озадаченность, и рот полуоткрыт.

[And the angels burst out laughing. Do you know how angels laugh? And they had promised to meet me, and didn't, and now they burst out laughing. Do you know how angels laugh? They are shameful creatures...should I tell you how they burst out laughing just now? A long time ago, in Lobnia—at the station—a man was cut up by a train, cut up in an unbelievable way: his whole lower half was crushed to smithereens and scattered over the road bed, but his upper half from the belt up remained as if alive, and stood by the tracks, the way busts of various pigs stand on pedestals. The train pulled away but he—that half of him—remained standing there, and on his face there was a sort of perplexity and his mouth half open.] (R121/E162–63)

The reader is confronted with a violent conundrum. The angels' vicious laughter in the last segment of the *poema* is problematic because it is so blatantly demonic. While the reader may puzzle over the ambiguous ending of *Moscow—Petushki*—does the I-narrator die a physical or a symbolic death? why does God remain silent?— and may eventually seek comfort in this ambiguity, the angels' laughter leaves no such loophole. Instead it is compared to the mockery of monstrous children at the spectacle of human suffering, a body cleaved in two. Their vicious laughter (after all, Lucifer was once the best among them) shocks the reader into appreciating the full horror of Venichka's alcoholized existence—the physical, psychological, and spiritual tolls exacted by a life of "intoxication and slaughter." This passage, the last in which the angels appear, graphically illustrates the degree to which alcohol has carved into our hapless dipsomaniac's body and psyche. Clearly identifying with the perplexed victim of the railroad accident whose body was mangled and riven in two, Venichka acknowledges that he also has been physically and psychologically mutilated. The grotesque image of a halved body underscores the degree to which his psyche has yielded to nightmare and hallucination, for even his beloved angels —God's messengers—have betrayed him. It may also reflect the violence inherent in and, ultimately, the futility of seeking spiritual transcendence through alcohol.

Moscow—Petushki surely emerges as the most strident work of its decade in its rejection of the realist's view that the world is deterministic, preeminently rational, and possessed of a stable unity. Erofeev leads his contemporaries in his pessimistic assessment of the human spirit. Not only does the I-narrator have to cope with hostility and aggression in the world at large, but throughout the course of his narrative he confronts as well the knowledge that these deadly impulses dwell within his very soul. Such is the effect of the Sacred/Monstrous polarity: a lethal internalization of violence in the world at large.

Endnotes

1. In his excellent study of Socialist Realism, Geoffrey Hosking describes the narrator of the Socialist Realist novel in the following manner: "The narrator is an Olympian figure, who understands completely the laws of history, and knows where each character fits into them and where he is going; he has, moreover, a privileged right of entry into the hearts and minds of each one of them, so that he can analyse as well as judge them." See Geoffrey Hosking, *Beyond Socialist Realism: Soviet Fiction Since Ivan Denisovich* (New York: Holmes and Meier, 1980), 19.

2. Katerina Clark, *The Soviet Novel: History as Ritual* (Chicago: University of Chicago Press, 1981), 35.

3. I am referring, of course, to the aged heroines of Village Prose, namely Matrena in Solzhenitsyn's *Matrenin dvor* [*Matrena's Home*] and Daria in Rasputin's *Proshchanie s Materoi* [*Farewell to Matera*].

4. In *Their Father's Voice*, Cynthia Simmons argues that of the following works—*Ozhog* [*The Burn*], *Moscow—Petushki*, *It's Me, Eddy*, and *A School for Fools*—Sokolov's novel is the most textually aberrant "with regards to the specific metafunctions of discourse"(4–5).

5. For an analysis of this theme in Russian literature, see Brown, *Russian Literature Since the Revolution*. "The individual person in his confrontation with social reality and social demand" (4) is one of the ways Brown articulates the theme of his book. For different approaches to this issue in the context of the grotesque see Wolfgang Kayser, *The Grotesque in Art and Literature*, trans. Ulrich Weisstein (Gloucester, MA: P. Smith, 1968); Bernard McElroy, *Fiction of the Modern Grotesque*

(New York: St. Martin's Press, 1989). In his introduction, McElroy states that grotesque fiction "is concerned mostly with the same issues as non-grotesque modern literature." He describes them in the following manner: "Man is usually presented as living in a vast, indifferent, meaningless universe in which his actions are without significance beyond his own, limited, personal sphere. The physical world of his immediate surroundings is alien and hostile, directing its energies to overwhelming the individual, denying him a place and identity even remotely commensurate with his needs, aspirations, surrounding him on every side with violence and brutalisation, offering him values that have lost their credibility, manipulating and dehumanising him through vast, faceless institutions, the most ominous of which are science, technology, and the socio-economic organisation" (17).

6. Simmons, "An Alcoholic Narrative as 'Time Out'," 159.

7. See Paperno and Gasparov, "'Vstan' i idi'," 389 and Zorin, "Prigorodnyi poezd," 257–58.

8. Eduard Limonov, *Eto ia — Edichka* (New York: Index Publishers, 1979), 53.

9. *NIKTO, Disangelie ot Marii Dementnoi, Grani*, no. 82 (December 1971): 34. Hereafter this work will be designated *No One*. Although this work was published anonymously, Josephine Woll lists its author as Nikolai Bokov. See Woll, *Soviet Dissident Literature*, 21.

10. Andrew Durkin, "Narrator, Metaphor, and Theme in Sinjavskij's *Fantastic Tales*," *Slavic and East European Journal* 24 (Summer 1980): 135.

11. This collection was published under Siniavskii's pseudonym, Abram Terts.

12. About the impossibility of neat, stable distinctions between the two halves of Sokolov's narrating schizophrenic, see Fred Moody, "Madness and the Pattern of Freedom in Sasha Sokolov's *A School for Fools*," *Russian Literature Triquarterly* 16 (1979): 11.

13. See D. Barton Johnson, "A Structural Analysis of Sasha Sokolov's *School for Fools*: A Paradigmatic Novel," in *Fiction and Drama in Eastern and Southeastern Europe*, ed. Henrick Birnbaum and Thomas Eckman (Columbus: Slavica, 1980), 207–37; Moody, "Madness and the Pattern of Freedom," 13; Paperno and Gasparov "'Vstan' i idi'," 396.

14. For a different interpretation of these epithets, see Simmons, "An Alcoholic Narrative as 'Time Out'." Simmons divides Venichka's doubles into two categories: those that "symbolize the narrator's escape from repression from banality and those that represent his quest for God, knowledge, or the self" (164).

15. In the *Teatr* memoirs several of Erofeev's acquaintances stress the "real life" Erofeev's characteristic gesture of covering his throat. See Frolova et al., "Neskol'ko monologov," 74–116, 119–22.

16. Paperno and Gasparov, "'Vstan' i idi'," 397; Simmons, "An Alcoholic Narrative as 'Time Out'," 164.

17. To add to the confusion, it sometimes becomes difficult, if not impossible, to determine just who is speaking: his double or his audience: "Я заходил по тамбуру в страшном волнении и все курил, курил... — И ты говоришь после этого, что ты одинок и непонят? Ты, у которого столько в душе и столько за душой!" [I paced around in the vestibule, smoking the whole time. "And you say that you're lonely and misunderstood? You who have so much in your soul and beyond it?"] (R48/E57). On the one hand, only the gentler self would suffer from solitude and misunderstanding; on the other hand—only the more aggressive half would turn stoic suffering into a truculent complaint.

18. Bokov, *NIKTO*, 3–4.

19. For an excellent, albeit brief, analysis of this work's fragmented structure, see G. S. Smith, "Vasilii Aksenov's *Ozhog*," *Radio Liberty Research*, 5 November 1981, 1–7.

20. What is curious about God's single utterance in *Moscow—Petushki* is that it is not conveyed in italics as are the utterances of the angels and the various references to Venichka's quest for godhood.

21. Gaiser-Shnitman, *Venedikt Erofeev*, 62.

22. Paperno and Gasparov associate the angels with death. See their article "'Vstan' i idi'," 400.

С потусторонней точки зрения: постмодернистская версия диалогизма

> *Позиция его, причудливая или просто*
> *чуднáя — как он говорил: "с моей*
> *потусторонней точки зрения" —*
> *глубоко последовательна.*
>
> Ольга Седакова
> *Из воспоминаний о Вен. Ерофееве*

О карнавальности поэмы Венедикта Ерофеева *Москва —
Петушки* сказано более чем достаточно. И действительно,
близость поэмы к "пиршественной традиции," к кощунственным
травестиям, сплетающим сакральные образы с мотивами
"телесного низа," к "серьезно-смеховым" спорам по последним
вопросам бытия и т.д., и т.п. — буквально бросается в глаза.
Однако показательно, что все критики, писавшие о ерофеевской
карнавализации, вынуждены были оговариваться насчет
специфической, нетрадиционной, *семантики* этих традиционных
форм в *Москве — Петушках*. Так, Светлана Гайсер-Шнитман,
указывая на связь поэмы с "памятью жанра" мениппеи, вместе с
тем отмечает, что не меньшую роль в поэтике поэмы играют
семантические структуры далеко не карнавальных жанров, типа
духовных странствий, стихотворений в прозе, баллад, мистерий.[1]
Андрей Зорин, ссылаясь на неприятие Бахтиным финала
восхитившей его поэмы Ерофеева (в нем, финале, ученый "видел
'энтропию'"), утверждает, что в *Москве — Петушках* "стихия

народного смеха в конце концов обманывает и исторгает героя...Карнавальному единству героя и народа...состояться не суждено."² А Михаил Эпштейн доказывает, что "у Вени ценности, раньше карнавально перевернутые, стали опять медленно переворачиваться...Но это уже и не сам карнавал, а его послебытие: все прежние свойства, опрокинутые карнавалом, теперь восстанавливаются в каком-то новом, 'ноуменальном' измерении...карнавал сам становится объектом карнавала, выводящим к новой области серьезного."³

Литературоведам неожиданно вторят авторы воспоминаний о Венедикте Ерофееве, неизменно подчеркивающие глубочайшую, программную, серьезность, пронизывавшую жизнь, условно говоря, "кабацкого ярыжки". "У Венички было ощущение, что благополучная, обыденная жизнь — это подмена настоящей жизни, он разрушал ее, и это разрушительство отчасти действительно имело религиозный оттенок" (Владимир Муравьев); "Наверное, так нельзя говорить, но я думаю, что он подражал Христу" (Галина Ерофеева); "Веничка прожил на краю жизни. И дело не в последней его болезни, не в обычных для пьющего человека опасностях, а в образе жизни, даже в образе внутренней жизни — 'ввиду конца'...Чувствовалось, что этот образ жизни — не тривиальное пьянство, а какая-то служба. Служба кабаку?" (Ольга Седакова).⁴

Приведенные суждения позволяют высказать гипотезу о парадоксальной серьезной и даже трагедийной карнавальности поэмы (и, по-видимому, всей жизненной философии) Ерофеева, осуществленной в рамках диалогической поэтики в целом. Можно также предположить, что такая трансформация связана с общей логикой постмодернистского диалога с хаосом, заставляющей художника отождествлять сам процесс творчества с созиданием заведомо фиктивных симулякров и даже со смертью. Однако сила воздействия *Москвы — Петушков* на все последующее развитие русского постмодернизма и современной русской литературы ("Венедикт Ерофеев стал признанным классиком русской литературы," — констатирует Андрей Зорин⁵) наводит на мысль о том, что этот писатель не просто оформил имплицитную постмодернистскую парадигму художественности, но и, придав ей глубоко оригинальное звучание, ввел ее в контекст русской культурной традиции. Как ему это удалось? Каков эстетический механизм этих трансформаций? Каков художественно-философский смысл этого синтеза (если он действительно состоялся)?

Попытаемся ответить на эти вопросы, сконцентрировав внимание прежде всего на семантике диалогизма ерофеевской поэмы.

Структура

Первая, наиболее очевидная, черта ерофеевского диалогизма — это, вероятно, стилистическая амбивалентность. Речь идет не только о "фамильяризации высокого стиля, неожиданных и комических мезальянсах."[6] Речь, скорее, следует вести о глубоко своеобразных сближениях высоких и низких стилистических пластов, при которых происходит подлинная встреча абсолютно несовместных смыслов. Характерный пример:

> А потом (слушайте), а потом, когда они узнали, отчего умер Пушкин, я дал им почитать "Соловьиный сад", поэму Александра Блока. Там, в центре поэмы, если, конечно, отбросить в сторону все эти благоуханные плеча и неозаренные туманы и розовые башни в дымных ризах, там в центре поэмы лирический персонаж, уволенный с работы за пьянку, блядки и прогулы. Я сказал им: "Очень своевременная книга, — сказал, — вы прочтете ее с большой пользой для себя". Что ж? они прочли. Но, вопреки всему, она на них сказалась удручающе: во всех магазинах враз пропала вся "Свежесть". Непонятно почему, но сика была забыта, вермут был забыт, международный аэропорт Шереметьево был забыт, — и восторжествовала "Свежесть", все пили только "Свежесть"!
> О беззаботность! О птицы небесные, не собирающие в житницы! О краше Соломона одетые полевые лилии! — Они выпили всю "Свежесть" от станции "Долгопрудный" до международного аэропорта Шереметьево! (33)

Стилистическую траекторию этого фрагмента можно представить в виде нисходящей параболы. В начале, в иронической интерпретации, воссоздается высокий поэтический стиль ("благоуханные плеча и неозаренные туманы и розовые башни в дымных ризах"), который затем резко снижается, во-первых, в вульгарное просторечие ("пьянку, блядки и прогулы") и, во-вторых, в пародию на расхожую ленинскую цитату ("Очень своевременная книга"). Но финальная часть фрагмента представляет собой возвышающее возвращение в поэтическую тональность, причем, название одеколона "Свежесть" ассоциативно рифмуется с "Соловьиным садом" ("восторжествовала 'Свежесть'") и вписано в библейский стилистический контекст ("О краше Соломона одетые полевые лилии..."). Здесь высокое снижается не дискредитации ради, а для обретения иной формы существования в "низовых" смыслах. Иначе говоря, высокое и низкое в стиле Ерофеева не разрушают, не отменяют друг друга, а образуют амбивалентное смысловое единство. Собственно, на таком диалогическом пересечении высоких и низких смыслов построены все наиболее яркие в стилевом отношении моменты поэмы: от знаменитых слов о плевках на каждую ступеньку общественной лестницы до главы о коктейлях, от описаний "белобрысой дьяволицы" до исследования икоты.

Этот же принцип определяет и логику построения образа культуры в поэме Ерофеева. Многочисленные культурные цитаты в тексте *Москвы — Петушков* подробно описаны Б. М. Гаспаровым и И. А. Паперно, Ю. И. Левиным, С. Гайсер-Шнитман, М. Г. Альтшуллером.[7] Обобщая сделанные этими исследователями наблюдения, можно отметить, что и тут не происходит однозначного снижения традиционных тем культуры. Даже в травестийном рассказе про неразделенную любовь к арфистке Ольге Эрдели — притом, что в роли арфистки в конце концов выступает рублевая "бабонька, не то, чтоб очень старая, но уже пьяная-пьяная" (73) — реализуется высокая тема воскресения через любовь, возникающая несколькими страницами ранее в рассказе Венички о собственном воскресении. А комический перечень писателей и композиторов, пьющих во имя творчества и из любви к народу, среди которых только "тайный советник Гете не пил ни грамма" (67), оборачивается формой авторской исповеди, подготавливающей трагический финал поэмы: "Он [Гете] остался жить, но *как бы* покончил с собой, и был вполне удовлетворен. Это даже хуже прямого самоубийства..." (67); не случайно в следующей главе черноусый скажет о самом Веничке: "у вас — все не как у людей, все, как у Гете!.." (69). Наиболее явно этот тип отношений с культурой проступает в том, как актуализируются в *Москве — Петушках* евангельские мотивы. И. А. Паперно и Б. М. Гаспаров, первыми проанализировавшие евангельский прасюжет поэмы, отмечают:

> Каждое событие существует одновременно в двух планах. Похмелье интерпретируется как казнь, смерть, распятие. Опохмеление — воскресение. После воскресения начинается жизнь — постепенное опьянение, приводящее в конце концов к новой казни. Герой прямо говорит об этом в конце повести: «Ибо жизнь человеческая не есть ли минутное окосение души?» Однако такая трактовка бытовых событий, в свою очередь оказывает обратное воздействие на евангельские мотивы в повести. Последние нередко обретают оттенок пародии, шутки, каламбура: высокое и трагическое неразрывно сплетается с комическим и непристойным. Кроме того, такое наложение сообщает евангельскому тексту циклический характер: одна и та же цепь событий повторяется снова и снова...Обратный, по сравнению с евангельским, порядок событий указывает на замкнутый круг, по которому они движутся.[8]

Важно отметить, что одни параллели с Новым Заветом предстают нарочито смещенными. Так, например, не Веничка-Иисус воскрешает Лазаря, а напротив самого Веничку воскрешает блудница — "плохая баба": "двенадцать недель тому назад: я был во гробе, я уж четыре года лежал во гробе, так что уже и смердеть перестал. А ей говорят: «Вот — он во гробе. И воскреси, если сможешь»" (71); а упоминание о звезде Вифлеема возникает только непосредственно перед последним распятием. Тогда как другие евангельские цитаты поражают своей скрупулезной точностью. Так, четверо убийц "с налетом чего-то классического" соотносимы с четверкой палачей из Евангелия: "Воины же, когда распяли Иисуса, взяли одежды его и разделили на четыре части, каждому воину по части..." (Иоан.,19:23). И — "как тогда была пятница" (Иоан., 19:31).

В данном случае можно говорить о сознательном комбинировании принципов цитатной точности и цитатного смещения. Образ культуры, создаваемый таким путем, сам попадает в зону "неготового контакта" с текущей, "низовой," реальностью: он оказывается одновременно каноническим и все еще *незавершенным*. Образ культуры лишается ореола эпического предания и становится объектом радикальной *романизации*. Собственно, того же эффекта средствами иронической рефлексии добивался и Битов в *Пушкинском доме*. Как и у Битова, у Ерофеева это, с одной стороны, приводит к релятивизации образа культуры, он лишается абсолютного значения, проблематизируется. Но оригинальность *Москвы — Петушков* видится в том, что здесь есть и другая сторона того же процесса: сам "низовой," полностью "внекультурный" контекст оказывается местом *непредсказуемого* свершения вечных культурных сюжетов. Забегая вперед, отметим, что непредсказуемость реализации евангельской линии проявляется прежде всего в том, что последнее распятие нового Иисуса не сопровождается воскресением: "...и с тех пор я не приходил в сознание, и никогда не приду" (122). Вот почему не только высокое и торжественное обязательно резко снижается Ерофеевым, но и наоборот: травестия неизбежно выводит к трагической серьезности.

Но стержневым воплощением диалогической амбивалентности становится центральная фигура поэмы — сам Веничка Ерофеев, одновременно и центральный герой, и повествователь, и двойник автора-творца. Последнее обстоятельство подчеркнуто полным тождеством имени писателя с именем персонажа, а также множеством автобиографических сигналов, типа указания места, где была написана поэма ("На кабельных работах в Шереметьево — Лобня") в прямом соседстве с описанием этих самых кабельных работ в истории недолгого бригадирства Венички (главы "Кусково — Новогиреево," "Новогиреево — Реутово"). Это удивительно цельный характер. Это внутренне оксюморонная цельность — в ее основе лежит культурный архетип *юродства*. Связь Венички Ерофеева с традицией русского юродства отмечалась С. Гайсер-Шнитман, М. Эпштейном. А вот что пишет об этом Ольга Седакова:

среди множества играющих контрастов *Петушков* есть самый глубокий контраст: эстетикой безобразия окружена совсем иная этика. Назвать ее этикой благообразия было бы слишком, но, во всяком случае, о каком-то странном, может быть, потустороннем благообразии можно говорить. Не для красного словца Веничка (имя героя, не автора) сообщает о своем целомудрии, о расширении сферы интимного, и стихи Песни Песен появляются в сцене пьяной "любви". Звезда Вифлеема над икотой и блевотиной (и доказательство бытия Божия на примере икоты...), искушение на крыше храма, перенесенное в тамбур электрички, и множество других библейских тем явно в малоудобном применении — не простое кощунство. Такое соседство не так странно для тех, кто читал, например, жития юродивых.[9]

С этой точки зрения раскрываются многие загадки ерофеевской поэмы. Да, и сама загадочность, парадоксальность поэмы соответствует эстетике юродства, в которой "парадоксальность выполняет функцию эстетической доминанты."[10] Так, например, проясняется *художественный* смысл пьянства главного героя. Питие Венички, описанное с таким тщанием и такими подробностями — это типичный символический жест "мудрейшего юродства," призванного обновить вечные истины с помощью кричащих парадоксов поведения. Это присущее юродивому "самоизвольное мученичество" — вроде бы и не нужное, но желанное, как упоминаемые в поэме "стигматы святой Терезы": "И весь в синих молниях, Господь мне ответил: — А для чего нужны стигматы святой Терезе? Они ведь ей тоже не нужны. Но они ей желанны. — Вот-вот!— отвечал я в восторге. — Вот и мне, и мне тоже — желанно мне это, но ничуть не нужно! 'Ну, раз желанно, Веничка, так и пей...'" (25–26). В то же время в пьянстве Венички проступают черты "священного безумия" юродивого, безумия, позволяющего напрямую и фамильярно беседовать с ангелами и даже обращаться к Господу с приглашением на выпивку (*Раздели со мной трапезу, Господи!* [26]). Именно в силу этих причин пьянство с таким постоянством описывается Ерофеевым в терминах религиозных, "божественных." "Что мне выпить во Имя

Твое?" (54) — вопрошает Веничка, и рядом с этим вопросом логично смотрятся и феерические рецепты коктейлей (не случайно многие из них носят библейские названия "Ханаанский бальзам," "Иорданские струи," "Звезда Вифлеема"), и сам *ритуал* их приготовления, в котором крайне важно, например, что "Слезу комсомолки" должно помешивать веткой жимолости, но ни в коем случае не повиликой; и тот сугубо *духовный* результат, который эти коктейли вызывают: "Уже после двух бокалов этого коктейля человек становится настолько одухотворенным, что можно подойти и целых полчаса, с расстояния полутора метров, плевать ему в харю, и он ничего тебе не скажет" (58). Примечательно, кстати, что обретенная "одухотворенность" сродни гиперболизированной кротости юродивого. А разве не вписываются в этот же ряд ангелы, уговаривающие Веничку не допивать бутылку, или сосед по вагону, произносящий после каждой дозы спиртного: "'Транс-цен-ден-тально!'" (27)? Характерно также, что, по наблюдениям А. М. Панченко, тяготы и страдания древнерусского юродивого содержат в себе непрямое напоминание о муках Спасителя,[11] что объясняет, почему так настойчивы параллели между Веничкиным путешествием и Евангелием. Да и сам сюжет путешествия соответствует традиции юродивого "скитания 'меж двор'." Не должна в данном случае смущать и "греховность" многих Веничкиных поступков и деклараций, ведь даже любовь к блуднице находит соответствия в житиях юродивых: "Осии повелел [Бог] пояти жену блужения и паки возлюбить жену любящую зло и любодеицу."[12]

Важно, что с не меньшим постоянством процесс пития окружен в поэме ассоциациями артистическими. Не зря, например, почти с фольклорной обязательностью повторяется одна и та же метафора: пил, "запрокинув голову, как пианист, и с сознанием величия того, что еще только начинается и чему еще предстоит быть" (38, см. также 45, 63). И дело не только в том, что юродство "есть своего рода форма, своего рода эстетизм, но как бы с обратным знаком."[13] Другое объяснение может быть связано с принципиальной театральностью, зрелищностью юродивого поведения[14] — на эту версию работают и многочисленные театральные метафоры поэмы, например: "Может, я там [то есть в тамбуре] что репетировал?...Может, я играл бессмертную драму 'Отелло, мавр венецианский'? Играл в одиночку и сразу во всех ролях?" (27). Но главное: таким образом "юродивая" позиция экстраполируется на процесс творчества. Не случайно в поэме сам процесс странствия описывается в литературоведческой терминологии: "Черт знает, в каком жанре я доеду до Петушков... От самой Москвы все были философские эссе и мемуары, все были стихотворения в прозе, как у Ивана Тургенева...Теперь начинается детективная повесть" (59). Полное совпадение имени персонажа с именем биографического автора делает такую экстраполяцию еще более зримой.

"Отзвуки идеи тождества царя и изгоя есть и в древнерусском юродстве," — пишет А. М. Панченко.[15] Это также один из ведущих мотивов поэмы. Он опять-таки отражен в соответствиях между запойным персонажем и всевластным, "надтекстовым," автором-творцом. Но не только. Веничка, вспоминая свое бригадирство, говорит о себе как о "маленьком принце" (33), собутыльники, возмущенные Веничкиным "безграничным расширением сферы интимного," то есть его отказом публично отправляться до ветру, говорят: "Брось считать, что ты выше других...что мы мелкая сошка, а ты Каин и Манфред..." (28); знаменитость Венички выражается в том, что он "за всю свою жизнь ни разу не пукнул..." (30). Это, казалось бы, типичные формы наоборотного, карнавального возвеличивания. Но рядом — постоянно звучат интонации, исполненные подлинно царского достоинства: "О эфемерность! О, самое бессильное и позорное время в жизни моего народа" (18); "все вы, рассеянные по моей земле" (24); "Мне нравится, что у народа моей страны глаза такие пустые и выпуклые...Мне нравится мой народ" (26-27).

Еще отчетливей ответственность Венички за *свой народ* (мы еще вернемся к другим коннотациям этого постоянно звучащего оборота) звучит в его постоянных проповедях и пророчествах. Это опять-таки парадоксальные, юродивые проповеди и пророчества. О том, что "Все на свете должно происходить медленно и неправильно, чтобы не сумел загордиться человек, чтобы человек был грустен и растерян" (17), о "всеобщем малодушии" как "предикате высочайшего совершенства" (21–22), о том, что "надо чтить, повторяю, потемки чужой души, надо смотреть в них, пусть даже там и нет ничего, пусть там дрянь одна — все равно: смотри и чти, смотри и не плюй..." (74), о том, что "Жалость и любовь к миру — едины" (75) и о том, как свершится день "избраннейший всех дней" (87). Общий смысл этих проповедей — глубоко диалогический. Так, ненависть к идее подвига и героизма (вообще характерная для Ерофеева[16]) вполне понятна именно в диалогическом контексте: праведник всецело завершен и закончен; он самодостаточен и поэтому абсолютно закрыт для диалогических отношений. Между тем греховность и малодушие, слабость и растерянность — это, как ни странно, залог открытости для понимания и жалости, первый признак незавершенности и готовности изменяться.

Обращает на себя внимание совпадение этой философии с концепцией Зигмунда Баумана о "случайности как судьбе." Речь, напомним, идет о том, что лежащий в основе постмодернистской ситуации кризис идей Единого Закона и Абсолютной Истины порождает принципиально новую жизненную стратегию. Приятие алогической случайностности существования как единственно возможной судьбы не только выступает в качестве главного условия внутренней свободы личности, но и порождает особого рода дискомфорт: "Жить в случайности значит жить без всяких гарантий, лишь с временной, прагматической, Пирровой уверенностью в чем бы то ни было... [ср. с Ерофеевским: "все должно идти медленно и неправильно" - М.Л.] Сознание случайности не вооружает своего носителя преимуществами протагониста в борьбе воль и целеустремлений, как впрочем, и в игре хитрости и удачи. Оно не ведет к доминированию и не поддерживает доминирования. Как будто для равновесия оно также не помогает и в борьбе против доминирования. Оно, если огрубить, безразлично к настоящим или будущим структурам силы и доминирования."[17] Эта философия свободы в беззаконной случайности мироустройства, свободы через слабость, свободы без гарантий, свободы, обрекающей на страдание — в высшей степени близка герою *Москвы — Петушков*, она и определяет смысл его юродства.[18]   Диалогизм же оказывается прямым выражением, практическим следствием этой свободы.

С "юродивой" точки зрения понятно, почему поэма Ерофеева не укладывается в рамки карнавально-праздничной смеховой культуры. Все дело в том, что юродивый балансирует на грани между смешным и серьезным, олицетворяя собой *"трагический вариант смехового мира"* (по определению А. М. Панченко).[19] Характерно, что и сам Веничка, называя себя дураком, блаженным (традиционные синонимы юродства) мотивирует эти самоопределения прежде всего "мировой скорбью" и "неутешным горем":

> ...я болен душой, но не подаю и вида. Потому что с тех пор, как помню себя, я только и делаю, что симулирую душевное здоровье, каждый миг, и на это расходую все (все без остатка) и умственные, и физические, и какие угодно силы. Вот оттого и скушен...
>
> Я не утверждаю, что мне — теперь — истина уже известна или что я вплотную к ней подошел. Вовсе нет. Но я уже на такое расстояние к ней подошел, с которого ее удобнее всего рассмотреть.
>
> И я смотрю и вижу, и поэтому скорбен. И я не верю, чтобы кто-нибудь еще из вас таскал в себе это горчайшее месиво — из чего это месиво, сказать затруднительно, да вы все равно не поймете — но больше всего в нем "скорби" и "страха". Назовем хоть так. Вот: "скорби" и "страха" больше всего и еще немоты. (39–40)

Средневековое юродство, как и античный кинизм, были для своих эпох чем-то вроде постмодернизма. "Жизнь юродивого, как и жизнь киника, — это сознательное отрицание красоты, опровержение общепринятого идеала прекрасного, точнее, перестановка его с ног на голову..." — обобщает А. М. Панченко.[20] Речь, собственно, идет о том, что юродивый, как и писатель-постмодернист, вступает в диалог с хаосом, стремясь среди грязи и похабства найти истину. "'Благодать почиет на худшем,' — вот что имеет в виду юродивый."[21] Не случайно модель юродивого сознания приобрела такое значение у Даниила Хармса, одного из самых радикальных предшественников русского постмодернизма. Этим типологическим родством стратегий, вероятно, объясняется тяготение Вен. Ерофеева и позднейших постмодернистов (имею в виду прежде всего Сашу Соколова и Евг. Попова) к культурному архетипу юродства.

Однако в случае с поэмой Ерофеева сказались и иные, а именно: историко-литературные факторы.

М. О. Чудакова писала по поводу булгаковского *Мастера и Маргариты*: "Сопротивление социальному уничижению личного, единичного, 'штучного,' выдающегося над однородностью, привело к тому, что герой (подчеркнуто сближенный, как было сказано, с автором) оказался приравнен ни более ни менее, как к Христу, а его уход оставлял возможности истолкования 'явления героя' как оставшегося неузнанным Второго пришествия. Это повторится потом в *Докторе Живаго*...Само собой ясно, что далее двигаться по этому пути было уже некуда. Назревала смена героя романа и смена цикла."[22] Вен. Ерофеев в своем герое, юродивом дублере Христа, одновременно и завершает эту великую традицию и разворачивает ее на 180 градусов. В *Москве — Петушках* тоже реализован мотив неузнанного Второго пришествия и нового распятия. Однако многоуровневая амбивалентность поэтики *Петушков* переводит эти мотивы в совершенно иное измерение: возникает новая парадигма, в которой высокое повторение пути Христа и пародия, травестия, снижающая Евангелие в сюрреальный быт русского алкоголика, *сливаются* воедино. Представить себе такую комбинацию у Булгакова или Пастернака — невозможно: для них евангельские контексты важны как хранители вечных и абсолютных ценностей. Для Ерофеева — и здесь существо разворота традиции — и евангельский сюжет становится предметом мениппейного "испытания идеи," и он тоже принципиально релятивен, текуч, лишен устойчивого ценностного смысла. Таким образом, поэма Ерофеева становится переходным мостиком от духовного учительства русской, преимущественно, реалистической классики XIX и XX веков (ориентация Булгакова на Гоголя, а Пастернака на Толстого общеизвестны) к безудержной игре постмодернизма. Позиция же юродивого, с одной стороны, как нельзя лучше соединяет в себе оба берега — нравственную проповедь и игровую свободу, а с другой —

возрождает оборвавшуюся на Хармсе традицию русского юродства, в свою очередь восходящую к Розанову, Ремизову, Лескову, Достоевскому, древнерусской классике.

Семантика

Макрообраз хаоса в поэме формируется как система из нескольких семантических ареалов. Во-первых, это все, что связано с "народной жизнью" — а именно, мотивы дна, пьянки, образы попутчиков Венички и т.д. Символическим концентратом этого ряда мотивов становится описание глаз народа в главе "Карачарово — Чухлинка" (в несколько перифразированном варианте оно повторится в главе "43-й километр — Храпуново"):

> Зато у моего народа — какие глаза! Они постоянно навыкате, но — никакого напряжения в них. Полное отсутствие всякого смысла — но зато какая мощь! (Какая духовная мощь!) Эти глаза не продадут. Ничего не продадут и ничего не купят. Что бы ни случилось с моей страной, во дни сомнений, во дни тягостных раздумий, в годину любых испытаний и бедствий, — эти глаза не сморгнут. Им все божья роса... (27)

В этом описании одна полуфраза фактически аннигилирует другую, и семантически, и стилистически. Нарисованное в этом и аналогичных фрагментах лицо народа оказывается зеркальным отражением *лица хаоса*: ничего не выражающего, и в то же время без связи, логики и смысла выражающего все что угодно. Определение "мой народ" здесь выступает не только как форма дистанции царя-юродивого от подданных, но еще в большей мере — как форма причастности. Последнее акцентируется Ерофеевым: "Мне нравится мой народ. Я счастлив, что родился и возмужал под взглядами этих глаз" (27); "Теперь, после пятисот кубанской, я был влюблен в эти глаза, влюблен, как безумец" (59). Именно на условиях "нераздельности и неслиянности" протекает диалог Венички с народным ликом хаоса. Показательно стремление Венички систематизировать, рационально упорядочить сам процесс выпивки.[23] Прямое порождение этой тактики — "пресловутые 'индивидуальные графики,'" которые Веничка вел, будучи бригадиром, или уже упомянутые рецепты коктейлей, комически сочетающие математическую точность и фантастичность ингредиентов. "Душу каждого мудака я теперь рассматривал со вниманием, пристально и в упор" (35), — вспоминает Веничка свое бригадирство. Но точно так же он рассматривает и свою душу, и на самого себя составляя "индивидуальный график" ("биение гордого сердца, песня о буревестнике и девятый вал" [35]), философски и экспериментально анализирует, почему "с первой дозы по пятую включительно я мужаю, то есть мужаю неодолимо, а вот уж начиная с шестой ... и включительно по девятую, — размягчаюсь. Настолько размягчаюсь, что от десятой смежаю глаза, так же неодолимо" (50). В последнем случае Веничка идет по иному пути внутренней гармонизации сугубого безобразия — это путь эстетических аналогий. Так, решение дозы спиртного от шестой до девятой *выпить сразу, одним махом* — но выпить *идеально*, то есть выпить только в воображении"(51) уподобляется симфониям Антонина Дворжака. А, например, во время вагонного симпосиона, где каждый рассказывает историю о любви ("как у Тургенева"), в каждой из этих историй иронически просвечивает культурный подтекст (история о воскресении у Черноусого; вагнеровский Лоэнгрин у Митрича; некий метасюжет русской классики, включающий Пушкина, Анну Каренину и Лизу Калитину, у "женщины трудной судьбы"), причем этот подтекст, как правило, серьезно усиливается Веничкой: "А я сидел и понимал старого Митрича, понимал его слезы: ему просто все и всех было жалко... Первая любовь или последняя жалость — какая разница?" (75).

Другой уровень хаоса — социально-политический — образован стереотипами советского официоза и советской ментальности в целом. И опять-таки эти стереотипы не только пародийно снижаются Веничкой. Он использует этот безобразный язык для собственных импровизаций о путешествиях по белу свету ("Игрушки идеологов монополий, марионетки пушечных королей — откуда у них такой аппетит?" [79]). Более того, не то сон, не то воспоминание Венички о Черкасовской революции (главы "Орехово-Зуево — Крутое," "Воиново —

Усад") свидетельствует о кратком, пародийном, и все же восприятии Веничкой логики исторического абсурда. По крайней мере, вся хроника Черкассовской революции со штурмами и декретами выглядит как травестированная копия Октября.

Но в поэме реализован еще один, возможно, важнейший уровень мирообраза Хаоса — *метафизический*. Он манифестирован прежде всего хронотопической структурой поэмы. Наиболее зримо формула мироздания *Петушков* воплощена в траектории пьяных блужданий Венички: как известно, направляясь к Кремлю, он неизменно оказывается на Курском вокзале, откуда уходит поезд в Петушки; однако реальная дорога в Петушки приводит Веничку к Кремлю, где он и находит свою страшную погибель. И если Петушки — это в полном смысле райская обитель ("Петушки — это место, где не умолкают птицы, ни днем, ни ночью, где ни зимой, ни летом не отцветает жасмин. Первородный грех, — может, он и был, — там никого не тяготит" [37]), то Кремль — противоположный полюс пространства поэмы, по верному истолкованию В. Курицына, вызывает прямую ассоциацию с адом.[24] Поэтому причудливость Веничкиных траекторий имеет вполне отчетливый метафизический смысл: любопытствующий об аде, здесь попадает в рай, устремленный к раю оказывается в аду.

Это логика зазеркалья, это пространство заколдованного, порочного круга. Только в этой, метафизически искаженной реальности могут возникать пространственно-временные образы такого типа: "Не то пять минут, не то семь минут, не то целую вечность — так и метался в четырех стенах, ухватив себя за горло, и умолял Бога моего не обижать меня" (26); "Наше завтра светлее, чем наше вчера и наше сегодня. Но кто поручится, что наше послезавтра не будет хуже нашего позавчера" (39), "Молодому тоже подали стакан — он радостно прижал его к левому соску правым бедром, и из обеих ноздрей его хлынули слезы..." (68). А на обратном, скорбном, пути из Петушков в Москву окончательно исчезает пространство, его заменяет абсолютный мрак за окном электрички, исчезает и время: "Да зачем тебе время, Веничка?...Был у тебя когда-то небесный рай, узнавал бы время в прошлую пятницу — а теперь небесного рая больше нет, зачем тебе время?" (116).

Совершенно очевидно, что этот, метафизический, лик хаоса не вызывает у Венички ничего похожего на упоение. Тут скорее онтологической ужас. Но при этом Веничка не отшатывается от абсурда мироустройства, он и его пробует *заговорить*.

Наиболее четко программа этого, метафизического, диалога выражена в рассуждении об икоте в главе "33-й километр — Электроугли." Пьяная икота предстает как чистый случай неупорядоченности и, соответственно, как модель жизни человека и человечества: "Не так ли в смене подъемов и падений, восторгов и бед каждого отдельного человека — нет ни малейшего намека на регулярность? Не так ли беспорядочно чередуются в жизни человечества его катастрофы? Закон — он выше всех нас. Икота — выше всякого закона" (54). Далее, икота уравнивается с Божьей Десницей, причем переход от икоты к Богу нарочито сглажен стилистически:

> ...*она* [икота] неисследима, а мы — беспомощны. Мы начисто лишены всякой свободы воли, мы во власти произвола, которому нет имени и спасения от которого — тоже нет.
> Мы — дрожащие твари, а *она* — всесильна. *Она*, то есть Божья Десница, которая над всеми нами занесена и пред которой не хотят склонить головы одни кретины и проходимцы. *Он* непостижим уму, а следовательно, *Он* есть." (54)

Иными словами, символ хаоса приобретает значение недоступной человеку высшей, Божьей, логики. И это примиряет с хаосом. Больше того, *вера* в то, что внутри хаоса запрятан Высший смысл придает Веничке силы и становится источником его личной *эпифании* (здесь это слово, произнесенное Джойсом по поводу *Улисса*, представляется как нельзя более уместным):

> Верящий в предопределение и ни о каком противоборстве не помышляющий, я верю в то, что Он благ, и сам я поэтому благ и светел.
> Он благ. Он ведет меня от страданий — к свету. От Москвы — к Петушкам. Через муки на Курском вокзале, через очищение в Кучино, через грезы в Купавне — к свету в Петушках. (54)

Осуществляется ли эта программа? Каковы последствия диалога с хаосом, в первую очередь, с хаосом метафизическим? Ответом на этот вопрос становится финальная часть поэмы, где, как и в начале, когда Веничка беседовал с ангелами и Богом, собеседниками Венички выступают "послы вечности," персонажи мифологические и легендарные.

В этой, финальной, части поэмы внутреннее напряжение действия держится на противоречии между все более иллюзорной линейностью движения (ведь и главы по-прежнему обозначаются названиями станций, лежащих на пути из Москвы в Петушки) и той стремительностью, с которой сворачивается в кольцо реальное пространство текста (финал этого процесса в главке, сводящей в одну точку оба конца Веничкиного маршрута: "Петушки. Садовое кольцо"). Эта метаморфоза проявляется не только в том, что электричка идет обратной дорогой, все ближе к Москве, но и в том, как симметрично прокручиваются здесь все важнейшие мотивы первой части:

— воспоминание о женщине и о младенце, "уже умеющем букву 'Ю'";

— мотив "Неутешного горя";

— христианские цитаты и перифразы (от отречения Петра до "лама савахвани");

— темы Гете и Шиллера;

— текстуально повторяются или незначительно перефразируются такие важные словесные формулы, как: "О эфемерность! О тщета! О, гнуснейшее, позорнейшее время в жизни моего народа!" (115); "Талифа куми, как сказала твоя Царица, когда ты лежал во гробе" (115); "'Почему же ты молчишь?' — спросит меня Господь весь в синих молниях" (116 — ср.: "И весь в синих молниях, Господь мне ответил...*Господь молчал*" [25–26]).

Докучающие Веничке в этой части явные посланцы хаоса: Эринии, Сатана, Сфинкс, понтийский царь Митридат с ножиком, скульптура "Рабочий и колхозница," четверка убийц — придают кольцеобразной структуре совершенно определенный смысл. Веничкины попытки организовать хаос изнутри проваливаются.

Посланцы хаоса убивают Веничку — без надежды на воскресение. Дурная бесконечность одолевает линию человеческой жизни.

На фоне этих повторов особенно заметны *смещения* образов Бога и ангелов, происходящие в этой части поэмы. Добрые ангелы не только уподобляются здесь злым детям, глумливо, дьявольски смеющимся над страшной смертью человека: "И ангелы — засмеялись...Это позорные твари, теперь я знаю — вам сказать, как они сейчас засмеялись?...Они смеялись, а Бог молчал" (121). Показательно, что в поэме это происходит после Веничкиного моления о Чаше ("Весь сотрясаясь, я сказал себе: 'Талифа куми!'...Это уже не 'талифа куми', то есть 'встань и приготовься к кончине', — это 'лама савахвани', то есть 'для чего, Господь, ты меня оставил?'" [121]), тогда как в Евангелие после моления о Чаше "явился же к Ему Ангел с небес и укреплял Его" (Лук., 22:43). Так что и в молчании Господа в этом эпизоде слышится безмолвное согласие с убийцами. Изменяется и Веничкино отношение к хаосу. Если еще в главе "Усад — 105-й километр" он произносит: "остается один выход: принять эту тьму" (99), — то в главе "Петушки. Вокзальная площадь" исход видится иначе: "И если я когда-нибудь умру — а я очень скоро умру, я знаю — умру, так и не приняв этого мира, постигнув его вблизи и издали, снаружи и изнутри постигнув, но не приняв" (115).

Почему же терпит поражение Веничкин диалог с хаосом? Почему его смерть окончательна и бесповоротна?

Первая и важнейшая причина связана с юродивой "нераздельностью и неслиянности" Венички по отношению к окружающему его хаосу. Дело в том, что Веничка *сбивается*, вычисляя запрятанную внутри хаоса логику. Он не может не сбиться, ибо такова расплата за "священное безумие," за вовлеченность в пьяный абсурд. Таков неизбежный результат диалогического *взаимодействия* с хаосом, а не монологического воздействия на него: диалог требует вовлеченности. Даже надежные числа оказываются на поверку двусмысленными. Не случайно сон, из-за которого Веничка пропускает рай Петушков, сваливает его после заведомо опасной шестой дозы спиртного. Действие поэмы происходит в пятницу во время тринадцатой поездки Венички в Петушки. В. Курицын интерпретирует "тринадцатую пятницу" как символ буйства дьявольских сил. Е. А. Смирнова видит здесь напоминание о 13-м нисана по древнееврейскому календарю, когда был предан, а затем и распят Иисус.[25] Но не менее важно в этом контексте и то, что 13 — это вообще число Христа, ведь он тринадцатый апостол. Иными словами: одно и то же число — для Венички существенный инструмент поиска прочности внутри хаоса — обладает и дьявольским, и божественным смыслом.

Виновен ли Веничка в том, что Хаос оказался сильнее его? Если да, то это чистый случай *трагической вины*. Причина поражения Венички не в его ошибке — ошибка, наоборот, результат правильности избранного пути. Вся художественная конструкция поэмы и прежде всего образные соответствия/смещения между первой (до Петушков) и второй (после) частями поэмы внятно свидетельствуют о том, что *буквально все, проникнутое божественным смыслом, оказывается в равной мере причастно к хаосу*. Действительно, евангельский сюжет свершается вновь. Но свершается *неправильно*. Нового Христа предает не Иуда (характерно, что даже упоминание об Иуде отсутствует в поэме, не говоря уж о каких бы то ни было персонажных соответствиях) — но Бог и ангелы. Иначе говоря, *запечатленные в этом вечном сюжете духовные ценности не выдерживают мениппейного испытания атмосферой тотальной амбивалентности*. Карнавальность, по Бахтину, воплощает "веселую относительность бытия." У Ерофеева эта же веселая относительность мироустройства переживается как *объективный* источник трагедии. Ведь даже эмблема самого чистого и светлого персонажа поэмы — младенца, сына Венички — превращается в финале поэмы в огненный знак смерти, кровавый символ абсурда: "Густая красная буква 'Ю' распласталась у меня в глазах, задрожала, и с тех пор я не приходил в сознание, и никогда не приду" (122).

Этот финал создает парадоксальную ситуацию: неоднократно подчеркиваемое тождество героя и автора-творца делает "смерть автора" буквально свершившимся эстетическим событием поэмы. Более того, нельзя не увидеть в этой концовке продолжение экспериментов русской метапрозы 1920–30х годов, ведь ретроспективно этот финал производит неожиданный эффект: получается, что перед нами исповедь человека, находящегося по ту сторону жизни, написанная буквально с "потусторонней точки зрения." Однако у Ерофеева "смерть автора" приобретает чрезвычайно важное семантическое наполнение. По сути дела, эта позиция становится той трагической ценностью, которая противопоставляет Веничку и его двойника-автора сплошь релятивному миру вокруг него. Ибо в этой реальности смерть оказывается единственно возможной *прочной, недвусмысленной* категорией. И взгляд из смерти обладает единственно возможной — трагической — подлинностью. В финале читатель получает возможность как бы заново воспринять и всю поэму, поняв ее парадоксы и прежде всего саму установку на диалог с хаосом как следствие обретенной автором-творцом и оплаченную ценой гибели героя "потусторонней точки зрения." Эта точка зрения и создает проявляющуюся лишь "постфактум," после финала, необходимую для поэмы дистанцию — "из прекрасного далека" — которая в полной мере оправдывает жанровое обозначение *Москвы — Петушков*.

Примечания

1. Гайсер-Шнитман, *Венедикт Ерофеев*, 257–65.
2. Зорин, "Опознавательный знак," 121.
3. Эпштейн, "После карнавала," *Золотой век*, 88–90.
4. Все цитаты из мемуаров о Ерофееве приводятся по публикации Фроловой и др., "Несколько монологов," 90, 89, 98.
5. Зорин, "Опознавательный знак," 119.
6. Гайсер-Шнитман, *Венедикт Ерофеев*, 257.
7. См.: Паперно и Гаспаров, "'Встань и иди'," 387–400; Левин, "Классические традиции в другой литературе," 45–50; Гайсер-Шнитман, *Венедикт Ерофеев*; Альтшуллер, "*Москва — Петушки* Венедикта Ерофеева," 142.
8. Паперно и Гаспаров, "'Встань и иди'," 389–90.
9. Седакова, "Несказанная речь," 264.
10. Д. С. Лихачев, А. М. Панченко, Н. В. Понырко, *Смех в Древней Руси* (Ленинград: Наука, 1984), 104.
11. Там же, 114.
12. Там же, 85.
13. М. М. Бахтин, *Проблемы поэтики Достоевского* (Москва:

Художественная литература, 1972), 397.

14. О зрелищности юродства см.: Лихачев, Панченко, Понырко, *Смех в Древней Руси*, 81–116.

15. Там же, 139.

16. Об этом вспоминает Ольга Седакова: "Еще непонятнее мне была другая сторона этого гуманизма: ненависть к героям и к подвигам. Чемпионом этой ненависти стала у него несчастная Зоя Космодемьянская...Он часто говорил не только о простительности, но о нормальности и даже похвальности малодушия, о том, что человек не должен быть испытан крайними испытаниями. Был ли это бунт против коммунистического стоицизма, против мужества и «безумства храбрых»?... Или мужество и жертвенность и в своем чистом виде были для Вени непереносимы? Я так и не знаю..." (Фролова и др., "Несколько монологов," 91).

17. Zygmunt Bauman, "Postmodernity, or Living with Ambivalence," in *A Postmodern Reader*, ed. J. Natoli and L. Hutcheon (New York: State University of New York Press, 1993), 15–16.

18. По-видимому, эта философия свободы была близка Венедикту Ерофееву вообще: "Самым главным в Ерофееве была свобода...," пишет Вл. Муравьев. "Конечно, он сам себя разрушил. Ну, что ж — он так и считал, что жизнь — это саморазрушение, самосгорание. Это цена свободы" (Фролова и др., "Несколько монологов," 94).

19. Лихачев, Панченко, Понырко, *Смех в Древней Руси*, 72.

20. Там же, 80.

21. Там же, 79.

22. М. О. Чудакова, "Пастернак и Булгаков: рубеж двух литературных циклов," *Литературное обозрение*, № 5 (1991): 16.

23. Вл. Муравьев вспоминает о Ерофееве: "он был большим поклонником разума (отсюда у него такое тяготение к абсурду)...Ерофеев жил и мыслил по законам рассудка, а не потому что у него правая пятка зачесалась. Очевидная анархичность его лишь означает, что он жил не под диктовку рассудка...Как у всякого рассудочного человека, если он при этом не дурак (а бывает и так), у него было тяготение к четким структурам, а не расплывчатым, к анализу" (Фролова и др., "Несколько монологов," 93). Напомню также, что пьеса Ерофеева *Вальпургиева ночь, или Шаги командора* написана с открытой ориентацией на классицистическую трагедию — своего рода образец эстетического рационализма.

24. См.: Курицын, "Мы поедем с тобою на 'а' и на 'ю'," 296–304.

25. Смирнова, "Венедикт Ерофеев глазами гоголеведа," 62.

Erofeev's Grief: Inconsolable and Otherwise

Karen Ryan-Hayes

In her reminiscences of Venedikt Erofeev, the poet Ol'ga Sedakova writes: "Grief was a real passion of Venia's. He proposed writing this word with a capital letter, like Tsvetaeva did: Grief..."[1] *Gore*—grief, sorrow, woe or misfortune—is indeed a leitmotif in *Moscow—Petushki*, Erofeev's *poema* (and only completed major work). Venia, Erofeev's narrator and alter ego, introduces the topos of grief on the second page of the text within a rhetorical explication of the experience of waking up with a hangover. From the outset, grief exerts a physical force on Venia; he tells us: "Я пошел направо, чуть покачиваясь от холода и от горя" [I turned right, staggering a bit from the cold and from grief] (R17/E15). A series of exclamations and questions follows this sentence, as Venia expands on the nature of grief; the reader learns that it is connected with nausea (perhaps of the metaphysical variety), exhaustion, sadness and stupefaction.

Erofeev's grief, then, is a highly subjective personification of the authorial narrator's own spiritual condition. Yet this mutifaceted and powerful entity is certainly derived from a number of identifiable cultural, literary and artistic sources. Personified Grief is a character in both *byliny* and in lyrical folk songs.[2] The folkloric concept of *gore* underlies the protagonist's character in Vasilii Shukshin's tale *Kalina krasnaia* [*Snowball Berry Red*] and provides a title for Chekhov's short story about irretrievable loss. Resonances from these sources in *Moscow—Petushki*, however, are tenuous and probably coincidental. A more significant source of the grief topos in Erofeev's work is Ivan Kramskoi's painting entitled *Neuteshnoe gore* [*Inconsolable Grief*], which he completed in 1884. Both straightforward and parodic links to this model illuminate the nature of Erofeev's curiously intense grief. They also support and develop the theme of spiritual alienation that informs the entire text and sharpens its satirical edge.

Venia refers explicitly to Kramskoi's painting twice in the course of the extended monologue that constitutes *Moscow—Petushki*. Kramskoi's solitary figure of a woman in mourning, gazing without seeing and pressing a handerchief to her lips is emblematic for Erofeev. The moment of overwhelming grief that the artist conveys in this work is, for Venia, a constant state of being: "У других, я знаю, у других это случается, если кто-нибудь вдруг умрет, если самое необходимое существо на свете вдруг умрет. Но у меня ведь это вечно! — хоть это-то поймите" [I know this happens with others if somebody dies suddenly, if the most necessary being on earth dies suddenly. But with me this is an eternal condition. At least understand this] (R40/E46–47). Moreover, Venia perceives the woman portrayed by Kramskoi as his double. In one of the more hallucinatory passages in the text, the narrator approaches her in a car of the commuter train and thinks "Ни дать, ни взять — копия с 'Неутешное горе', копия с тебя, Ерофеев" [Like two peas in a pod: a copy of *Inconsolable Grief*, a copy of you, Erofeev] (R107/E143). The image of the mourning wife or mother provides a consistent visual representation of Venia's state of being.

Inconsolable Grief occupies a significant place both within Kramskoi's oeuvre and in the history of nineteenth-century art. For Erofeev's purposes, what is extraordinary about this work is how it conveys a profound emotion through a single figure. Kramskoi's paintings often focus on one subject—his portraits of Tolstoy and Saltykov-Shchedrin and the canvas entitled *Khristos v pustyne* [*Christ in the Desert*] are well-known examples. In *Inconsolable Grief*, however, he depicts a subject who is not famous and therefore bears no associations aside from what her portrait expresses. Because there are no extraneous figures depicted, all of the emotion is both concentrated in and emanates from this woman.[3] Venia, the narrator of *Moscow—Petushki*, is a textual analogue of Kramskoi's figure in mourning. He is, we are told, the embodiment of grief, the one whose grief is most profound and most constant. This enables him and requires him to become, like Kramskoi's subject, a vessel or depository for everyone's grief (remembered, present or potential).

Kramskoi originally called his work *Vdova* [*The Widow*], and this has naturally led some commentators to conclude that the woman portrayed is in mourning for her husband. However, Kramskoi's statement that while working on the canvas, he "sincerely sympathized with maternal grief"[4] has supported an alternative interpretation of the work as a portrayal of a mother grieving for her dead child. The very ambiguity of the cause of the woman's sorrow, the impossibility of determining the "plot" of the picture serves Erofeev well. Just as the precise nature of the woman's loss is not the most important dimension of the painting, the source of Venichka's grief is not the primary riddle to be solved in *Moscow—Petushki*. Instead, Erofeev (like Kramskoi) seeks to express the universality of grief and the powerful, visceral experience of that emotion through a single suffering figure.

In *Inconsolable Grief*, Kramskoi captures the physical manifestations of grief in a naturalistic, almost photographic manner. The figure before us in the painting is slightly disheveled; her greying hair is loose, her face is puffy and her eyes are red from tears. None of this, however, detracts from the dignity and grace of the grieving woman.[5] Erofeev's procedure in the verbal medium is analogous: he consistently trains his unflattering objective lens on his authorial narrator Venia, the personification of inconsolable grief. As one might expect, the first-person narrative viewpoint of *Moscow—Petushki* conveys a perception of the world that is partial and prejudiced, but the limitations of Venia's viewpoint do not shape our apprehension of him positively. Omission and selection are generally employed to a first-person narrator's advantage; he or she will often attempt to gain the reader's sympathy by presenting himself in the best possible light. Venia, by contrast, tends to expound upon his worst traits and to concentrate on his represensible behavior—his alcoholic binges, his neglect of his small son, his failure to keep a job, and so on. In order for us to fathom the intensity and profundity of Venichka's grief, it is essential that we apprehend him not as a larger-than-life hero, but drawn to scale. While he occupies the foreground of the text, Erofeev as the verbal portraitist consistently concentrates on his flaws, his defects, his least attractive qualities. Venichka's grief is thus given a human face and gains immediacy.

All of this is not to say that Erofeev is concerned with establishing sympathy or empathy on the part of the reader. Indeed, the impossibility of emotional or spiritual bonding is a recurrent theme of *Moscow—Petushki*. Erofeev's treatment of the topos of spiritual isolation is also enriched by references to Kramskoi's *Inconsolable Grief*. Commentators on this portrait note the artist's highly effective use of *emptiness*. This emptiness—what V. I. Porudominskii calls *deistvuiushchaia pustota*, or "active emptiness" —separates the grieving woman portrayed from the observer spatially and emotionally:

> A woman in a black dress has irrefutably simply, naturally stopped next to a box with flowers, one step away from the observer; one fatal step, which separates grief from the person who sympathizes with grief. This emptiness—which is only *projected* by one's gaze —is remarkably visibly and definitively situated in front of the woman in the painting. The woman's gaze...powerfully attracts the gaze of the observer, but does not respond to it.[6]

Venichka too perceives only a void around him and this separates him from those with whom he works, travels and even drinks. In his own explication of Kramskoi's model, Venia stresses the grieving woman's distance from everyday concerns. He speculates about how she might react if a cat should by chance smash some piece of priceless porcelain or shred an expensive peignor; he concludes that she would not storm or flail, that her grief elevates her above such banality. Examining his own psyche, Venichka realizes that grief has also set him apart from others. As he considers the impossibility of spiritual communion, he poses a series of rhetorical questions: "...разве суета мне твоя нужна? люди разве твои нужны? До того ли мне теперь?...что мне до этих суетящихся и постылых?" [...do I really need all this fuss of yours? Are your people really necessary? What does it matter to me?...what do these vain and repellent creatures have to do with me?] (R18/E16). And just as the woman's spiritual isolation makes her seem "boring" and "frivolous" to others (so Venia tells us), his own alienation leads people to regard him as tiresome and gloomy. It explains why he appears to be "легковеснее всех идиотов, но и мрачнее всякого дерьма" [more frivolous than all idiots, but also gloomier than any shitass] (R41/E47).

Erofeev, like Kramskoi, insists on the profound privacy of the experience of grief. Moreover, the fragility and the vulnerability that characterize grief place it in direct opposition to the values of optimism and valor that pervade official Socialist Realist art as late as the seventies. Venichka defends man's right to solitary tears; observing his double, Kramskoi's woman in mourning on the commuter train, he muses "Когда человек плачет, он просто не хочет, чтобы кто-нибудь был сопричастен его слезам. И правильно делает, ибо есть ли что-нибудь на свете выше безутешности?" [When a man cries he simply does not want anyone to be privy to his tears. And he's justified, for is there anything on earth higher than that which is inconsolable?] (R107–108/E144). Art historians have traced the development of Kramskoi's work through preparatory sketches and studies. By gradually removing superfluous figures and revising the stance of the central figure, the artist conveyed the grief of the woman with increasing subtlety and restraint.[7] It is precisely these qualities that find a resonance in Erofeev's world view. Venichka champions delicacy and understatement in opposition to artificially imposed cheerfulness on a monumental scale.

The Tale of Grief - Misfortune

Another source of Erofeev's treatment of grief in *Moscow—Petushki* is the seventeenth-century *Povest' o Gore-Zlochastii* [*Tale of Grief-Misfortune*]. Although there are no explicit indicators of the tale's significance as a model in the text (as is the case with Kramskoi's painting), both thematic and stylistic echoes of *The Tale of Grief-Misfortune* may be found in the *poema*. These resonances in turn help to illuminate Erofeev's particular conception of grief and its meaning for the work as a whole.

In *The Tale of Grief-Misfortune*, grief is personified as an independent entity which acts forcefully upon the life of the hero, the unnamed *molodets*, or "youth." The image of grief in the tale is dichotomous; it is both a manifestation of external fate and a symbol of the young man's internal spiritual condition.[8] Gore-Zlochastie, or Grief-Misfortune, first appears to the youth in a dream, suggesting that this phenomenon is a product of a disturbance in his own psychic equilibrium. According to Dmitrii Likhachev, this constitutes a distinct departure from the folkloric model of grief, where *Gore*/Grief acts independently of humans' behavior.[9] Here Gore-Zlochastie is summoned up and delineated by the hero's opting to live "какъ ему любо" [as he listed].[10] Counseled carefully by his parents to eschew drinking, boasting and carousing with women, he willfully chooses to disobey virtually all of their precepts. At this point personified grief attaches itself to him, saying "А хто родителей своих на добро учения не слушаетъ, / того выучю я, Горе злочастное" [But he who will not listen to the good teaching of his parents / will be taught by me, Misery - Luckless - Plight!] (R36/E419).

Venichka's grief has a dual nature; it too is both externally imposed and internally created. On one level, *Moscow—Petushki* is an extended hallucination, and the action of the *poema* takes place entirely within the narrator's mind. Venia believes that he is aboard a commuter train speeding toward Petushki, but he actually never leaves his entranceway at all. In this reading, the text is circular and closed and Venichka's grief is entirely a manifestation of internal disturbances. If, on the other hand, we regard the action of the text as taking place on some plane of reality outside of the narrator's mind, then Venichka's grief acquires a different character. According to this interpretation, Venia actively rejects the moral and social precepts offered him and thus summons or conjures up *Gore*/Grief. Indeed, the values endorsed by Soviet culture are satirized and debased in Erofeev's vision. Labor, idealized and celebrated by the Party and the press, is an onerous burden for Venichka. Working six or seven hours a day brings on terrible depression and compels one to drink from early morning to ease the psychological pain. Courage is similarly devalued by Venichka. He yearns for "universal chicken-heartedness" (*vseobshchee malodushie*) (R21/E21) and he finds brave heroes offensive. Finally, he avoids the Kremlin, for him a place of punishment synonymous with hell. The Kremlin is, of course, a potent symbol of ideology and authority, so that Venichka's managing never to see it despite living in Moscow for years constitutes denial, an individualistic rebellion against established power. Venichka opts to defy social strictures and like the *molodets* of *The Tale of Grief-Misfortune*, he is consequently pursued by *Gore*/Grief and punished for his disobedience.

In the prologue to *The Tale of Grief-Misfortune*, the anonymous author tells us that the "forbidden fruit" in paradise was the fruit of the vine; this variant of the Genesis account of original sin is, William Brown notes, entirely appropriate to the story.[11]

А въ началѣ вѣ ка сего тлѣннаго
сотворил *бог* небо и землю,
сотворил богъ Адама и Евву,
повелѣлъ имъ жити во святомъ раю,
дал имъ заповѣдь божественну:
не повелѣл вкушати плода винограднаго
от едемскаго древа великаго.
[In the beginning of this passing age
God created heaven and earth,
God created Adam and Eve.
He ordered them to live in holy paradise,
and gave them this divine command:

He told them not to eat the fruit of the grapevine,
from the great tree of Eden.] (R28/E410)

The *molodets* of the tale proper receives a similar admonition from his parents, who counsel him "не ходи, чадо, в пиры и в братчныы" [Go not, child, to feasts and carousings] and "не пей, чадо, двух чар за едину" [drink not two beakers at once] (R29/E411). Of course, he acts against their good advice, and his carousing is subsequently described in considerable detail. Urged on by his new companions, he consumes green wine, sweet mead and "heady beer" (*pivo p'ianoe*) (R30/E413), all of which leads to his becoming inebriated and falling asleep. His false friends then abandon him and take with them all his belongings, leaving him in rags.

Inebriation is a pervasive theme in *Moscow—Petushki*; according to Paperno and Gasparov, Erofeev originally intended to entitle the text *P'ianitsy* [*Drunkards*].[17] Venia's drinking may be interpreted as a celebration of independence, individualism and freedom from social constraint in the carnival tradition. He dwells at length (one might say ad nauseum) on the variety, quality and price of the alcoholic beverages that he consumes. On the first page of the text, he informs the reader that he has drunk "Стакан зубровки. А потом — на Каляевской — другой стакан, только уже не зубровки, а кориандровой..." [A glass of Zubrovka. Then later, on Kaliaevskii Street, another, only not Zubrovka this time but coriander...] and shortly thereafter "добавил еще две кружки жигулевского пива и из горлышка альб-де-десерт" [I added two mugs of Zhiguli beer and an Albe de dessert port straight from the bottle] (R16/E13). Venichka also provides us with cocktail recipes that include ingredients such as varnish, cologne, nail polish, mouthwash and dandruff treatment. These listings and the repetitions of these listings may derive from the exotic catalogue of drinks consumed by the rebellious *molodets* of the *Tale*. (It is worth noting in this regard that the *molodets'* combination of green wine, sweet mead and heady beer is repeated with minor variations four times in twenty-

heady beer is repeated with minor variations four times in twenty-four lines of the tale.)

Just as the seventeenth-century hero's drinking is an attempt to achieve fraternity or "symposium,"[13] Venia's binging is connected with his desire to establish bonds with his fellow travellers. He states his philosophy simply:

"Человек не должен быть одинок" — таково мое мнение. Человек должен отдавать себя людям, даже если его и брать не хотят. А если он все-таки одинок, он должен пройти по вагонам. Он должен найти людей и сказать им: "Вот. Я одинок. Я отдаю себя вам без остатка. (Потому что остаток только что попил, ха-ха!)."

["Man should not be lonely"—that's my opinion. Man should give himself to people, even if they don't want to take him. But if he is lonely anyway, he should go through the cars. He should find people and tell them: "Look. I'm lonely. I'll give myself to the last drop. (Because I just drank up the last drop, ha, ha!)"] (R107/E143)

However, the passengers on the Moscow—Petushki commuter train —like the trusted friend of the *molodets*—desert Venichka and steal his bottles. As he approaches his destination, he realizes that symposium is an unachievable ideal and that there is only emptiness: "Что тебе осталось? утром — стон, вечером — плач, ночью — скрежет зубовный..." [What's left to you? In the morning to moan, in the evening to weep, at night to grind your teeth...] (R116/E156).

A particularized echo of *The Tale of Grief-Misfortune* in Erofeev's text is Venia's attempt to buy sherry at the Kursk Station restaurant. In the *Tale*, the *molodets* displays exemplary polite behavior upon entering a banquet hall and is accordingly treated well by the good people at the feast. This situation is itself reminiscent of *byliny* but, as Brown notes, the hero of *The Tale of Grief-Misfortune* is far from a *bogatyr* and the setting is commonplace, not epic.[14] Erofeev revises this topos of the *bylina* further. In his literary universe, courtesy and reticence meet with incomprehension or overt hostility. Venichka's polite attempts to order some sherry to ease his hangover are scorned, and they soon become plaintive and obtuse. Although he agrees to wait quietly until some sherry appears, the waiters are disgusted and physically eject him from the restaurant. In the seventeenth-century model, obedience and compliance—albeit somewhat after the fact—allow the *molodets* to gain respect and honor; Venichka, by contrast, cannot save himself from *Gore*/Grief in this manner.

In general, these parodic resonances from *The Tale of Grief-Misfortune* in *Moscow—Petushki* in respect to drunkenness underscore an important difference in Erofeev's conception of grief. In Venichka's world, it is not drinking that gives rise to *Gore*/Grief; rather, drinking is normative, a symptom of the endemic spiritual illness that is grief. To exist in this world means to drink, and the only alternatives that present themselves are those of degree.

The development of the motif of the paradisical Garden in *Moscow—Petushki* borrows heavily from *The Tale of Grief-Misfortune*. The *Tale* begins with a brief account of Adam's fall and exile from Eden. Although the tale moves from the general to the particular with the introduction of the *molodets*, the story told is archetypal; the hero's wanderings recount man's journey through life.[15] Moreover, the tale ends with a petition to God to give mankind access to paradise: "Избави, господи, вѣчныя муки, / а дай намъ, господи, свѣтлы рай" [Lord, preserve us from eternal torment, / and give us, O Lord, the light of paradise!] (R38/E422).

The goal of Venichka's trip on the commuter train is to return to Petushki, his own private Eden. In Petushki, he tells us, the birds never cease singing, the jasmine never stops blooming and "Первородный грех, — может, он и был, — там никого не тяготит" [Perhaps there is original sin, but no one feels threatened by it there] (R37/E43). Venia's sojourn through hell in an attempt to regain entry to paradise parallels that of the *molodets* of *The Tale of Grief-Misfortune*; certainly it derives from Dante's *Divine Comedy* and Gogol's *Mertvye dushi* [*Dead Souls*] as well. As it turns out, there can be no return; Petushki may be only an illusion. Addressing himself, Venichka says "Был у тебя когда-то небесный рай...а теперь небесного рая больше нет" [Once you had a heavenly paradise…but now your heavenly paradise is no more] (R116/E155). The Sphinx whom Venichka encounters mocks him, informing him that he can never reenter paradise. The answer to one of the Sphinx' nonsensical riddles is "в Петушки, ха-ха, вообще никто не попадет!.." [Nobody in general, ha, ha, will end up in Petushki!] (R105/E140). Venichka's realization that his expulsion from the Garden is a permanent condition underlies his spiritual alienation and loneliness. And just as the nameless *molodets* of *The Tale of Grief-Misfortune* is a kind of Everyman, Venichka may be a *geroi nashego vremeni*, or "hero of our time," for the post-Thaw generation.

It has been pointed out that *The Tale of Grief-Misfortune* departs from its folkloric models in allowing the hero to escape *Gore*/Grief by entering a monastery; in folk songs, only the grave provides refuge from *Gore*/Grief.[16] Furthermore, it is significant that the *molodets* of the tale is treated with sympathy by the author. He is not merely a sinner, but an unfortunate victim compelled to renounce the freedom that he has chosen. And while *Gore*/Grief's primary function may not be the salvation of the youth's soul,[17] it does propel him into the monastery.

In Erofeev's parodic version, there is no possibility of redemption, no escape from grief. Venichka's journey takes him from light to darkness; he resigns himself to this, concluding "Ну, так и нечего требовать света за окном, если за окном тьма…" [Well, then, there's no demanding light beyond the window if beyond the window it is dark] (R99–100/E132). There is no monastery—symbolically speaking, no haven of faith—where Venichka might find refuge. The world to which Venichka has been exiled following his expulsion from the Garden is an utterly unholy place. Upon arriving at the Kremlin, he realizes:

Нет, это не Петушки! Если Он навсегда покинул мою землю, но видит каждого из нас, — Он в эту сторону ни разу и не взглянул. А если Он никогда земли моей не покидал, если всю ее исходил

босой и в рабском виде, — Он это место обогнул и прошел
стороной.
[No, this isn't Petushki! If He has left the earth forever but sees each
one of us, He never once looked in this direction. And if He never
left the earth, if He has passed through it barefoot and dressed as a
slave, He went around this place and passed by to the side.]
(R119/E160)

Venichka is hunted down and murdered by four figures. These four
are unnamed, but they have "classical profiles" and inspire
convulsive terror in Venia. It is worth noting that as *Gore*/Grief
pursues the *molodets* in *The Tale of Grief-Misfortune*, it undergoes
four transformations to counter those accomplished by the hero; it
takes on four distinct guises but remains personified grief. (A fifth
transformation does take place, but this is separated in the text by
several lines and stands apart.) So while it is quite possible to see the
four murderers in *Moscow—Petushki* as Marx, Engels, Lenin and
Stalin,[18] I would suggest that we regard them as variable
manifestations of Venichka's Grief.

Erofeev's fickle angels are also, it seems, derived from models in
the medieval tale. In the *Tale*, Gore-Zlochastie's relations are a
multitudinous race: "Не одно я, Горе, еще сродники, / а вся родня наша
добрая, / всѣ мы гладкие, умилныя" [And not I, Misery, alone, but all
my relatives, / and there is a godly race of them: / we are all gentle
and insinuating] (R37/E421). Though Gore-Zlochastie is
foregrounded, its relatives implicitly pursue, tempt and deceive men
as well. The angels of *Moscow—Petushki* are, it turns out, equally
duplicitous. They initially speak to Venichka "gently" and "quietly"
(*laskovo-laskovo; tikho-tikho*) (R18/E16), recalling the relatives of
Gore-Zlochastie. They promise to accompany Venichka on his trip
until he smiles and they speak to him from time to time. However, at
the moment when the four murderers are approaching, the angels
definitively desert Venia and—even worse—exit laughing. Erofeev
describes the angels' laughter at this point as diabolical and obscene.
For Erofeev, laughter is associated with the public or official realm
(in contradistinction to tears, which are private and personal).

Venichka's angels, then, may be manifestations of the external conditions that give rise to his grief.

The image of Venichka's lover in *Moscow—Petushki* is probably to some extent derived from *The Tale of Grief-Misfortune* as well. In both texts, the bride or girlfriend of the hero is a dual figure, associated variously with good and evil, virtue and vice. In the *Tale*, Gore-Zlochastie appears to the *molodets* in a dream and tells him that his "beloved bride" (*nevesta liubimaia*) (R34/E417) is dangerous; Gore-Zlochastie warns the youth that she will poison and strangle him and steal his gold and silver. Although the *molodets* does not believe this dream, the notion of woman as *sosud d'iavola*, or "vessel of the devil," is implanted[19] and the next time that Gore-Zlochastie appears to him, he is willing to be convinced that he should spend all his wealth on drink to avoid the complications and dangers of being rich. Venichka's lover in *Moscow—Petushki* is closely associated with the image of the Garden, with Edenic Petushki. She is described in terms of whiteness, the traditional color of purity and innocence: "И потом — эта мутная, эта сучья белизна в зрачках, белее, чем бред и седьмое небо!" [And then, that turbid, bitchy whiteness of her pupils, whiter than delirium, whiter than seventh heaven!] (R47/E55).[20] However, Venichka also calls her *d'iavolitsa* [she-devil] and notes that she is sometimes "venemous" (*iadovitaia*) (R47/E56); recalling a passionate encounter, he writes "А я, раздавленный желанием, ждал *греха*, задыхаясь" [And I, crushed by desire, awaited *sin*, gasping for breath] (R46/E54) (emphasis mine). Finally, and very significantly, she "laughs ecstatically" (*vostorzhenno smeetsia*) (R47/E56), which suggests her affinity with Venichka's diabolical angels. Erofeev's feminine figure, like the bride of the *molodets*, remains an ambiguous abstraction. This is in part because she, like Petushki, is illusory and unattainable, an impossible construct of Venichka's alcohol-inspired ecstasy. But the slippery duality of her character also owes something to the model of the stylized bride in the seventeenth-century tale.

Children are employed peripherally in Erofeev's text, as in *The Tale of Grief-Misfortune*, to illustrate ideas. In the *Tale*, children embody both innocence and evil (as does the bride figure). The *molodets* remembers his own childhood in a song, in which he is the object of love and admiration; his mother says of him:

> Безпечална мати меня породила,
> гребешкомъ кудерцы розчесывала,
> драгими порты меня одѣяла
> и отшед под ручку посмотрила,
> хорошо ли мое чадо въ драгих портах? —
> А въ драгих портах чаду и цѣны нѣтъ.
> [Sorrowless mother has borne me:
> with a comb she combed my little locks,
> dressed me in costly garments,
> and stepping aside shaded her eyes
> and looked at me:
> 'Does my child look well in costly garments?
> In costly garments my child is a priceless child!'] (R37/E420)

On the other hand, children have the potential of causing distress and unhappiness in *The Tale of Grief-Misfortune*. When the *molodets* is invited to a great feast, the host sees that he is gloomy and asks if perhaps children have insulted him or treated him unkindly.

These two aspects of children play an important role in Erofeev's text as well, and he develops the dichotomy. Venia's son, who lives in Petushki (the Garden), epitomizes innocence and vulnerability. He is characterized in several simple strokes: he is sickly, he is expecting treats, he delights in his ability to write the letter ю. An image that is related to Venia's thoughts of his son is his recollection of the death of two little boys on the Moscow—Petushki commuter train. The boys are crushed in a stampede to avoid the conductor; Venichka remembers: "были насмерть раздавлены — так и остались лежать в проходе, в посиневших руках сжимая свои билеты" [they were crushed to death. They lay as they fell between cars; their hands, turning blue, still clutched their tickets] (R85/E110). But there are other children in Venia's memory who seem to be genuinely evil.

Their response to an equally grotesque incident is telling in this regard. A man's body is severed by a train and his torso remains standing; the children run around him, stick a lighted cigarette butt in his mouth and—most significantly—laugh. Their laughter links them with the "whitish one," with the treacherous angels, and by extention, with *Gore*/Grief, for grief is the embodiment of spiritual brutalization for Erofeev.

Several specific textual features of *Moscow—Petushki* appear to be resonances of stylistic elements of *The Tale of Grief-Misfortune*. One of these is the text's defiance of generic classification. *Moscow—Petushki* is an extraordinarily eclectic work, drawing on a number of genre traditions. (Erofeev subtitled it a *poema*, and while this term suggests interesting parallels with Dante and Gogol, it is not very useful in refining the expections that we bring to the text.) *The Tale of Grief-Misfortune* is an appropriate model in this regard, for it too is "a mélange of genres,"21 a *povest'* in name but in fact a sui generis work combining many forms.

The repetition of words, epithets and entire phrases by Erofeev also recalls the composition of the *Tale* (as well as that of *byliny*). A particularly interesting case of repetition in the medieval text that seems to be echoed in *Moscow—Petushki* is words denoting or connoting grief. The *molodets* of the *Tale* is twice described as "кручиноватъ, скорбенъ, нерадостенъ" [gloomy, sorrowful, joyless] (R32/E414–15) and he recounts his misfortune in similar terms:

и на мою бѣдность великия
многия скорби неисцѣлныя
и печали неутѣшныя,
скудость и недостатки и нищета послѣдняя.
[and to my poverty were added
many great and incurable sorrows
and sadness without comfort,
want, and misery, and extreme wretchedness.] (R33/E415)

Erofeev's use of synonyms to develop and emphasize the topos of grief is more diffuse, but there is nevertheless a high frequency of words built on the roots *gor-* and *tosk-* (*toska, toskovat', zatoskovat'* [melancholy, to be melancholy, to become melancholy]); there are also repetitions of *skorb'* [sorrow] and *skorbnyi, grustnyi* and *mrachnyi* [sorrowful, sad, gloomy]. A few examples of these variants should suffice:

Сколько лишних седни оно вплело во всех нас, в бездомных и тоскующих шатенов!
[How many unnecessary gray hairs it has caused us homeless and grieving brunets!] (R18/E15)

Разве по *этому* тоскует моя душа? Вот что дали мне люди взамен того, по чему тоскует душа!
[Truly is this what my soul is longing for? This is what people have given me instead of that which my soul is longing for!] (R25/E26)

...я выпил пива и затосковал. Просто: лежал и тосковал.
[...I had drunk some beer and started grieving. So I simply lay there and grieved.] (R28/E30)

И я смотрю и вижу, и поэтому скорбен.
[And I look, and I see, and for that reason, I'm sorrowful.] (R40/E46)

И так от этого грустно! А они нашей грусти — не понимают...
[And it's sad because of that. But they don't understand our sorrow.]
(R80/E103)

The creation of compound words—a technique Gudzii calls "tautological combination" (*tavtologicheskoe sochetanie*)[22]—is a source of stylistic parody for Erofeev. In *The Tale of Grief-Misfortune*, forms such as *ukrasti-ograbiti, iasti-kushati, rod-plemia, obmanut'-solgat'* [steal-rob, eat-eat, race-tribe, deceive-lie] and even the name *Gore-Zlochastie* [Grief-Misfortune] provide emphasis and serve as rhetorical flourishes. Erofeev creates compound forms (quite possibly on this model) but uses them to give the text a primitive, even infantile quality. As was noted previously, the angels speak *laskovo-laskovo* [gently-gently] and *tikho-tikho* [quietly-quietly] (R18–19/E16) to Venichka; he mentally names two of his travelling companions on the commuter train *tupoi-tupoi* [Stupid-Stupid] and *umnyi-umnyi* [Smart-Smart] (R59/E73), striking the same childish note. Alternately, Erofeev's verbal combinations can be strikingly original and incongruous; he asks himself "Быть ли мне вкрадчиво-нежным? Быть ли мне пленительно-грубым?" [Should I be tender in an insinuating way? Should I be crude in a captivating way?] (R46/E54).

The repetition of entire phrases serves a similar function in *The Tale of Grief-Misfortune* and in *Moscow—Petushki*. Erofeev, like the anonymous author of the seventeenth-century tale, uses repetition of seminal statements and questions to raise the rhetorical level of the text and to establish a mood of solemnity. However, the procedure in the *Tale* is straightforward. Erofeev's usage of iteration, by contrast, is often tinged with irony. The following extended repetition, for example, is both meaningful (in that it focuses on the topos of laughter) and utterly banal; it approximates the speech of a stuttering drunk:

И ангелы — засмеялись. Вы знаете, как смеются ангелы? И они обещали встретить меня, и не встретили, и вот теперь засмеялись, — вы знаете, как они смеются? Это позорные твари, теперь я знаю — вам сказать, как они сейчас засмеялись?

[And the angels burst out laughing. Do you know how angels laugh? And they promised to meet me and they didn't meet me, and now they've burst out laughing. Do you know how they laugh? They are shameless creatures, now I know. Shall I tell you how they burst out laughing just now?] (R121/E162)

Conclusions

I have attempted to demonstrate that both Kramskoi's painting *Inconsolable Grief* and the seventeenth-century *Tale of Grief-Misfortune* are probable sources of Erofeev's treatment of the image of *Gore*/Grief in *Moscow—Petushki*. These particular models are productive because they both express how grief compels one to withdraw from the world, to focus inward, to isolate oneself. Determining the origins of Erofeev's aesthetic conception may provide a key to understanding the narrator's extreme alienation and loneliness. On the basis of multiple thematic and stylistic parallels with these two models, we can see more clearly that Erofeev's grief stems from both internal and external causes. Venichka's narcisissism is motivated by its internal locus; Gore/Grief is within him, an utterly private and intimate experience (as it clearly was for Kramskoi). His nonconformity, on the other hand, stems from externally imposed grief. Like the hero of *The Tale of Grief-Misfortune*, Venichka stands alone in opposition to those who represent a morally and spiritually bankrupt society and suffers because of his inability or unwillingness to conform to its standards.

Regarding Erofeev's grief as a composite image derived from these two sources supports a reading of *Moscow—Petushki* as an expression of the widespread ennui of the *zastoi* period. *Inconsolable Grief* and *The Tale of Grief-Misfortune* both eloquently convey the general through the particular. The woman depicted in Kramskoi's work embodies human grief, regardless of the specific causes of her suffering. *The Tale of Grief-Misfortune* examines the acute need for spiritual regeneration in a period of pessimism and doubt.[23] Just as the central figures in these works express a broader human or social condition, Erofeev's Venichka is Everyman for the Brezhnev era. A bizarre anecdote which Venia relates to his travelling companions illustrates the distortion of values and the alienation that pervade his world:

> — Вы мне напоминаете одного старичка в Петушках. Он — тоже,
> он пил на чужбинку, он пил только краденое: утащит, например,
> в аптеке флакон тройного одеколона, пойдет в туалет у вокзала и
> там тихонько выпьет. Он называл это "пить на брудершафт", он
> был серьезно убежден, что это и есть "пить на брудершафт", он
> так и умер в своем заблуждении...Так что же? значит, и вы
> решили — на брудершафт?..

Они все раскачивались и плакали, а внучек — тот даже заморгал от горя, всеми своими подышками...

["You remind me of a little old man in Petushki. He, too, drank only other people's stuff, he drank only stolen stuff. For example, he'd swipe a bottle of Triple eau de cologne from the pharmacy, go into the toilet at the station, and drink it on the sly. He called this 'drinking *Brüderschaft*'; he was seriously convinced that this actually was 'drinking *Brüderschaft*' and he died like that, in his delusion...So, what's up? Did you too decide to drink *Brüderschaft*?"

They rocked back and forth and cried, and the grandson even started to blink his arm-pits from grief.] (R62/E77)

Venia's fellow travellers, like the old man in the anecdote, cannot even grasp the concepts of communion, symposium and friendship and they too are doomed to disintegrate in the void. It is significant that the grandson and other characters in Erofeev's text suffer the effects of *Gore*/Grief too. This suggests that Venichka's repeated references to *moi narod* [my people] are not entirely ironic. Erofeev's narrator is indeed on some level archetypal; he is a representative of his people, and of his time and place, for he both embodies and articulates a great and inconsolable grief.

Endnotes

1. Frolova et al., "Neskol'ko monologov," 100.
2. On popular sources of the image of *Gore*/Grief, see N. K. Gudzii, *Istoriia drevnei russkoi literatury* (Moskva: Gosudarstvennoe uchebno-pedagogicheskoe izdatel'stvo, 1945), 408; V. V. Kuskov, *Istoriia drevnerusskoi literatury* (Moskva: Vysshaia shkola, 1989), 239.
3. V. Porudominskii, *I. N. Kramskoi* (Moskva: Iskusstvo, 1974), 178–79.
4. Ibid., 180.
5. Kramskoi's model for *Inconsolable Grief* was his wife, Sof'ia Nikolaevna. The painting was completed in the aftermath of the deaths of two of Kramskoi's children in Paris (see Porudominskii, *I. N. Kramskoi*, 180; T. I. Kurochkina, *Ivan Nikolaevich Kramskoi* [Moskva: Izobrazitel'noe iskusstvo, 1980], 176).
6. Porudominskii, *I. N. Kramskoi*, 183.
7. N. A. Iakovleva, *Ivan Nikolaevich Kramskoi 1837–1887* (Leningrad: Khudozhnik RSFSR, 1990), 105–106.

8. William Edward Brown, *A History of Seventeenth-Century Russian Literature* (Ann Arbor: Ardis, 1980), 89; Gudzii, *Istoriia drevnei russkoi literatury*,406.

9. Dmitrii Likhachev, *Velikoe nasledie* (Moskva: Sovremennik, 1975), 330.

10. *Povest' o Gore-Zlochastii*, in *Pamiatniki literatury drevnei Rusi*, ed. A. A. Dmitriev (Moskva: Khudozhestvennaia literatura, 1988), 30. Translation from *Misery-Luckless-Plight*, in *Medieval Russia's Epics, Chronicles, and Tales*, ed. and trans. Serge A. Zenkovsky (New York: Dutton, 1963), 412. Hereafter citations from *The Tale of Grief-Misfortune* will be indicated in parentheses.

11. Brown, *A History of Seventeenth-Century Russian Literature*, 87.

12. Paperno and Gasparov, "'Vstan' i idi'," 391. Kaganskaia ("Shutovskoi khorovod," 181) refers to Erofeev's text by this title.

13. R. W. B. Lewis, in *The Picaresque Saint. Representative Figures in Contemporary Fiction* (London: Victor Gollancz, 1960), 29, defines "symposium" in its original meaning as drinking together in a celebration of companionship.

14. Brown, *A History of Seventeenth-Century Russian Literature*, 87.

15. "The later biography of the *molodets* is a typical case of the cheerless life of the whole human race." (Likhachev, *Velikoe nasledie*, 314.)

16. Likhachev, *Velikoe nasledie*, 328.

17. Brown argues convincingly that there is no evidence that *Gore*/Grief's conscious goal is the salvation of the *molodets*. Indeed, it is unclear which power—divine or infernal—*Gore*/Grief serves. (*A History of Seventeenth-Century Russian Literature*, 90.)

18. Gaiser-Shnitman (*Venedikt Erofeev*, 270) asserts that the killing of Venichka with an awl is a reference to Stalin, whose father was a shoemaker. Muravnik ("Ispoved' rossiianina," 103) takes this line of interpretation further and suggests that we can easily decode the identity of all of the bandits once the allusion to Stalin is grasped. Presumably the others are Marx, Engels and Lenin.

19. "In the consciousness of the *molodets* traditional conceptions are still active. So he cannot overcome the old view of woman as 'vessel of the devil,' the source of all man's troubles and mishaps. He is faithful to the religious beliefs of his forefathers." (Kuskov, *Istoriia drevnerusskoi literatury*, 238.)

20. In Eastern Slavic folklore, the color white does not have positive connotations, but rather is invested with diabolic associations. I am indebted to my colleague Natalie Kononenko for pointing out this additional ambiguity in the depiction of Venichka's lover.

21. Brown (*A History of Seventeenth-Century Russian Literature*, 87) notes that this mixing of genre conventions distinguishes *The Tale of Grief-Misfortune* from genuine popular works.

22. Gudzii, *Istoriia drevnei russkoi literatury*, 407.

23. Zenkovsky, in his introduction to his translation of *The Tale of Grief-Misfortune* (*Medieval Russia's Epics*, 409), writes that the tale "belongs to the middle of the seventeenth century, when the problem of religious regeneration became so acute during the period of the movement of the Seekers After God and the Great Schism." Likhachev (*Velikoe nasledie*, 328) also locates the source of the tale's theme in its sociopolitical context: "One should, perhaps, connect the deep pessimism of the plot of *The Tale of Grief-Misfortune* with what its author observed in actual Russian reality of the second half of the seventeenth century."

Venichka Erofeev's Grief and Solitude: Existentialist Motifs in the *Poema*[1]

Konstantin Kustanovich

Tears Through Laughter

The reader of Venedikt Erofeev's *poema Moscow—Petushki* will find him or herself puzzled by the confusing impression the book creates. On the one hand, the reader will immensely enjoy funny witticisms and parodies which abound in the book. On the other hand, the reader's entire reading will be accompanied by a deep sense of the tragic. In this article I seek the explanation of this duality of the comic and the tragic in the combination of postmodernist and existentialist tendencies in the *poema* respectively, and it is the latter aspect that I will examine in greater detail. Before engaging in the analysis of existentialist themes I will also briefly consider other possible interpretations of the tragic in the *poema*.

The *poema* is saturated with associations, allusions, and intertexts which lead the reader into a maze of rich cultural and political context. In modern literature such a wealth of references would suggest profound meanings. A tree in Tolstoy's *Voina i mir* [*War and Peace*] or in Pasternak's *Doktor Zhivago* [*Doctor Zhivago*] or in Sartre's *Nausea*—carries an important symbolic load. The text of Bely's *Peterburg* [*Petersburg*] rests on the foundation of anthroposophy which sprouts here and there throughout the novel. So many critics enjoy finding hidden meanings in Joyce's *Ulysses* that "more than a hundred studies and reviews appear every year as new approaches and evaluations develop."[2] One also expects to find plenty of nutrients for the mind in the bowl of mixed references in Erofeev's *poema,* and yet, when asked what the *poema* is about, one will hardly find a more profound answer than the remark Galina Erofeeva (Erofeev's widow) heard from the critic Yurii Aikhenval'd: "it is simply about an alcoholic who rides on a train."[3] Thus, on closer observation, mixed nuts turn out to be empty shells which mock one's desire for a healthy diet to feed one's hermeneutic sensibilities.

On the other hand, the book does give the impression, if only intuitive, of a greater meaningfulness than one would expect from a work of fiction with such a protagonist and plot. The reader feels that *Moscow—Petushki* offers more than simply a menu of imaginable and unimaginable concoctions with which to intoxicate oneself, and that it is more than a postmodernist collage of cultural bric-a-brac. This impression stems, at least in part, from the fact that the book is simultaneously funny and tragic. Similar blending of the comic and the tragic was seen in Russian literature prior to Erofeev, particularly in the works of Gogol and Bulgakov. The functions of the comic and the tragic aspects in their works are different, however. One might say that Gogol is more ontological, while Bulgakov is more phenomenological. The comic in the latter has a satirical nature—the writer attacks specific events, people, and socio-political aspects of Soviet life in the twenties and thirties. The tragic in Bulgakov also emerges mostly as a result of interaction between people or between people and the political system (this is not to deny the significance of religious and philosophical themes in *Master i Margarita* [*The Master and Margarita*]).

Gogol, thanks to the Russian critic Vissarion Belinsky and the entire revolutionary-democratic tradition in Russian literary criticism, had been regarded for more than a century as a great realist and satirist. No one had listened to Gogol himself who insisted that those monsters of his dwelt in our "spiritual city" rather than in society. Melancholy, which we encounter even in Gogol's happiest stories of his early period, breaks through not because of some sad events or occurrences, but because of the feeling that nothing can avert the coming of old age (the ending in "Sorochinskaia iarmarka" ["The Fair of Sorochinets"]) and death ("Starosvetskie pomeshchiki" ["Old-Fashioned Landowners"]). Few critics now subscribe to the interpretation originated by Belinsky that Gogol exposed the harsh and oppressive life under Nicholas I. Gogol's grief was about what *life* does to people rather than what a tsar does to them. His sadness is about the human condition, as an existentialist would say. Virtually all of Gogol's works have in them an archetypal motif of the futility of human striving for happiness. He once wrote in his notebook, "The old rule: one wants to reach, to grasp with his hand, but suddenly—an obstacle, and the desired object moves away to a great distance."[4] Akakii Akakievich's dream overcoat slips away from him at the very moment it seems he has overcome all the barriers on the way to this cherished possession. The mayor and his family in *Revizor* [*The Inspector General*] experience a similar blow of fate at the climax of their happiness. Chichikov's life story at the end of *Mertvye dushi* [*Dead Souls*] may serve as a modern rendering of the myth of Sisyphus. The artist Piskarev in the short story "Nevskii prospekt" ["Nevsky Prospect"] is struck speechless by the beauty of a woman whom he follows only to find out that she is a prostitute. In *Svad'ba* [*The Wedding*], Agaf'ia Tikhonovna's fiancé flees at the last moment through a window. And the wealth in "Portret" ["The Portrait"] and in "Vecher nakanune Ivana Kupala" ["St. John's Eve"] comes from the evil one and brings only ruin and death.

Functions of the Comic and the Tragic

The world that Erofeev creates in *Moscow—Petushki* is closer to Gogol's artistic world than to Bulgakov's.[5] To affirm this, one should look into the character and function of the comic and tragic aspects in the *poema*. The main device Erofeev uses to produce the comic effect is based on bringing together the profane and the sacred. The meaning of "the sacred" here is not limited to religious references—which are abundant in the *poema*—but it also includes elements of the cultural and political context of Soviet life in the 1960s. In this context the government sanctified the teachings of the communist founding fathers and its own regime, while the intelligentsia worshipped high culture, especially pre-revolutionary, dissident, and Western literature, as the only means of eluding oppressive government control. Therefore, the importance of politics and culture was unduly aggrandized—made "sacred"—in post-Stalinist Russia. Erofeev in his *poema* undoes this sanctification through a postmodernist blending of carnivalesque elements (carousing, bodily functions, copulation, etc.) with a smorgasbord of religious, cultural, and political intertexts. Thus, next to the parallel between the stigmata of St. Theresa and a cheap wine which Venichka procured for his trip to Petushki, we find mock research on the unpredictability of hiccuping paired with a reference to Marx and Engels. The drinking habits of Schiller and Goethe become a topic of heated discussion among the group of alcoholics traveling on the same train as Venichka. And poor Pushkin, who is perhaps still turning in his grave from the treatment by the great Kharms and Bulgakov, is coalesced in *Moscow—Petushki* with Evgenii Evtushenko into a monstrous creature, Evtiushkin. The list of examples can be continued ad infinitum. Such a broad range of topics subjected to Erofeev's comic treatment suggests that none of them is a specific target for a satirical attack—the comic here has little or no satirical function. To reiterate: the main function of the comic in Erofeev's *poema* is a postmodernist downgrading of cultural and political idols. It also has another function: it creates an environment in which the tragic could survive without inducing terrible boredom on the Soviet reader of the sixties who had become allergic to melodrama, graveness, and solemnity.

The "Moral" Interpretation

The *poema*'s tragic impression comes not from tragic events (with the exception of the last episode) but from the recurrent motif of Venichka's *skorb'* [grief]. That grief is one of the main themes here is an assertion that would elicit few objections. The question is: What causes grief in Venichka and what is its nature? Several answers can be suggested. The one which lies on the surface of the text is the protagonist's addiction to alcohol (and his drinking practices).

Venichka suffers from a hangover; he suffers when he drinks too little or too much; he suffers from depression caused by alcohol and from the social troubles that drinking entails. There is no need to quote from the book to support this interpretation—one can find dozens of examples. It is sufficient to remember just one aphoristic phrase Venichka coins: "О, самое бессильное и позорное время в жизни моего народа — время от рассвета до открытия магазинов!" [Oh, the most helpless and shameful time in the life of my people— the time from the dawn to the moment when stores open!] (R18/E15).

Some influential critics of Russian literature, among them Vladimir Lakshin, took this moralistic approach to Erofeev's *poema*. The *poema* was published in Russia for the first time in 1988–89 in the journal *Trezvost' i kul'tura* [*Sobriety and Culture*].[6] In his review of this publication Lakshin even provided statistical information on the growth of alcohol consumption in Russia from 1950 through 1973. According to him, Erofeev's genius manifests itself first of all in his ability to "profoundly and monumentally (*krupno*)" depict his narrow topic—"drinking, vodka, and the life of a Russian alcoholic."[7] Lakshin also suggests that Erofeev's work:

> provides useful material for contemplation, why the strictest decrees and quick and adroit measures against drinking cannot succeed....You take away vodka, they will drink moonshine; take away moonshine, they will target drugs or stupefying, over-the-counter chemical goods...[8]

Yet Erofeev's Venichka would forgo vodka for all kinds of unimaginable concoctions even when vodka was in abundance. He would scorn the primitive Kubanskaia and create an alcoholic "poem"—a "Tear of a Komsomol Girl" or "Aunt Klava's Kiss"— from furniture polish, nail polish, perfume, eau de cologne, mouthwash, dandruff lotion, lotion to prevent foot odor, etc. This contradiction, however, would not bother a reader who believes that the world of a literary work has rules of its own which often are quite different from the rules and laws of empirical reality. In the world of *Moscow—Petushki*, alcohol is not a curse ruining the bodies and souls of millions of men and women in Russia, but literally aqua vitae, a substance vital for the normal, nay, spiritual existence of everybody, from a feeble-minded boy and his grandfather traveling on the train together with Venichka, to Schiller and Goethe.

Venichka and the Kremlin

Another tempting interpretation for a critic in search of the source of Venichka's grief is the protagonist's relationship with the Soviet system. Venichka's statement in the opening lines of the *poema*, that he has never seen the Kremlin although he has crossed Moscow a thousand times "с севера на юг, с запада на восток, из конца в конец, насквозь и как попало" [from the north to the south, from the west to the east, from one side to another, through and in any other way] (R16/E13), indicates that there is something wrong between him and the regime that the Kremlin represents. One can interpret this statement as an expanded metaphor contained in the slang phrase *ia tebia v upor ne vizhu* [I don't see you point-blank], meaning "I completely ignore you" or "I don't give a damn about you" or similar. In another marked place, at the end of the *poema*, the theme of the Kremlin appears again. Venichka finally sees it, but at the most terrible moment of his life, several minutes before he is murdered by four thugs. They catch up with him on Red Square, start beating him, and then finish him off in the doorway of a building nearby. Thus the Kremlin, which looms high above the scene of Venichka's murder, and which Venichka sees the first time in his life, is directly associated with his death and may be considered its cause. The question of the identity of the four murderers is an intriguing one, and there have been several suggestions as to who they are. If Erofeev indeed had actual people in mind for Venichka's murderers, then the four whose profiles were on the red banners that appeared in Stalinist times during each Soviet holiday—Marx, Engels, Lenin and Stalin—are the most obvious solution of the riddle.[9] Fleeing from the thugs, Venichka tries to remember in which newspapers he saw their mugs. One of them wears boots as Stalin always did, and their classical profiles are mentioned in their description by Venichka.

Between the beginning and end references to the encounter (or non-encounter) with the Kremlin, Venichka's conflict with the Soviet regime seems to be manifested in numerous mocking quotations of and allusions to characters, events, and the culture of the Soviet period. The Revolution, the hundredth anniversary of Lenin's birth, the attempt on Lenin's life, his funeral, allusions to Soviet literary figures including Gorky, Nikolai Ostrovskii and Evtushenko and to political events such as the Arab-Israeli conflict provide a rich socio-political context of Soviet life in the late 1960s. In his early review of the *poema* a leading Russian literary critic, Andrei Zorin, sees this context as "a battlefield on which the Moscow Don Quixote fights his monster"—the Kremlin, "the main symbol of state power."[10] Yet, as has been noted above, while many of the cultural and political references in the *poema* mock the Soviet establishment, others, in the same mocking way, allude to the Bible—Erofeev's favorite book according to some accounts—and to works of Russian and Western literature and music. One should not conclude from this, however, that Erofeev's book is a crusade against not only the Soviet system, but also against the entire world culture. Critical works that attribute an anti-Soviet function to Erofeev's book fall victims to inertia—we expect a Soviet writer who does not follow the precepts of Socialist Realism, but allows him or herself some kind of disrespect for Soviet values, to be actually an anti-Soviet writer, a dissident. Here, I think, lies the explanation for the popularity of a parallel between Erofeev and a Russian liberal of the eighteenth century, Aleksandr Radishchev—a parallel which, in my opinion, does not hold water. True, the formats of both *Moscow—Petushki* and Radishchev's *Puteshestvie iz Peterburga v Moskvu* [*A Journey from Petersburg to Moscow*] are similar. Radishchev, however, is mainly concerned about the lack of social justice and the tragic fate of the lower classes in Catherine's Russia. His work is a typical ideological piece which in its passionate denunciation of the existing system is more akin to the writings of Erofeev's contemporary, Aleksandr Solzhenitsyn. We find nothing like Radishchev's and

Solzhenitsyn's ardent exposé in Erofeev's *poema*. Erofeev seems to have accepted the system within which he lived, although he might have disliked it with all his heart. One of Erofeev's best friends, Vladimir Murav'ev, writes in his penetrating memoirs:

> One should not consider Erofeev as a most miserable alcoholic—a victim of the contortions of Soviet reality. He was not a victim. He was in Soviet reality like a fish in water.[11]

Not all decent people in the Soviet Union had enough resolve and courage to become dissidents—whether in action or in spirit. Most preferred to leave the Soviet system outside their personal lives and respond to its crimes with disgust but also with a certain degree of detachment. Erofeev was one of them. His relations with the system can be represented by the words of one of the characters in his unfinished play *Dissidenty, ili Fanni Kaplan* [*Dissidents, or Fanni Kaplan*]: "Ну, что же, большевики — это атмосферическое явление, и относиться к нему следует как ко всякому явлению атмосферическому" [Well, Bolsheviks are an atmospheric phenomenon and one should treat them as just an atmospheric phenomenon].[12]

Moscow—Petushki has suffered the same kind of misinterpretation as Pasternak's *Doctor Zhivago*. Venichka's relationship with the Soviet regime is similar to that of Yurii Zhivago. They both might have fallen victim to it, but neither considered the system an intimate part of his life. Lara's farewell words over Zhivago's coffin can also apply to Venichka's philosophical stance (if we allow for the difference in lifestyles between Zhivago and Venichka):

> The riddle of life, the riddle of death, the enchantment of genius, the enchantment of unadorned beauty—yes, yes, these things were ours. But the small problems of practical life—things like the reshaping of the planet—these things, no thank you, they are not for us.[13]

Soviet power in both works is not a source of death, it is a tool of death. Man is predestined to die, and whether he is killed by a totalitarian system or by nature does not really matter. Here the comparison with an "atmospheric phenomenon" seems very appropriate. Undoubtedly, there is a difference between the philosophy of Pasternak's book and Erofeev's one, which lies in Pasternak's ultimate optimism—death in the life cycle is always followed by resurrection—and Erofeev's pessimistic stance. In the words of another friend of his, the poet Ol'ga Sedakova, Erofeev "seems not to have read beyond Good Friday....The worn-out famous phrase by Nietzsche 'God is dead' would sound in Venia's edition 'God is murdered'."[14]

Two years after his first review of the *poema*, Zorin published another article in which he replaces his earlier emphasis on the ideological character of *Moscow—Petushki* with an emphasis on the personal one:

"The homebound, intimate, and circle-oriented semantics" (Iu. Tynianov) of *Moscow—Petushki* prophetically pointed to the deep shift in the gravitational center of the emotional (I'd rather abstain from saying "spiritual") life of the generation from the public to the private. The sphere of realization and manifestation of an individual becomes a group of friends rather than a social group.[15]

At the end of the article Zorin concludes:

Moscow—Petushki is one of the most consistently anti-ideological books in all our literature; and the claims of any ideological constructions to be significant, to occupy the mind and heart, are disgusting and boring for the writer....Venichka indeed "has never seen the Kremlin." And although he was destined to die near the Kremlin wall, his ability to...pass the center of the country and symbol of power had a great liberating meaning.[16]

The shift noted by Zorin began with the waning of the Thaw in the late fifties and early sixties. The intelligentsia's decisive turn away from social life took place in 1968, after the invasion of

Czechoslovakia, which marked the loss of hope for liberalization and the beginning of the stagnation period in Soviet history. It was only natural that in this atmosphere of utter hopelessness, interest in the ultimate questions of personal existence reached its maximum; it is in these questions rather than in social aspects of life that one finds the key to the interpretation of Venichka's grief.

Existential Grief

In my analysis of the nature of Venichka's grief I will occasionally turn to the character and biography of the author, Venedikt Erofeev, in order to facilitate my understanding of his protagonist, Venichka. I believe that in this particular case such an approach is justified—for the author and his friends the book was not a work of fiction but another medium for continuous discourse. Lidiia Liubchikova writes that, for a long time, she "could not perceive it [the *poema*] as fiction, but read it as a diary in which all the names are familiar."[17] I, however, will separate the author and protagonist by using different names: Erofeev and Venichka, respectively.

I would also like to propose a specific method of reading Erofeev's *poema*. Two tendencies prevailing in contemporary Russian literature merge in Erofeev's book and beget the combination of the comic and the tragic. One of them is avoiding, by any means, what is called in Russian *pafos* and which is defined in a Russian dictionary as "воодушевление, энтузиазм, вызываемые какой-л. высокой идеей" [fervor and enthusiasm caused by a high idea].[18] In a discussion of Erofeev's book in *Literaturnaia gazeta* [*The Literary Gazette*], Boris Khazanov noted that:

> contemporary literature flees from *pafos*—the *pafos* of morality, the *pafos* of piousness, the *pafos* of patriotism—as from fire. They [young authors] are afraid of *pafos* because they feel that it has turned into kitsch.[19]

The shift away from *pafos* was a reaction to the graveness and solemnity of Socialist Realism. The surest way to kill solemnity was all-permeating irony which filled the pages of early post-Stalinist fiction, especially the Youth Prose, settled down on the last page of *The Literary Gazette*, and culminated in the seventies and eighties in the Russian brand of postmodernism—the works of the Conceptualist poets (Prigov, Rubinstein and Kibirov), the prose of Vladimir Sorokin, the late fiction of Evgenii Popov and the art of Komar and Melamid, Il'ia Kabakov and others. (Simone de Beauvoir describes a similar scorn for *pafos* among Sartre and his friends who "derided every inflated idealism, laughed to scorn delicate souls, noble souls, all souls and any kind of souls, inner life itself..."[20]).

Yet, people have not lost the ability to experience deep and serious emotions and these demand an appropriate means of expression. With *pafos* dead and irony dominating, the logical way would be to harness irony for the purpose of expressing these emotions. This second function of irony—revealing unobtrusively "tears through laughter"—is far less conspicuous than the first, anti-*pafos* one. In Erofeev's *poema*, however, it takes upon itself the main burden of meaning. In his article "Posle karnavala, ili vechnyi Venichka" ["After Carnival, or the Eternal Venichka"], Mikhail Epstein refers to this use of irony as "anti-irony":

> Irony turns inside out the meaning of the direct, serious word, while anti-irony turns inside out the meaning of irony itself, re-establishing the seriousness, but without directness and unequivocalness.[21]

Anti-irony also plays an important role in other postmodernist works, carrying out a nostalgic function. Bakhyt Kenzheev's cycle of poems *Epistles* can serve as an example of postmodernism going nostalgic. The imitation of nineteenth-century style creates an ironic veil which hides, but does not eliminate, the persona's emotions. Without this veil the poet would have a hard time finding an adequate means of expression for the feelings which Pushkin could express by simply exclaiming: "My friends! How wonderful our union is!" Erofeev, too, covers the tragic with the veil of the comic, and yet we always feel the tragic's strong presence. Hence the duality of the *poema* and the protagonist's discourse. Venichka himself notices this duality of his: "я легковеснее всех идиотов, но и мрачнее всякого дерьма....я и дурак, и демон, и пустомеля разом" [I am lighter than all the idiots, but I am also gloomier than any shit....I am a fool and a demon and a chatterbox at the same time] (R41/E47). The words "I am a fool and a demon[22] and a chatterbox" create an image of a lone man who wants to pour his heart out, to confess the most intimate thoughts that torment him, to invite the reader (listener) to weep together over his grief and solitude; and he even begins his tragic outpouring, but then his shyness (here one pictures Erofeev's famous gesture: closing and holding the collar of his shirt with his hand out of shyness) stops him dead in his tracks and he switches to sheer buffoonery masking his momentous openness. Thus, to reach the text's tragic core one should see beyond the surface buffoonery.

The one day in Venichka's life and his death described in the *poema* can be viewed as a metaphor for life in general occupied with an existential search for salvation—the search which fails and brings the protagonist to despair and death. Venichka's ultimate goal is Petushki—Eden complete with Eve—an expert in sexual matters in the bargain—and with the beloved son living close by. The protagonist, however, never reaches Petushki. His trip ends in the empty train, submerged in darkness, flying through the night with no direction and time. Darkness with no sense of space and time is death. The last sentence of the *poema* clearly indicates that there will be no resurrection. Venichka's entrance into paradise is denied. In fact, his entire existence, as it is presented in the *poema*, is the story of continuous rejection. The episode in the restaurant serves as a prelude depicting Venichka's first attempt to reach paradise. "Saint Peter" (the restaurant doorman) grudgingly admits him but later he is thrown out by the restaurant staff in white gowns (angels). He is rejected in the Sorbonne and in the British Library. The most important rejection, though, is his rejection by God. Venichka's relationship with God is intimate, but one-sided.

Venichka often talks to God, trying to solicit His help, but God, in most cases, is silent. Only once He responds to Venichka's supplications, but only in a short and strict admonition. The angels —the "real" ones, not those in white robes who threw Venichka out of the restaurant—behave like cruel children: they laugh at Venichka and abandon him in the middle of his trip.

Thus the true source of Venichka's grief lies in his feeling of what the Russian existentialist thinker Nikolai Berdiaev calls *bogoostavlennnost'* [abandonment by God] and sees as *razorvannost', razdel'nost', otchuzhdennost', pokinutost'* [division, separation, alienation, desertion] of the individual.[23] In Heidegger's words Venichka can be characterized as an "entity, endangered and abandoned to itself."[24] Venichka's "abandonment by God" can be best viewed in the episode describing how he takes inventory of his precious possessions. He carries in his briefcase several bottles of cheap liquor and a sandwich. Having observed the sandwich and a bottle of Rosé Strong (*rozovoe krepkoe*) at one rouble, thirty-seven kopeks[25] he calls to God in desperation:

> Господь, вот ты видишь, чем я обладаю. Но разве *это* мне нужно? Разве по *этому* тоскует моя душа? Вот что дали мне люди взамен того, по чему тоскует душа! А если б они мне дали *того*, разве нуждался бы я в *этом*?
>
> [Lord, you see what I possess. But is *this* what I need? Is *this* what my soul pines for? This is what people have given to me instead of that for which my soul pines. And if they had given me *that* would I need *this*?] (R25/E26)

Here we deal with the *poema*'s typical ambivalence—the tragic veiled by the comic. The combination of gethsemanic agony with what causes this agony, to wit, Rosé Strong and Kubanskaia vodka, produces the comic effect. There are, however, the two contexts in which this passage should be read and its meaning understood. The immediate context is the description of the protagonist examining his briefcase and contemplating its content. This context is responsible for the comic effect. On the other hand, the broader context is based on the protagonist's grief and fear as a recurrent motif. This context provides the reader with a reason to perceive Venichka's appeal to God literally. Then the emphasized "this" and "that" do not refer to cheap stuff and better stuff to drink, but rather to senseless and meaningful being respectively. The passage then presents an image of a spirit in agony longing for a higher meaning of existence and not finding it.

There are many passages in the *poema* which work in a similar way. At the beginning of the *poema* Venichka wanders around the Kremlin trying to reach Kursk Station. He just woke up after a drunken slumber somewhere in an entryway. He is overwhelmed with a bad hangover and is looking for a way to procure a drink.

> Я пошел направо, чуть покачиваясь от холода и от горя. О, эта утренняя ноша в сердце! о, иллюзорность бедствия! о, непоправимость! Чего в ней больше, в этой ноше, которую еще никто не назвал по имени, чего в ней больше: паралича или тошноты? истощения нервов или смертной тоски где-то неподалеку от сердца?
>
> [I went to the right, slightly swaying from cold and grief. Oh, this morning burden in the heart! Oh, illusion of calamity! Oh, irreparability! What is there more of in this burden which no one has been able to name yet? What is there more of in it—paralysis or nausea? Exhaustion of nerves or deadly despair somewhere in the vicinity of the heart?] (R17–18/E15)

The three "Oh" exclamations at the beginning, the moaning and groaning combined with the high-style rhetoric, and the immediate context of this particular episode could lead the reader to see in this passage a hangover raised to the level of *Weltschmerz* for some postmodernist fun. On a closer examination of the *poema*'s text and other sources, however, such an interpretation appears superficial. Even the "Oh"s cease to be a buffoonish element as we learn from memoirs of Erofeev's friends that the "Oh" in exclamatory addresses was a typical feature of Erofeev's speech, even when he was serious.[26] Moreover, if one looks at this passage, separating it from its narrow context, one will find in it not the suffering from the morning hangover but existential despair caused by the "burden which no one has been able to name yet" and which is akin to what Sartre calls "nothingness." And nausea, as we see in Sartre's novel with the same title and in his other works, can be caused by experiencing nothingness—pure existence stripped of any essence— rather than by overindulging in alcohol. When you have this experience, when "existence invades you suddenly, masters you, weighs heavily on your heart like a great motionless beast,"[27] then the sense of absurdity overwhelms you. Antoine Roquentin, the protagonist of *Nausea*, has this sickening experience of nothingness and concludes:

> Without formulating anything clearly, I understood that I had found the key to Existence, the key to my Nauseas, to my own life. In fact, all that I could grasp beyond that returns to this fundamental absurdity.[28]

V nichka would not, perhaps, subscribe to the grave tone of this statement, but, in his own way and style, he expresses the same notion of the absurdity of life:

> Помню, еще очень давно, когда при мне заводили речь или спор о каком-нибудь вздоре, я говорил: "Э! И хочется это вам толковать об этом вздоре!" А мне удивлялись и говорили: "Какой же это вздор? Если и это вздор, то что же тогда не вздор?" А я говорил: "О, не знаю, не знаю! Но есть".
>
> [I remember, a long time ago, when they talked or argued about some kind of nonsense in my presence, I would say, "Eh, why would you even want to talk about this nonsense?" And they would get surprised with me and say, "What do you mean, nonsense? If this is nonsense, then what is not?" And I would say, "Oh, I don't know, don't know, but some things aren't."] (R40/E46)

What seems extremely important to Venichka's friends is nonsense for him. There is some profound truth which is meaningful for Venichka, but what is it? Venichka does not know himself. He approaches this truth with some kind of intuitive knowledge, but the foreboding of it aggravates his grief even more. The following passage again has Erofeev's usual duality of buffoonery and graveness. At the beginning the author mocks Hegel's concept of approaching, but never reaching the absolute truth, while the second paragraph points at a very important condition of Venichka's—the condition of "grief and fear."

> — Я не утверждаю, что мне — теперь — истина уже известна или что я вплотную к ней подошел. Вовсе нет. Но я уже на такое расстояние к ней подошел, с которого ее удобнее всего рассмотреть.
>
> И я смотрю и вижу, и поэтому скорбен. И я не верю, чтобы кто-нибудь еще из вас таскал в себе это горчайшее месиво — из чего это месиво, сказать затруднительно, да вы все равно не поймете — но больше всего в нем "скорби" и "страха". Назовем хоть так. Вот: "скорби" и "страха" больше всего, и еще немоты. И каждый день, с утра, "мое прекрасное сердце" источает этот настой и купается в нем до вечера. У других, я знаю, у других это случается, если кто-нибудь вдруг умрет, если самое необходимое существо на свете вдруг умрет. Но у меня-то ведь это вечно! — хоть это-то поймите.
>
> [I don't really say that now I know the truth or that I have approached it extremely close. Not at all. But I have approached it close enough to be able to examine it in the most convenient way.
>
> And I look at it and see and therefore I grieve. And I don't believe that anyone else among you carries as bitter a mixture as I do. Hard to tell what kind of mixture it is—and you wouldn't understand it anyway—but it consists most of all of "grief" and "fear." Yes, we can put it this way. Here, "grief" and "fear" there are most of all, and also muteness. And every day, from the very morning "my wonderful heart" oozes this balm and bathes in it till evening. With others—I know—with others it happens if someone suddenly dies, if the most needed being in the world suddenly dies. But with me—it is perpetual, try to, at least, understand that.] (R40/E46–47)

We see here many elements which connect Venichka's condition with existentialist themes: intuitive, rather than rational, knowledge;

grief and fear as a permanent condition rather than a product of a specific event; experience of death as an impetus arousing grief; muteness; and alienation—the opposition between Venichka and those nameless "you."

Grief and fear in the face of death as a permanent condition constitutes one of the main premises of existentialism. Sartre's proposition that "man is condemned to freedom" and therefore must face and make choices at every moment of his life leads to the conclusion that one should live as if one is to die tomorrow. This proposition informs both Venichka's and Erofeev's lives. Venichka compares his condition with the grief of the woman in Kramskoi's painting *Neuteshnoe gore* [*Inconsolable Grief*] caused apparently by someone's death, but stresses that he permanently carries this grief in himself. As for Erofeev, his friend Ol'ga Sedakova remembers:

Venia's real passion was grief. He suggested that this word be written with a capital G, as Tsvetaeva did: Grief.[29]

For many years, actually for all the years that I knew him (and it is —scary to even say it—twenty years) Venichka lived at the edge of life. And it was not a matter of the last illness of his or dangers usual for a drinking person, but rather of the way of life "in view of the end."[30]

Existential Solitude

The opposition between Venichka and the nameless "you" noted above brings us to another important existentialist theme— alienation and solitude. Venichka's solitude can perhaps be best explained in terms of Heidegger's concept of authentic and inauthentic Dasein.

In each case Dasein is mine to be in one way or another. Dasein has always made some sort of decision as to the way in which it is in each case mine. That entity which in its Being has this very Being as an issue, comports itself towards its Being as its ownmost possibility. In each case Dasein *is* its possibility, and it 'has' this possibility but not just as a property, as something present-at-hand would. And because Dasein is in each case essentially its own possibility, it *can*, in its very Being, 'choose' itself and win itself; it can also lose itself and never win itself; or only 'seem' to do so. But only in so far as it is essentially something which can be *authentic* —that is, something of its own—can it have lost itself and not yet won itself. As modes of Being, *authenticity* and *inauthenticity*...are both grounded in the fact that any Dasein whatsoever is characterized by mineness. But the inauthenticity of Dasein does not signify any 'less' Being or any 'lower' degree of Being. Rather it is the case that even in its fullest concretion Dasein can be characterized by inauthenticity—when busy, when excited, when interested, when ready for enjoyment.[31]

Venichka's solitude results from the fact that his is an authentic Being among inauthentic Beings. He "chose" himself, his "ownmost possibility" instead of merging with the crowd in life of "busy, exited, interested, and ready for enjoyment" essences. Heidegger's concept of authentic and inauthentic Being resembles strikingly Kierkegaard's analysis of forms of despair in his book *Sickness unto Death*. Heidegger's inauthentic Being is equivalent to Kierkegaard's "immediacy." Both states imply not finding or losing one's own self and striving to be absorbed by others in order to flee despair of Being. Kierkegaard describes the immediate man as follows:

The *immediate* man...is a something included along with "the other" in the compass of the temporal and the worldly, and it has only an illusory appearance of possessing in it something eternal. Thus the self coheres immediately with "the other," wishing, desiring, enjoying, etc.[32]

Unlike Heidegger, who does not attach a value judgment to authentic and inauthentic Beings, Kierkegaard proposes a scale in which the despair of the immediate man is the lowest kind of despair.

This form of despair is: in despair at not willing to be oneself; or still lower, in despair at not willing to be a self; or lowest of all, in despair at willing to be another than himself. Properly speaking, immediacy has no self, it does not recognize itself...[33]

A higher form of despair—when the "despairer" "despairs about the eternal and over oneself"[34]—makes the despairer feel a need of solitude.

> The fact that he feels this vital necessity more than other men is also a sign that he has a deeper nature. Generally the need of solitude is a sign that there is spirit in a man after all, and it is a measure for what spirit there is. The purely twaddling inhuman and too-human men are to such a degree without feeling for the need of solitude that, like a certain species of social birds (the so-called love birds), they promptly die if for an instant they have to be alone. As the little child must be put to sleep by a lullaby, so these men need the tranquilizing hum of society before they are able to eat, drink, sleep, pray, fall in love, etc.[35]

We also find solitary figures in works of other recognized forefathers of existentialism. One of the recurrent motifs in Nietzsche's *Thus Spake Zarathustra* is the opposition between the human herd and the solitary Zarathustra who teaches that the Christian call for "loving one's neighbor" comes from the ancient tradition, when "Creating ones were first of all peoples, and only in late times individuals."[36] Nietzsche would agree with Kierkegaard that the desire to become a member of a herd comes from one fleeing from oneself:

> Ye crowd around your neighbour, and have fine words for it. But I say unto you: your neighbour-love is your bad love of yourselves.
>   You flee unto your neighbour from yourselves, and would fain make a virtue thereof: but I fathom your "unselfishness."[37]

But to separate oneself from the herd is not simple. Only through suffering one can leave the herd and find oneself.

> "He who seeketh may easily get lost himself. All isolation is wrong": so say the herd. And long didst thou belong to the herd.

> The voice of the herd will still echo in thee. And when thou
> sayest, "I have no longer a conscience in common with you," then
> will it be a plaint and a pain.[38]

In Russian literature precursors of existentialist "loners"—the "superfluous men"—can be found as early as the Romantic period of the nineteenth century. Pechorin, in his withdrawal from people and life, experiences existential alienation rather than simply romantic boredom and satiation with life. His creator's exclamation that "life is...such an empty and silly thing" is more a manifestation of existential despair than a romantic posture. While Pechorin is merely a step that a romantic hero makes toward existentialist *Weltanschauung*, Dostoevsky's Underground Man has clearly gone all the way in this direction. His solitude is the solitude of the "authentic Dasein." He rejects rationalist, objective, mass thinking and insists on the "ownmost possibility" of human being. When his loneliness drives him to attempt a union with others he fails miserably. But he is unwilling to give up his authenticity in order to belong to a social group and therefore remains alone. In twentieth-century Russian literature a literary character who experiences existential alienation is Kavalerov, the protagonist of Olesha's novel *Zavist'* [*Envy*]. The title may mislead the reader and make it easy to attribute Kavalerov's alienation to his inability to adjust to the new culture—the fate that befalls Edichka in Limonov's novel *Eto ia — Edichka* [*It's Me, Eddie*]. Kavalerov, however, is bitter not because he is rejected by the new society and at the same time yearns for participation in it, as is the case with Limonov's protagonist. Kavalerov himself rejects society which forces "inauthentification" of Dasein on the individual. He is as repelled by the culture oriented toward mass production, mass entertainment, and mass emotions, as Dostoevsky's Underground Man is repelled by rationalism.

When Erofeev was writing *Moscow—Petushki* in the winter of 1970, existentialism was well-known and fashionable among Russian intellectuals. Works by Kierkegaard and Nietzsche circulated either in *samizdat* or in pre-revolutionary editions. Heidegger's name became a familiar feature in intellectual discussions. Individual works by Camus, Sartre and Kafka had appeared in the journal *Inostrannaia literatura* [*Foreign Literature*] and in separate book editions. A collection of critical articles, *Sovremennyi ekzistentsializm* [*Contemporary Existentialism*], was published in 1966, and a translation of a monograph by an American Marxist, Sidney Finkelstein, *Existentialism and Alienation in American Literature*, came out in 1967. Erofeev, who was, according to his sister, an avid reader of *sam-* and *tamizdat*,[39] knew about existentialism perhaps much earlier, in the early sixties. When he showed one of his early works, *Blagaia vest'* [*Good News*, written in 1962] to his friends, they characterized it as existentialist and Nietzschian.[40] Perhaps he knew Nietzsche's works very well. The style of *Moscow—Petushki* often approaches the sermonic style of *Thus Spake Zarathustra*. He also might have known Kierkegaard's works or about Kierkegaard. During his short stay at the Vladimir Pedagogical Institute, he worked with great interest and enthusiasm on articles about his "compatriots"—he was born and grew up in the northern Russian city of Murmansk — Hamsun, Björnson and Ibsen. Björnson and Ibsen were strongly influenced by Kierkegaard and this alone may have compelled Erofeev to seek out and read the Russian translations of Kierkegaard's works published in St. Petersburg around the turn of the century.

Yet it appears that Erofeev's existential mentality is deeply rooted in his character rather than drawn from fashionable theories. He, like his protagonist, knows and understands something that others do not; he is different and he, like his protagonist, could say to others: "Все, о чем вы говорите, все, что повседневно вас занимает, — мне бесконечно посторонне" [Everything you talk about, everything which always occupies your minds is infinitely alien to me] (R39/E46).[41] Erofeev's entire life was a succession of deviations from the "normal path." At seventeen he passed the entrance exams to Moscow University (MGU) with flying colors. His knowledge of Russian literature was perhaps much broader and deeper than that of not only other students but of some professors as well. In his second year of studies, however, he was thrown out of MGU for not taking finals. When he enrolled in the Vladimir Pedagogical Institute he was immediately awarded a special Lebedev-Polianskii personal stipend—an honor rarely accessible to freshmen. He was expelled from there, too. He lived in the Soviet Union—a place where each person had to be registered and accounted for—without a passport and a military registration card. When he was thirty he wrote a book which made him famous around the world. For the remaining twenty years of his life he wrote practically nothing else of the same literary value.

Murav'ev may have written the best explanation of Erofeev's self-destructive way of life: "Venichka had the feeling that a comfortable, ordinary life is a surrogate of a real life, and he was destroying it..."[42] Real life versus comfortable, everyday life is exactly the Heideggerian opposition between authentic and inauthentic Beings, between existence and essence. When existence "invaded" Erofeev, living a "normal" life became an intolerable burden for him, especially in the Soviet Union, where each aspect of life had a rigid essence attached to it by the state. But again, whether it was a communist essence or a capitalist one did not matter to Erofeev. When he was asked during his interview with *Kontinent* [*Continent*] about his relationship with Soviet power, he became very defensive, and angrily answered:

> Я люблю мою власть....Я все в ней люблю. Это вам вольно рассуждать о моей власти, е...а мать. Это вам вольно валять дурака, а я дурака не валяю, я очень люблю свою власть, и никто так не любит свою власть, ни один гаденыш не любит так мою власть.
>
> [I love my government....I love everything in it. You are fucking free to discuss my government. You are free to kid around, but I don't kid around. I love my government very much, and no one so loves his government, not a single son-of-a-bitch so loves my government.][43]

Did he really love "his government" so much? It is doubtful. Simply, when *Continent* made an attempt to foist on Erofeev a different essence, the anti-Soviet one, he rejected it as he did the Soviet essence.

Erofeev thought and lived differently from even his best friends. Hence his solitude. Erofeev's friends acknowledge that he was different. Liubchikova, the wife of one of his friends, says:

> Even my mom who was not very keen about drunkards was charmed by him and tried to convince him "not to mix with those good-for-nothings who are not equals to you." (That was a very precise remark about equals; "good-for-nothings" were Vladimirians. There were intelligent and original people among them—and yet, not equals.)[44]

Erofeev's widow Galina Erofeeva corroborates: "There were practically no people who were his equals. Maybe only Murav'ev. And, well, he also much respected Averintsev."[45] Perhaps Liubchikova and Erofeeva refer not only to his superior intellect, but also to something more deep and unique that distinguished him from others, something that they saw and felt but could not define because they, too, were those others. However intelligent and educated his friends were, they still remained on the other, inauthentic side of Being. Therefore Erofeev felt lonely even among his closest friends. Venichka's thirtieth birthday was, most probably, taken from Erofeev's own experience. Best friends came, and yet Venichka felt so lonely that he almost sobbed. The friends described in this episode are those whose memoirs we read more than twenty years later in *Teatr* [*Theater*]: Vadim Tikhonov with his wife Lidiia Liubchikova, Boris Sorokin with Ol'ga Sedakova ("a crazy poetess"), and Vladimir Murav'ev. We find the most telling example of Erofeev's isolation in the midst of his friends in an anecdote related by Erofeev's translator J. R. Dorrell, supplied to Dorrell by Erofeev's acquaintance, Mikhail Burdzhelian.

> "I invited Erofeev to a party in Moscow. He turned up in the company of a short man, ill-dressed, who introduced himself as 'the hero of Erofeev's *Moscow Circles*'. Throughout the evening Erofeev sat silent, while his 'hero' became ever more voluble

[Heidegger's 'idle talk' - K. K.]. At the end of the evening, they left, Erofeev still silent and sober, his 'hero' noisy and drunk [Heidegger's 'excited, interested, ready for enjoyment' - K. K.]."[46]

Liubchikova also notes Erofeev's alienation even in the middle of a most jovial party with close friends: "Ben, as it were, did not participate [in mischievous pranks]. He was simply present and was just thinking something to himself....I often felt that he was alienated from people, even from those who had good relationships with him."[47]

If Erofeev was lonely among his friends, what should he feel amidst the "herd"? He could have repeated after Kierkegaard: "A crowd is untruth." He wrote in his notebook:

Мне ненавистен "простой человек", т.е. ненавистен постоянно и глубоко, противен и в занятости и в досуге, в радости и в слезах, в привязанности и в злости, и все его вкусы, и манеры, и вся его "простота", наконец.
[I hate the "common man," that is, I hate him constantly and deeply. He disgusts me in his labor or leisure, in his happiness and tears, in his love and anger; and his tastes and manners disgust me too, and his "commonness" as well.][48]

This dislike for simple people was certainly not a class hatred. Erofeev's social status was even lower than that of "simple people" who surrounded him. He disliked in simple people, or masses, or "herd," their lack of individuality, their prejudices, their intolerance for everything that lay outside of their narrow notions of right and wrong or, in existentialist terms, the fact that essence preceded existence in their lives.

A vivid example of Venichka's existential conflict with the masses is the bathroom incident at the dormitory. His roommates denounce and reject him because in his bathroom habits Venichka displays his individuality. Because of his inability to conform, he "вечно буде[т] одиноким и несчастным" [will always be lonely and miserable] (R30/E33). Here Venichka clashes with "the immediate man" who finds refuge from existence in the distractions of inauthentic Being—excitement, curiosity, and idle talk, or what Nietzsche calls "the noise of the great actors, and the buzzing of the poison-flies."[49] The protagonist of Camus' *The Stranger* also behaved in a way that was either strange or unacceptable to other people. He did not show any grief at his mother's funeral. He passively accepted his social and professional status without striving to improve them. Most of the time he was lonely and bored. The murder he committed and his own imminent execution did not stir any significant emotions in him. Venichka could also identify with Antoine Roquentin's words:

> I am alone in the midst of these happy, reasonable voices. All these creatures spend their time explaining, realizing happily that they agree with each other. In Heaven's name, why is it so important to think the same things all together?[50]

Another example of Venichka's inadvertent confrontation with "immediacy" is his short tenure as a brigade leader. He was demoted not because he had sent fake plans to the administration, and not because the members of the brigade, including himself, never worked but only drank, played cards and slept; he was demoted for the behavior that betrayed in him *l'etranger*. The graphs that showed the drinking habits of the brigade members were an intolerable intrusion of individual creativity (however humorous) in the dull routine of collective indolence and corruption. The incident with the graphs, also a parody of rational thinking, provides one more connection between the *poema* and existentialist discourse. Venichka's statistical study of hiccuping is another such parody which perhaps can be traced to an anti-rationalist discussion in Dostoevsky's *Zapiski iz podpol'ia* [*Notes from Underground*]. Mocking rationalism was quite appropriate in "the most rational system" that did not work. One should not forget that Marxist-Leninist dialectic had its beginning in the coupling of the rationalist Hegel with the materialist Feuerbach.

The immediate man not only flees from existence into the essence, or "normal life," but he will also prosecute any deviation from the "norm," since such a deviation would break a thin, protective shell of his essence and expose him to existence. Venichka, on the contrary, never shows any totalitarian inclinations. As soon as he becomes the brigade leader he eliminates those few remaining operations which could still qualify as work. If before Venichka's promotion to brigade leader the brigade did unroll the cable and lay it underground every day only to unearth and discard it next morning, under Venichka, the cable is left alone and the workers only drink, sleep and play cards. Thus, Venichka does away with the very part of the brigade's life that justifies his being the leader.

In his dream toward the end of the trip, Venichka sees himself as the president of a rebellious "republic." The whole episode, at first glance, appears as just another buffoonish element in the *poema's* postmodernist collage. It is, however, marked by its unusual length —it is the longest cohesive story here—and it also stands out structurally—inserted without any contextual justification. It seems that the author is trying to make a specific point. The dream is clearly a parody of the October Revolution, and Venichka plays the role of Lenin here; the point, however, is not anti-Revolutionary, but anti-totalitarian in general. What Erofeev mocks here is not the concrete actions of Lenin or the Soviet government, but the institution of power itself, the idea that there could be a solution suitable for people en masse. A superficial reader will object at this point that the author does mock changing the calendar and eliminating the letter ѣ from the Russian alphabet in 1918 and therefore the episode is directed against a specific target. Erofeev, however, denounces not *these* particular decrees—they were, perhaps, the most logical and needed of all the decisions produced by the new government—but rather *any* revolutionary actions. A revolution changes the existing way of life in an organized and forceful manner. It is made by the masses and for the masses, and its leaders claim rationality as the basis of their totalitarian actions. Rationality is what a genuine existentialist mind cannot accept.

Totalitarianism rejects the right of the individual to find his or her own self; it undermines existence and glorifies essence.

Perhaps Camus and Sartre would condemn Venichka's irresponsible behavior in his capacity as a revolutionary leader. They themselves had a taste for revolution and communist ideals. Venichka would also fail a test for a bona fide existentialist because he still cherishes a hope to find salvation in his love for his son and the "red-haired bitch," and he clings to his life, pleas for mercy, and desperately attempts to flee from the four murderous thugs. Erofeev was very impressed by the story of St. Francis who, having learnt that he was terminally ill, said "Welcome, our sister Death." And he despaired over the fact that *We* are different."[51] A real existentialist should "die cleanly,"[52] "rid himself of hope...and open himself to the gentle indifference of the world"[53]—only then one becomes free. But after all, Venichka was never admitted to the Sorbonne.

Endnotes

1. I would like to express my gratitude to the Vanderbilt University Research Council for a summer fellowship that supported my research for this article.

2. Richard M. Kain, *Fabulous Voyager: James Joyce's Ulysses* (New York: Viking Press, 1959), ix.

3. Frolova et al., "Neskol'ko monologov," 87.

4. Quoted from Yurii Mann, "Dramaturgiia Gogolia," in N. V. Gogol, *Sobranie sochinenii,* vol. 4 (Moskva: Khudozhestvennaia literatura, 1977), 414.

5. According to Erofeev's friend Vladimir Murav'ev, Erofeev hated *The Master and Margarita* and managed to read only the first fifteen pages. The difference in the inner philosophies between the two writers may account for such a strong rejection of Bulgakov's novel by Erofeev. See Frolova et al., "Neskol'ko monologov," 93.

6. The fact of publication of Erofeev's work in the journal with such a title speaks for itself. Even a more striking example of such an interpretation of Erofeev's *poema* is its publication in a collection together with three journalistic pieces describing drug addicts, prostitutes, and AIDS. See *Ispoved' proroka* (Stavropol': Stavropol'skoe knizhnoe izdatel'stvo, 1991).

7. Lakshin, "Bezzakonnyi meteor," 225–26.

8. Ibid., 227.
9. See Paperno and Gasparov, "'Vstan' i idi'," 390.
10. Zorin, "Prigorodnyi poezd," 258.
11. Frolova et al., "Neskol'ko monologov," 94.
12. Erofeev, *Dissidenty, ili Fanni Kaplan*, in *Ostav'te moiu dushu v pokoe*, 274.
13. Boris Pasternak, *Doctor Zhivago*, trans. Max Hayward and Manya Harari (New York: Ballantine, 1981), 505.
14. Frolova et al., "Neskol'ko monologov," 102.
15. Ibid., 120.
16. Ibid., 122.
17. Ibid., 86.
18. *Slovar' russkogo iazyka v chetyrekh tomakh*, ed. A. P. Evgen'eva, vol. III (Moskva: Russkii iazyk, 1983).
19. Pomerants and Khazanov, "Pod sen'iu Venichki Erofeeva," 5.
20. Simone de Beauvoir, *Memoirs of a Dutiful Daughter* (Paris: Callimard, 1958), 335, quoted in Patrick McCarthy, *Albert Camus, The Stranger* (Cambridge: Cambridge University Press, 1988), 7.
21. Mikhail Epshtein, "Posle karnavala," in *Ostav'te moiu dushu v pokoe*, 14. He, in turn, borrows this term in reference to Erofeev's book from Erofeev's friend Vladimir Murav'ev.
22. The English word "demon" lacks the associational load which the Russian word has and which originates in Lermontov's poem of the same name. The poem, in turn, inspired Vrubel''s paintings. Erofeev uses this word in the Lermontovian and Vrubelian sense—a gloomy and lone, rather than evil, spirit.
23. N. Berdiaev, *Ekzistentsial'naia dialektika bozhestvennogo i chelovecheskogo* (Paris: YMCA-Press, 1952), 80–81.
24. Martin Heidegger, *Being and Time*, trans. John Macquarrie and Edward Robinson (New York: Harper and Row, 1962), 180.
25. A cheap, 40-proof fortified wine, a regular fare of Russian alcoholics desperate for a drink, but short of funds to buy a less deadly beverage.
26. See Frolova et al., "Neskol'ko monologov," 84, 105.
27. Jean-Paul Sartre, *Nausea*, trans. Lloyd Alexander (Cambridge, Mass.: Robert Bentley, 1979), 132.
28. Ibid., 129.
29. Frolova et al., "Neskol'ko monologov," 100.
30. Ibid., 98.
31. Heidegger, *Being and Time*, 68.
32. Soren Kierkegaard, *Sickness unto Death*, in *A Kierkegaard Anthology*, ed. Robert Bretall (Princeton: Princeton University Press, 1951), 351–52.

33. Ibid., 353.

34. Ibid., 360.

35. Ibid.

36. Friedrich Nietzsche, *Thus Spake Zarathustra*, in *The Philosophy of Nietzsche* (New York: Random House, 1927), 61. A very important theme in Pasternak's *Doctor Zhivago*—the predominance of the nation over the individual in pre-Christian times, in particular among Romans and Jews, and the emphasis on the individual in Christianity—may have been a product of Pasternak's polemic with Nietzsche's anti-Christian stance.

37. Nietzsche, *Thus Spake Zarathustra*, 63.

38. Ibid., 65.

39. Frolova et al., "Neskol'ko monologov," 77.

40. See Aikhenval'd, "Strasti po Venediktu Erofeevu," 75.

41. I would like to note that *mne postoronne* is not the best Russian language, and Erofeev is usually a very sensitive writer as far as language is concerned. A possible explanation for using this word is that Camus' *L'Etranger* was translated into Russian as *Postoronnii*.

42. Frolova et al., "Neskol'ko monologov," 90.

43. Ibid., 95.

44. Ibid., 82.

45. Ibid., 88.

46. Dorrell, "Translator's Preface," 3.

47. Frolova et al., "Neskol'ko monologov," 83, 85.

48. Erofeev, "Iz zapisnykh knizhek," in *Ostav'te moiu dushu v pokoe*, 297.

49. Nietzsche, *Thus Spake Zarathustra*, 52.

50. Sartre, *Nausea*, 8.

51. Frolova et al., "Neskol'ko monologov," 100.

52. Jean-Paul Sartre, "The Wall," in *The Wall and Other Stories*, trans. Lloyd Alexander (n.p.: New Directions, 1948), 29.

53. Albert Camus, *The Stranger*, trans. Matthew Ward (New York: Knopf, 1988), 122.

The Story of Russian

Marie R. Martin

А что ты делал в огнедышащую эпоху?
Из дневников Ерофеева

Но муза, правду соблюдая,
Глядит, а на весах у ней
Вот эта книжка небольшая
Томов немногих тяжелей.
А. Фет

Russian language, the great pride of Russian culture, plays a special role in Erofeev's poetics, where it is not so much the means of communication between the sketchy characters as the *langue* of contemporary culture in its entirety. The techniques of characterization are such that we perceive *Moscow—Petushki* as a portrait of different social groups in contemporary Russia. This portrait is created through social languages or social dialects, such as the speech of a bureaucrat filled with the language of political propaganda, or the literary and grammatically correct speech of a well-read member of the intelligentisia, or the substandard speech of poorly educated people.

Language becomes the main element in the grand scope of Erofeev's poetics. In this respect, *Moscow—Petushki* is the story of the greatness of the Russian language, its demise in the Soviet years, and its subsequent rebirth. The link between linguistic past, present and future is created through a unique usage of parody.

When Russia embraced *perestroika*, a great change was long overdue not only in people's lives, but also in the language. During the Soviet years the Russian language, from the "great and powerful" (*velikii i moguchii*), turned into a spent, limp and clichéd form filled with meaningless expressions, often naming non-existent phenomena. It did not go unnoticed. A number of such words, which cannot be translated, because they have no meaning, were collected by Isidore Geld in her *Dictionary of Omissions*.¹ Put another way, there were forms without content, or signifiers without signifieds. In *Moscow—Petushki* Erofeev also exposes the nonsense of some phrases very popular in the media. An example is the adverbial phrase *tselikom i polnost'iu*, used to speak about the total eradication of some social vice. Both adverbs mean the same thing, making this phrase redundant. Erofeev creates such a context for this expression that not only its redundancy but also its nonsense becomes obvious. Using this phrase, Venichka comments on the eradication of homosexuality in Soviet Russia.

А надо вам заметить, что гомосексуализм в нашей стране изжит хоть и окончательно, но не целиком. Вернее, целиком, но не полностью. А вернее даже так: целиком и полностью, но не окончательно. У публики ведь что сейчас на уме? Один только гомосексуализм.
[Let me point out to you that homosexuality in our country has been eradicated completely but not entirely. Or to be more precise, entirely but not fully. Or to be even more precise: completely and entirely but not fully. Really, what do people have on their minds these days? Nothing but homosexuality.] (R88/E114)

By breaking up the two adverbs *tselikom i polnost'iu* it becomes obvious that this phrase is not only nonsensical but also can be preposterous, as in the above example with homosexuality. Although the Soviet media might assert that a vice is eradicated, it is not eradicated as long as there exists a word signifying this phenomenon. A word will unmistakably invoke a phenomenon in the minds of the people. A phenomenon is only eradicated if the word signifying it is erased from memory.

The Soviet Russian language had become quite different from its classical predecessor, which is distinguished for clarity, simplicity and eloquence. In Erofeev's unique language, called "Venediktianstvo,"[2] the Soviet language undergoes such a seismic transformation that it is not able to return to its old ways, a phenomenon which we witness in the Russian literary language today. This study will focus on the process and mechanism of change aimed at returning lost greatness to the Russian language. I will further expound on each of the above statements.

Since the characters are depicted broadly, with just glimpses into their lives and no stories to tell, the artistic language becomes the most striking feature in Erofeev's not voluminous but all-inclusive art. Indeed, the characterization is done in the form of sketchy humorous portraits of society. Here we see mustachioed male and female faces, toothless smiles and empty gazes, identical berets and drab clothing, there a waitress' legs dressed in boring stockings ("without even a seam" [*bezo vsiakogo shva*], exclaims Venichka, according to whom an appealing seam would at least be something worth noticing [R21/E20]). The threesome in white who throw Venichka out of the restaurant are so like everybody else, that to Venichka their eyes are expressionless and blank. All the characters eventually blend into a uniform grey mass. The four killers crown this grey portrait with their "classical profiles" familiar to everyone since their portraits are displayed all over the Russian land. The extraordinary pundit Venichka—whose portrait is not given—is wisdom personified. Conversations that take place on the train are variations on the themes popular in contemporary Russian society, for example discussions of love a là Turgenev, or discussions of politics.

Moscow—Petushki can be viewed as a novel made up of voices[3] in which the characters become mouthpieces for society. Eternal Russian questions—individuality and society, the intelligentsia and the common people, the intelligentsia and political power, literature and society—are illuminated in *Moscow—Petushki* in the sphere of language.

Erofeev's language is unique not only because it incorporates an extraordinary number of well-known texts from Soviet pop culture, Soviet media, Socialist Realist literature, Russian classical literature, foreign literature widely read in Russia, musical works, and the Bible,[4] in other words, the entire arsenal of present-day Soviet culture,[5] but because out of these well-known expressions he created a language like no other. Vail' and Genis, commenting on the nature of Erofeev's style of writing, pointed to the fact that Erofeev collected all the books that had been written before him and from them constructed his story:

> And Venichka took all the books that had existed before him. And from each one of them he took a little of the best and of the worst. He didn't forget anybody: from Antonín Dvorzhák to Nikolai Ostrovskii. He gathered all of them in one and told a didactic story, "a moral for our forefathers,"[6] about the suffering and torment of the human spirit.[7]

In spite of such voluminous incorporation of other texts, it is nevertheless a language like no other. Bella Akhmadulina made the following statement about Erofeev's style:

> People don't live, speak or write like this. Only Venedikt Erofeev can do this. It is only his life which equals his style, his speech which is always direct, his talent. It is such a joy that this talent exists! It is sad to know what he will have to go through, this lucky possessor of such a talent...[8]

Critics inevitably make statements about Erofeev's extraordinary language (mostly in *Moscow—Petushki*). It has been called "exalted [and] transcendent...with many literary allusions," aphoristic and witty, and aesthetically interesting.[9]

According to Pawel Pawlikowski, the producer of a BBC documentary about Venedikt Erofeev, Erofeev believed in a cult of language. He listened carefully and evaluated people by the way they spoke. Language was an escape. "All the joking, the punning, was a way of coping with the world."[10] Just as Soviet commentators had previously, a reviewer writing in *Kontinent* [*Continent*] remarked on the indecent (*neprilichnyi*) language, but concluded that the work was "one of the most chaste (*tselomudrennyi*), most tragic, and most honest (*pravdivyi*) works of our time."[11] "The genius of verbal synthesis" is yet another characteristic of Erofeev's craft.[12] The famous saying "Homo sum; humani nihil a me alienum puto," which is usually translated, "I am a man, nothing human is foreign to me," for Erofeev's literary personage, Venichka, might well read: "my life is an utterance, therefore nothing in discourse is foreign to me."

I will strive to demonstrate that Erofeev's linguistic craftsmanship and cultural breadth are achieved through a masterful engagement of parody, which has been recognized as "the common denominator" of contemporary modernistic literature through the nineties.[13] Parody in this study is understood as defined by Linda Hutcheon in her *Theory of Parody*; it is "the repetition with difference with the pragmatic ethos ranging from the reverential to the playful to the scornful."[14] The parody which interests us in this study is the "elevating" type (my term), i.e. it elevates the parodying text to the level of the parodied.

I agree with theorists of parody that a parody may stand on its own (as in the case of *Don Quixote*[15]). However, I believe that in such a case the text is not read as parody, which limits the scope of interpretation. Often parody is nothing more than a scaffolding around the work.[16] But in Erofeev's case parody plays not only a reflective and contemplative role, but, most significantly, parody serves to regenerate the language. We should also point out the viability of parody in Russian culture, which generally views its present as inextricably bound with its past.

Since the new is only new when we are familiar with the old, it is only in comparison to background texts that we are able to perceive the novelty of Erofeev's verbal craft. His twisting and bending of words becomes apparent only if we know the common usage of these expressions.

Erofeev's parody is remarkable because through a guessing game with the reader it not only brings forth the parodied text but also comments on the usage of this parodied text in contemporary culture. Erofeev's parody does not negate a parodied text, instead it introduces a multifaceted outlook on the parodied text. The following examples from *Moscow—Petushki* will give us a glimpse of Erofeev's verbal craft:

> Я согласился бы жить на земле целую вечность, если бы прежде мне показали уголок, где не всегда есть место подвигам.
> [I would agree to live on the earth for an eternity if they'd show me first a corner where there's not always room for heroic deeds.]
> (R21/E21)

Venichka's above statement reworks Gorky's phrase from the romantic tale *Starukha Izergil'* [*The Old Woman Izergil'*]: "В жизни, знаешь ли ты, всегда есть место подвигам" [In life there is always room for heroic deeds].[17] This phrase became famous in Soviet ideology due to its valorization of everyday life and the simple man engaged in a glorious effort to build a communist society. It is apparent from Venichka's statement that he does not deny the fact that glory should have a place in life; rather he states that life does not amount to glory alone.

Another example of a non-negating parody is a reworking of the famous Soviet slogan and propaganda cliché *nashe svetloe zavtra* [our bright tomorrow], ideologically devised in an attempt to orient the whole culture toward future goals and achievements, disregarding chaos, shortages and disillusionment reigning in the here and now.

> Пусть светел твой сегодняшний день. Пусть твое завтра будет еще светлее....Почему же ангелы смущаются и молчат? Мое завтра светло. Да. Наше завтра светлее, чем наше вчера и наше сегодня. Но кто поручится, что наше послезавтра не будет хуже нашего позавчера?

[Let your today be bright. Let your tomorrow be even brighter....Why are the angels troubled? Why are they silent? My tomorrow is bright. Yes, our tomorrow is brighter than our yesterday and our today. But who will see to it that our day after tomorrow won't be worse than our day before yesterday?] (R39/E45)

We see a verbal game Erofeev creates around this famous Soviet slogan. He turns a metaphorical "tomorrow" into a calendar "tomorrow," followed by the day after tomorrow and preceded by the day before yesterday. And again, as in the previous example, there is no denigrating or negating the fact that the future might be bright. Such optimism should be cautious, Venichka suggests, considering two things: how much ugliness there is all around him and the fact that the angels are silent.

By parodying without denigrating the language which the culture regards as elevated, Venichka's speech rises to the level of greatness ascribed by cultural context to these well-known "winged expressions" and slogans. Such parodies involve the two texts in a dialogue rather than in competition between the parodied and the parodying.

Another characteristic of Erofeev's elevating parody is that he transforms very familiar slogans, proverbs and myths into his own language of proverbs and witty aphorisms. His witticisms are often published in contemporary newspapers and quoted by readers. In his desire to embrace the whole of humanity, Venichka exclaims in a proverbial way:

Надо чтить, повторяю, потемки чужой души, надо смотреть в них, пусть даже там и нет ничего, пусть там дрянь одна — все равно: смотри и не плюй...
[We must honor, I repeat, the dark reaches of another's soul. We must look into them even if there's nothing there, even if there's only trash there; it doesn't matter: you should look and honor it, look and don't spit.] (R74/E94)

The original proverb *chuzhaia dusha — potemki* implies fear of the unknown darkness deep inside a soul. Erofeev's parodic proverb looks at fearful darkness as plain nothingness which is then not scary because of the lack of substance. In this parody Erofeev not only rises to the level of conventional mythology, but goes beyond and broadens its scope. Unlike the original proverb, Erofeev's proverb introduces a Christian concept of brotherly love, commanding respect toward another, even if this other does not seem worthy of it.

Both the "well-said" quality of Erofeev's writings and their philosophical aspect perhaps explain their immense popularity in Russia. In this respect, Vail' writes, "He [Erofeev] presented us with a vast collection of aphorisms and sayings that are always practical and ready for usage."[18]

Another source of Erofeev's aphoristic language is the eloquent language of classical literature. When Erofeev parodies famous quotes from literature (by Tolstoy, Dostoevsky, Pushkin, Gogol, Blok and many other writers), his narrator assumes a point of view on the same elevated cultural level vis-à-vis the great writers. Such a stance gives the narrator *authority* to judge and question these cultural assumptions.

Here is an excerpt with quite an array of cultural icons. On the way to Petushki Venichka stops at the restaurant at Kursk Station for badly needed imbibement. When the waitress snaps that there is no alcohol, he exclaims in disbelief:

Нет ничего спиртного! Царица небесная! Ведь, если верить ангелам, здесь не переводится херес. А теперь — только музыка, да и музыка-то с какими-то песьими модуляциями. Это ведь и в самом деле Иван Козловский поет, я сразу узнал, мерзее этого голоса нет. Все голоса у всех певцов одинаково мерзкие, но мерзкие у каждого по-своему. Я поэтому легко их на слух различаю...Ну, конечно, Иван Козловский... "О-о-о, чаша моих прэ-э-эдков..." "О-о-о, дай мне наглядеться на тебя при свете зве-о-о-озд ночных..." Ну, конечно, Иван Козловский... "О-о-о, для чего тобой я околдо-о-ован... Не отверга-а-ай..."

[Nothing to drink! Mother of God! Indeed, if you believe the angels, sherry never stops flowing here. But now there's only music and even this music has some kind of mangy harmonics. Yes, that's Ivan

Kozlovskii all right. I recognized him right away; there is no one else with a voice that nasty. All singers have equally nasty voices, but every one of them is nasty in its own way. That's why I can identify them so easily. Of course, it's Ivan Kozlovskii. "Oh, Chalice of my forebearers, Oh, let me gaze for–e–ever upon you by star–r–r–r light." It's Ivan Kozlovskii for sure... "Oh, why am I smi–i–tten so with you. Don't reje–e–ect me."] (R20/E19)

In this passage we find reference to angels who follow Venichka everywhere he goes, and to Ivan Kozlovskii, a renowned tenor, singing two arias: the first from Wagner's opera *Lohengrin* and the second from Gounod's opera *Faust*. There is also a parody of a popular sixties song performed by the pop-singer Edita P'iekha: "Смерти не будет, будет музыка,/ Только музыка, вечная музыка,/ Музыка, только музыка" [There will be no death, there will be music,/ Only music, eternal music,/ Music, only music]. A parody of Tolstoy's famous opening phrase from *Anna Karenina*, "Все счастливые семьи похожи друг на друга, каждая несчастливая семья несчастлива по-своему" [All happy families are like one another; each unhappy family is unhappy in its own way],[19] is used as well.

The purpose of the above parodic passage, in my view, is to further separate Venichka from society. Every line of the above quotation designates what is greatly revered and admired in Russian culture. The comic atmosphere arises not from ridiculing the background texts but from a dare-devil attitude towards the familiar and conventional. In order to make his statement of taste concerning the voices of singers trustworthy, Venichka uses the form of Tolstoy's famous dictum as an instrument to prove the authority of his own statement. Using the structure of the venerated phrase, Venichka fills it like a vessel with his own content. As a result, Venichka's saying sounds as authoritative as Tolstoy's.

The juxtaposition of high culture with the crude physical reality of the restaurant famous for its lack of sherry and an abundance of udder and beef Stroganoff, for curt waitresses and ominous crystal chandeliers threatening to crush you, discloses how out of place beauty and art are when face to face with ugliness.

Erofeev's parodies are ambivalent because they do not affirm or negate cultural assumptions. In his philosophical search for a higher meaning of life, and for an expression capable of describing it, Erofeev through parody broadens society's outlook on culture and by doing so he opens possible venues for future writers.

I stated above that Erofeev's parodies comment not on the parodied text but rather on the usage of this text in modern culture. Let us see how Venichka talks about the hypocrisy of people's critical view of the material side of life. For this parody he uses a famous phrase from *Brat'ia Karamazovy* [*The Brothers Karamazov*]:

Сначала отточи свою мысль — а уж потом чемоданчик. Мысль разрешить или миллион? Конечно, сначала мысль, а уж потом — миллион.
[First, sharpen your thought, then worry about your suitcase. So what is it going to be: a thought or a million in cash? Of course, first the thought, then the million.] (R107/E142)

In Dostoevsky's phrase the spiritual aspect of life unequivocally negates the materialistic:

В нем мысль великая и неразрешенная. Он из тех, которым не надобно миллионов, а надобно мысль разрешить.
[In him there is a great and unsolved thought. He is one of those who doesn't need millions but needs to solve a thought.][20]

This phrase formulates an important postulate of Russian intelligentsia culture. It became a "winged expression" because it was quoted on many occasions by spokesmen of official socialist culture which drew on the classics in order to underscore the importance of material wealth. In Erofeev's phrase both spiritual and material sides are expressed as equal. Furthermore, the narrator hints that in contemporary culture it is certainly more in vogue to speak about the spiritual, as long as in real life it is not detrimental to the material.

Erofeev's works are tragic and comic at the same time. Such a mixture is the result of parodic techniques which the writer uses quite extensively and masterfully. We find similar parodic ambiguity when Pushkin is mentioned in the grotesque story of the Komsomol leader Evtiushkin, who beat up his girlfriend, broke her skull and knocked out her teeth. All this he does because of his great love for Pushkin, probably caused by the fact that the name Evtiushkin rhymes with Pushkin.

The passage is interspersed with parodic reworking of Pushkin's works. Svetlana Gaiser-Shnitman, noting some references from this excerpt, suggests that the image of the Komsomol leader Evtiushkin is modeled on the poet Evgenii Evtushenko.[21] Guy Houk investigates this issue in his detailed study of Evtushenko and Erofeev,[22] where he discovers several parodies of Evtushenko's poetry and of his social views in *Moscow—Petushki*.

However, this passage is saturated with parodic reworkings of Pushkin's poetry. The story of Evtiushkin and Dasha parodies Evgenii's and Tat'iana's story from *Evgenii Onegin*, since Evtiushkin speaks Tat'iana's words[23] in his love declaration to Dasha:

— Все с Пушкина и началось. К нам прислали комсорга Евтюшкина, он все щипался и читал стихи, а раз как-то ухватил меня за икры и спрашивает: "Мой чудный взгляд тебя томил?" Я говорю: "Ну, допустим, томил..." А он опять за икры: "В душе мой голос раздавался?...Тут он схватил меня в охапку и куда-то поволок. А когда уже выволок — я ходила все дни сама не своя, все твердила: "Пушкин - Евтюшкин - томил - раздавался". "Раздавался - томил-Евтюшкин - Пушкин". А потом опять: "Пушкин - Евтюшкин..."

[Everything started with Pushkin. They sent us a Komsomol organizer, Evtiushkin, he was always pinching me and reciting poetry, and once he catches hold of me by the calves and asks: "Has my wondrous gaze tormented thee?" I say, "What if it has?" But, by the calves again: "Has my voice resounded in thy soul?"...Then he grabs me in his arms and drags me off somewhere. And when he drags me out again I go around, days, not myself, repeating over and over: "Pushkin... Evtiushkin... tormented... resounded," "Resounded...

tormented... Evtiushkin... Pushkin." And then again: "Pushkin... Evtiushkin."] (R76/E97–98)

When Erofeev's drunk and riotous characters pronounce Pushkin's poetic lines as their own, we see the effects of an educational system which drilled into students that Pushkin is a great Russian writer. Pushkin's lines became separated from original contexts so forcefully that the original context is forgotten. Nothing is really left of Pushkin except for such rhymes as "Evtiushkin."

Pushkin is dehumanized in Russian culture to such an extent that even the lines from his personal correspondence become "winged expressions" and penetrate the stories of the ill-fated Dasha and her Komsomol organizer. Dasha tells about another violent incident in her love affair with Evtiushkin-Pushkin, using Pushkin's letter to his wife:

"Ты придешь прощения ко мне просить, а я выйду во всем черном, обаятельная такая, и тебе всю морду исцарапаю, собственным своим кукишем! Уходи!!" А потом кричу: "Ты хоть душу-то любишь во мне? Душу — любишь?" А он все трясется и чернеет: "Сердцем, — орет, — сердцем да, сердцем люблю твою душу, но душою — нет, не люблю!!"

И как-то дико, по-оперному, рассмеялся, схватил меня, проломил мне череп и уехал во Владимир-на-Клязьме. Зачем уехал? К кому уехал?

["You'll come to beg forgiveness from me and I'll come out all in black, all enchanting, and I'll give you the finger and scratch your eyes out with it. Go away!" And then I scream: "Do you at least love the soul in me? The soul?" And he shakes all over and turns black: "With my heart," he yells, "with my heart, yes, with my heart I love your soul, but, no, I don't love your soul with my soul!!"

And wild somehow, like in an opera, he burst out laughing and grabbed me and broke my skull and left for Vladimir-on-the-Kliazma. Why did he leave? To whom did he go?] (R77/E99)

In a letter (dated August 21, 1833) to Natal'ia Goncharova, Pushkin wrote a phrase which penetrated into the above passage:

Гляделась ли ты в зеркало, и уверилась ли ты, что с твоим лицом ничего сравнить нельзя на свете, а душу твою люблю я еще более твоего лица.

[Have you looked at yourself in the mirror? Have you seen that nothing in the world can be compared to your face? And your soul, I love your soul even more than your face.]24

These parodies cast judgment on the image of Pushkin in contemporary culture. Pushkin's name is repeated so often that it becomes a common name, as in the colloquial phrase: "Who is going to do this for you? Pushkin?" Persistent, out-of-place mentioning of Pushkin's name by people who have no idea about Pushkin infuriates the erudite Venichka, for whom Pushkin is not a sanctified classic of Russian literature, but a man of genius. Venichka insists many times that people not only do not know anything about Pushkin's greatness, but also they do not even know why Pushkin died. Poking fun at the burden of "greatness," Erofeev stated:

Пришедший к абсолюту, т.е. с этих пор обреченный ни разу не поковырять в носу или почесать в затылке.

[The one who discovered absolute truth is destined never to pick his nose or scratch his head.]25

Greatness and magnificence which are removed from physical reality—an essential part of life—do not amount to much. Three sides of human life: the physical, spiritual and super-spiritual are supposed to interract, according to Venichka. In order to speak with God, Venichka searches for a genuine form of expression which would incorporate the three sides of being. Then he turns to the language of the great writers and to Biblical language, elevating his own speech through a peculiar kind of parody. The Bible is the source of the greatest number of parodies. It offers the structure, the stylistic peculiarities and debatable content for genuine expression to soul-searching Venichka, who sees God and angels as interlocutors and friends in need.

In the following passage, pondering over his life, Venichka addresses God as a friend:

Господь, вот ты видишь, чем я обладаю. Но разве *это* мне нужно? Разве по *этому* тоскует моя душа? Вот что дали мне люди взамен того, по чему тоскует душа! А если б они мне дали *того*, разве нуждался бы я в *этом*? Смотри, Господь, вот: розовое крепкое за рупь тридцать семь...

И весь в синих молниях, Господь мне ответил:

— А для чего нужны стигматы святой Терезе? Они ведь ей тоже не нужны. Но они ей желанны.

— Вот-вот! — отвечал я в восторге. — Вот и мне, и мне тоже — желанно мне это, но ничуть не нужно!

"Ну, раз желанно, Веничка, так и пей," — тихо подумал я, но все медлил. Скажет мне Господь еще что-нибудь или не скажет?

Господь молчал.

[Lord, you see what I possess. But truly is *this* necessary to me? Truly is *this* what my soul is pained over? This is what people have given me in exchange for that over which my soul is pained! But if they had given me *that*, would I really be in need of *this*? Look, Lord, here's the stout rosé at a rub' thirty-seven...

And, all in blue flashes of lightning, the Lord answered me:

"So what did St. Teresa need her stigmata for? It, too, was unnecessary, yet she desired it."

"That's the point," I answered in ecstasy. "Me, too, I desire this, but it's not at all necessary."

"Well, since it's desired, Venichka, go on and drink," I said to myself, but took my time. To see if perhaps the Lord had anything else to say.

The Lord was silent.] (R25–26/E26–27)

Addressing God in a dialogical sense is symbolic in prayers, for no verbal answer is expected. God answers in actions. Hence, understanding the impossibility of a dialogue with God, Job pronounces: "For he is not a man, as I am, that I should answer him, and we should come together in judgment" (Job 9:32). In *Moscow—Petushki*, when Venichka addresses *Gospod'* as a friend, he receives an answer. Naturally, offering God a meal of "vodka and a sandwich" sounds sacrilegious. On the other hand, in the context of contemporary Soviet culture, it is respectful and can be viewed as a sign of communion with God. Parody of the Bible is created through transforming an absolute word into a dialogical word. Venichka's prayer is parodic of a Biblical prayer because the language of a prayer turns from absolute into dialogic. Based on Bakhtin's theory, Morson formulates the following distinction between an absolute word and a dialogical word:

> In the kingdom of words, there are two kinds of subjects: one speaks to other words, the other does not. The first answers what has been spoken before and itself anticipates an answer. Aware of its audience, it knows that it is heard against its social and historical background and evaluated in terms of its speaker's personality. It knows it can be paraphrased, for it paraphrases others constantly. The second kind of word refuses to be paraphrased. It does not say, it is a saying. Admitting no authorship, it condescends to no dialogue. It can only be cited, and recited. When spoken, it belongs to no one, when written, it is Scripture.[26]

Erofeev's parodies of the great writers are ambiguous, as are his Biblical parodies. In the above parody, in spite of a transformation of absolute language into dialogic language, prayerful mystery is not removed. Through a dialogue with God, Venichka places himself on equal terms with the divine. Venichka's soliloquies are imbued with the beauty of Biblical language when he talks about Petushki, about his red-head, and about his son, using the language of the Song of Songs. Venichka's "Biblical passages" are genuine and touching, and they override the ugly reality of Moscow, making the *poema* the most "chaste" work of our times.

In a move contrary to the heroic and bombastic language of culture Venichka attempts to find his own true expression to describe his experience in this world and reach God. As we have seen above, in attempting to do this he reaches out to the classics, to proverbs, and to the absolute language of the Bible. He also transforms the existing language. Familiar words acquire new, unfamiliar meanings. For example, such a transformation takes place in the word *malodushie* in the following excerpt:

О, если бы весь мир, если бы каждый в мире был бы, как я сейчас, тих и боязлив и был бы так же ни в чем не уверен: ни в себе, ни в серьезности своего места под небом — как хорошо бы! Никаких энтузиастов, никаких подвигов, никакой одержимости! — всеобщее *малодушие*. Я согласился бы жить на земле целую вечность, если бы прежде мне показали уголок, где не всегда есть место подвигам. "Всеобщее *малодушие*" — да ведь это спасение от всех бед, это панацея, это предикат величайшего совершенства!

[Oh, if only the whole world, if everyone were like I am now, quiet and afraid and never sure about anything, not sure of himself nor of the seriousness of his place in this world—oh, how good it would be! No enthusiasts, no heroic deeds, nothing obsessive! Just universal *chicken-heartedness*. I'd agree to live on the earth for an eternity if they'd show me first a corner where there is not always room for heroic deeds. "Universal *chicken-heartedness*"—yes, yes, this is salvation, this is the panacea, this is the predicate to sublime perfection!] (R21/E20–21) (Emphasis added)

In the opening of the above passage Erofeev parodies Soviet phraseology characterized by exalted, heroic style. Phrases such as *uveren v sebe, v ser'eznosti svoego mesta pod nebom, entuziasty, podvigi, oderzhimost', ugolok gde vsegda est' mesto podvigam* are stock words describing a strong hero of a Socialist Realist novel, as well as an exemplary person in real life. We can find numerous examples of these clichés in newspapers of the time.

To a hero—a person "with a big soul"—the narrator opposes *malodushnyi chelovek*. Through such juxtaposition Erofeev accentuates the internal form of the word *malodushie*, i.e. the meaning of both its roots, "small" and "soul." Thus, Venichka's *malodushie*, meaning "to have a small soul" or "meekness" becomes a parody of the usual meaning of the word *malodushie*, which in its "naked form" (Bakhtin's term)[27] is "cowardice." In such a new meaning *vseobshchee malodushie — spasenie* corresponds to the Biblical "Blessed are the meek, for they shall inherit the earth" (Matt. 5:5). That is why a translation of *malodushie* as "universal chicken-heartedness" does not convey what the word really means in Erofeev's text.

Another example which is commonly misinterpreted is the word *pervenets*. *Moscow—Petushki* is dedicated to Vadim Tikhonov, whom Erofeev calls *moi lyubimyi pervenets*. Here the word *pervenets* is used not in its usual meaning of "first-born son," but as simply "the first," which could be the first reader, or the first disciple. Vladimir Murav'ev, Erofeev's close friend, writes about the misinterpretation of this word in Western criticism:

> Tikhonov is now commemorated for sure. Nobody understands that in Erofeev's texts *pervenets* is the first student, the first who understood and so on. There was even a commentary that Erofeev dedicated his work of genius to his first-born son.[28]

It is important to keep in mind when we read Erofeev's texts that he turns upside down and inside out usual ideas and notions. The real Tikhonov worked with Erofeev as a cable-fitter. In his letter to Gaiser-Shnitman, Erofeev mentions that in the seventies he entertained himself by writing textbooks for his son in geography, history, philosophy and literature (none of which are preserved) where he turned around all the customary notions. Erofeev writes that for this he is indebted to Tikhonov (Erofeev refers to him as *napersnik* [close friend and confidant]), who could never keep things straight. Tikhonov kept confusing "Henry Ford with Ernest Rutherford, Offenbach and Feuerbach, Rembrandt and Willy Brandt, Georges Marchais and Jerome Beaumarchais..."[29]

Another peculiar example of redefinition of words is the case of *nichtozhestvo*. In *Moscow—Petushki* the passages about Venichka's son, although few, are emotional and touching. Venichka, talking about his son being ill, calls him *nichtozhestvo*, ordinarily a negative word, an insult. However, in the context of Venichka's narration which is filled with tenderness, via accentuation of the root *nichto*, this word becomes "a delicate, fragile human being."

Да, да, когда я в прошлый раз приехал, мне сказали: он спит. Мне сказали: он болен и лежит в жару. Я пил лимонную у его кроватки, и меня оставили с ним одного. Он и в самом деле был в жару, и даже ямка на щеке вся была в жару, и было диковинно, что вот у такого *ничтожества* еще может быть жар...

[Yes, when I arrived the last time, they told me he was asleep; he was sick and had a fever. I drank lemon vodka by his crib and they left me alone with him. He really did have a fever—even the dimple on his cheek was all warm, and it was curious that such *a little nothing* could have a fever.] (R42/E49) (Emphasis added)

Erofeev constructs a context in such a way that the norm is constantly violated, and the words become redefined according to their context. Ordinarily negative words acquire positive connotation, as the examples with *malodushie* and *nichtozhestvo* show. Through his daring revolutionary language Erofeev shows that cultural constraints are artificial and can be broken.

By defying cultural assumptions in regard to what is considered great, Erofeev demonstrates that the lexicon of greatness which inflated the Russian language during the sixties and seventies[30] does not withstand his test for honesty. He shows that there is nothing in common between the language of greatness and Soviet reality. In the seventies, when the *poema Moscow—Petushki* was written, there was a sharp rise of exalted vocabulary.[31] Panegyrical language was intermixed in the official language of the media and gradually became a part of conversational language.

The tradition of panegyric style can be traced back to the Old Russian literary style of "word weaving" which had a real purpose. Word weaving (*pletenie sloves*) was used as an expression of verbal inadequacy and was intimately bound up with the prayerful search for inspired words. Epiphanius' word weaving in *Zhitie Stefana Permskogo* [*The Life of St. Stefan of Perm'*] has been regarded as the Russian facet of a pan-Orthodox Slavic mode of literary expression.

Words of pathos, mostly epithets of a hyperbolic nature gravitating either to praise or to curse, comprise the lexical material of the Soviet panegyrical style. The panegyrical style, when not supported by physical reality, leads to cynicism. Great words become sham symbols, stylistic Potemkin Villages. Such are the expressions *velikii narod*, *velikii russkii iazyk*, *dukhovnaia moshch' velikogo naroda*.

Through the vehicle of parody, Erofeev masterfully reveals the emptiness of the panegyric lexicon of Soviet culture. Contemplating the correlation between reality and the language describing it, he shows that the language is praising a phenomenon which does not exist, thus destroying the linguistic Potemkin Villages. Erofeev records in his diary:

> Нет на свете ни пути зла, ни пути добра. Нет на свете ни зла, ни добра. Но есть нечестная игра и честная игра.
> [There is no evil or good way in life. There is no evil or good in life. But there is a dishonest game and an honest game.][32]

Similarly without accusations or admonitions, Venichka compares reality and the language which describes this reality according to whether it is an honest or dishonest description. And he puts to an ad absurdum test vocabulary of an exalted reverential nature. Here is an example of such a parody. The narrator uses Soviet newspaper clichés and Turgenev's poem in prose, *Russkii iazyk* [*The Russian Language*], in which the poet says that the great Russian language is given to a great people[33]:

> Мне это нравится. Мне нравится, что у народа моей страны глаза такие пустые и выпуклые. Это вселяет в меня чувство законной гордости...Можно себе представить, какие глаза там. Где все продается и все покупается: ...глубоко спрятанные, притаившиеся, хищные и перепуганные глаза....Девальвация, безработица, пауперизм...Смотрят исподлобья, с неутихающей заботой и мукой — вот какие глаза в мире чистогана...
> Зато у моего народа — какие глаза! Они постоянно навыкате, но — никакого напряжения в них. Полное отсутствие всякого смысла — но зато какая мощь! (Какая духовная мощь!) Эти глаза не продадут. Ничего не продадут и ничего не купят. Что бы ни случилось с моей страной, во дни сомнений, во дни тягостных

раздумий, в годину любых испытаний и бедствий, — эти глаза не сморгнут. Им все божья роса...

[I like that. I like it that my country's people have such empty, bulging eyes. This instills in me a feeling of legitimate pride. You can imagine what the eyes are like where everthing is bought and sold—deeply hidden, secretive, predatory and frightened. Devaluation, unemployment, pauperism...People look at you distrustfully, with restless anxiety and torment. That's the kind of eyes they have in the world of Ready Cash.

On the other hand, my people have such eyes! They're constantly bulging but with no tension of any kind in them. There's complete lack of any sense but, then, what power! (What spiritual power!) These eyes will not sell out. They'll not sell or buy anything, whatever happens to my country. In days of doubt, in days of burdensome reflection, at the time of any trial or calamity, these eyes will not blink. They don't give a good goddamn about anything.] (R26–27/E28)

The phrase *velikii russkii narod* was used so frequently in the media that the epithet *velikii* became inseparable from *russkii narod*. In this parody Erofeev uses typical negative expressions from Soviet newspapers to describe the cruel and cold Western consciousness. Then he portrays the *russkii narod* with lexical opposites of these negative phrases. However, the created opposites are even more negative in their connotation than the original newspaper clichés. For example: Russian *pustye glaza* are opposed to Western eyes, which "смотрят исподлобья, с неутихающей заботой и мукой" [empty eyes vs. eyes which look at you distrustfully, with restless anxiety and torment]. *Vypuklye glaza* are juxtaposed with "глубоко спрятанные, притаившиеся, хищные и перепуганные глаза" [bulging eyes vs. deeply hidden, secretive, predatory and frightened eyes].

In the above quotation Erofeev stylistically destroys a convention of well-known metaphors from the myth of an inferior Western culture, which was created by Soviet propaganda. As a result, *dukhovnaia moshch' velikogo naroda* does not stand for anything; it is just an empty phrase, a sham symbol. He also satirizes the simplicity and conventionality of propaganda consciousness which divides the world into two parts: "here" and "there."

Exposing sham symbols of spiritual culture, Venichka notices everything that is real, and he is able to characterize its reality. Physical reality, feelings of compassion, anger, human emotions are all very much real to the inquisitive and attentive Venichka; he finds the language to describe the physical world around him. Hence physical reality is characterized by paralysis, nausea, nervous exhaustion, terrible sadness, stupor, fever, drink, beef Stroganoff, cake, udder, sherry; even obscenities are used in his search for true expression. Obscene words are the ones which pertain to the ugliest, lowest reality. Sometimes physical reality is so ugly that "человеческий язык не повернется выразить" [the human tongue cannot move to describe it] (R22/E22), or so complicated that it is impossible to express; such cases should be honored with a minute of silence, Venichka urges. He concludes that being has ugly fangs and later in the novel he wonders where is that happiness they write about in newspapers.

In the context of *Moscow—Petushki*, a minute of silence honors a dead spiritual culture which Venichka mourns. The mere fact that the words of greatness are a part of contemporary language means that great events occurred, and values existed. Inviting readers from all over his land to join him in the wake, Venichka opens a world of Biblical dimensions. It is felt especially acutely if we consider that *rasseiannye po moei zemle* is based on the Bible: "and let us make us a name, lest we be scattered abroad upon the face of the whole earth" (Gen. 11:4).

By parodying the language of greatness which gradually lost its content, not only does Erofeev imbue these empty forms with new context, but he also revives the texts where these forms originated. Parody, according to Bakhtin, is one of the most ancient and widespread forms for representing the direct word of another.[34] In the case of Soviet-speak these direct words stopped being viewed in any context other than Soviet. In other words, these expressions lost the individuality of interpretation which they had had in their contexts; they began to mean only one thing. Roland Barthes calls this cultural phenomenon "mythologization," which he defines as follows:

> "Mythologization" is the process whereby an object or idea is taken from its original context and turned into an ideological model: myth has the task of giving a historical intention a natural justification, and making contingency appear eternal. In passing from history to nature, myth acts economically: it abolishes the complexity of human acts, it gives them the simplicity of essences, it does away with all dialects, with any going back beyond what is immediately visible, it organizes a world which is without contradictions because it is without depth, a world, wide open and wallowing in the evident, it establishes a blissful clarity: things appear to mean something by themselves.[35]

In Russia, however, the process of mythologization is constant; it is strong and pervasive. I agree with Andrew Wachtel's keen observation that Russian society has been consistently defining its ideological positions by recourse to works of art. Wachtel writes:

> ...ideas that are initially advanced in linguistics, historical, or literary texts gradually become divorced from their original contexts and begin to be perceived as free-floating ideological positions. The resulting ideologies take on a life of their own—a life that is often only tangentially related to the concerns of the artistic work or works that originated the process.[36]

Erofeev's stylistic achievement carries out the process of "demythologization." Through the game of detection of parodied sources the reader is forced to place quoted phrases into their original contexts where they recover their complexity and multitude of interpretations.

As a result of its cultural and philosophical depth, Erofeev's language can be perceived as knowledge, as a metaphor for the fruit from the Tree of Knowledge. Indeed, in the *uvedomlenie* [preface] to *Moscow—Petushki*, Erofeev—the writer—hints that he treats his artistic word as The Word. Just as the Creator forewarns Adam and Eve not to taste the forbidden fruit, Erofeev forewarns his readers to skip the chapter "Serp i Molot—Karacharovo" ["Hammer and

Sickle—Karacharovo"] which was supposedly written as pure obscenity, except for only one decent sentence: "and I drank it immediately" (*I nemedlenno vypil*). By this honest warning, Erofeev writes, he only achieved the opposite effect: all the readers, especially women, went first for the "bad" chapter. The situation shows human nature. It echoes the protostory of Adam and Eve, and perhaps the poetic reference to it in Pushkin's *Evgenii Onegin*,[37] memorized at school. The passage from *Evgenii Onegin* is so well known that it became a part of the vocabularly of "winged expressions."[38] If in the introduction Erofeev suggests the divine significance of his word, in the body of the work he shows that his word is capable of a dialogue with God.

Moreover, at the end of the story when Venichka's throat is pierced with an awl, he dies but his Word continues to speak and finishes the story, proving that the language is the main player in *Moscow—Petushki.*

I have attempted to show *how* Erofeev in his parodies uses *bytovoi* language permeated with cultural context. Through parody Erofeev breaks the stiff fetters of cultural constraints and creates an original form of expression. Playing the game of detection of parodied sources, the reader is forced to place quoted phrases into their original contexts where they recover their complexity and multitude of interpretations. As a result of this process of "demythologization" the language regains its equilibrium of signifier and signified, as the above examples demonstrates.

Erofeev's elevating parody takes us even further back beyond Russian classical literature, to the Biblical roots when "at the beginning there was the Word," thus regenerating Russian memory in the union of past, present and future in the eternal time of *bytie* where as Erofeev's narrator says, parodying the phrase from *Anna Karenina*, "Все смешалось, чтобы только начаться" [Everything was all mixed up, only to start anew] (R47/E56).[39] In such a way Erofeev's language undergoes a metamorphosis from *byt* to *bytie*—an eternal question of Russian culture.

Endnotes

1. Isidore Geld, *Dictionary of Omissions for Russian Translators with Examples from Scientific Texts* (Columbus: Slavica, 1993). "Omissions" are words or phrases that are not to be translated when turning a Russian text into English, e.g. the word *dostatochno* in the phrase: "Не предложено достаточно убедительное объяснение."

2. Velichanskii, "Fenomen Erofeeva," 125.

3. Porter, *Russia's Alternative Prose*, 73.

4. See Gaiser-Shnitman, *Venedikt Erofeev*. Gaiser-Shnitman identifies about 200 texts in *Moscow—Petushki*.

5. Al'tshuller, "*Moskva — Petushki* Venedikta Erofeeva," 75.

6. This is quoted from Erofeev, *Moscow—Petushki*, R23/E22.

7. Vail' and Genis, "Strasti po Erofeevu," *Knizhnoe obozrenie*, 8.

8. Akhmadulina et al., Afterword to *Moskva Petushki i pr.*, 123.

9. E. Brown, quoted in Kasack, *Dictionary of Russian Literature*, 471; Vail', "Zhabo iz lyka," 5; Maryniak, "A Hero of Our Time," 9.

10. Maryniak, "A Hero of Our Time," 9.

11. Review of *Moskva — Petushki*, *Kontinent*, 371.

12. Vail' and Genis, "Strasti po Erofeevu," *Ekho*, 110.

13. Porter, *Russia's Alternative Prose*, 20.

14. Linda Hutcheon, *A Theory of Parody. The Teachings of Twentieth-Century Art Forms* (London: Methuen, 1985), 60.

15. Hutcheon discusses some parodic works, like *Don Quixote*, which actually manage to free themselves from the background text enough to create an autonomous form.

16. Porter, *Russia's Alternative Prose*, 26.

17. M. Gor'kii, "Starukha Izergil'," in *Izbrannye proizvedeniia v trekh tomakh*, vol. 1 (Kiev: Dnipro, 1987), 45.

18. Vail', "Zhabo iz lyka," 5.

19. L. N. Tolstoi, *Anna Karenina. Roman v vos'mi chastiakh* (Leningrad: Khudozhestvennaia literatura, 1987), 3.

20. F. M. Dostoevskii, *Brat'ia Karamazovy*, in *Polnoe sobranie sochinenii v tridtsati tomakh*, vol. 14 (Leningrad: Nauka, 1976), 76.

21. Gaiser-Shnitman, *Venedikt Erofeev*, 180.

22. See Guy Houk's article "Erofeev and Evtushenko" included in this volume.

23. Compare this passage to Tat'iana's letter to Evgenii:

Ты в сновиденьях мне являлся,

Незримый, ты мне был уж мил,

Твой чудный взор меня томил,

В душе твой голос раздавался.

[You appeared to me in my dreams.

Unseen, you were already clear to me.

Your wondrous gaze tormented me.

Your voice resounded in my soul.]

A. S. Pushkin, *Evgenii Onegin*, in *Polnoe sobraniie sochinenii*, vol. 5 (Leningrad: Nauka, 1978), 61.

24. V. V. Kunin, ed., *Druz'ia Pushkina: perepiska, vospominaniia, dnevniki v dvukh tomakh*, vol. 2 (Moskva: Pravda, 1986), 447.

25. Erofeev, "Iz zapisnykh knizhek," *Literaturnaia gazeta*, 6.

26. Gary Saul Morson, "Tolstoy's Absolute Language," in *Bakhtin, Essays and Dialogues on His Work* (Chicago: University of Chicago Press, 1986), 123.

27. Bakhtin stressed that there is an "enormous difference between naked words out of context and words as they are exploited in social situations. Isolated words constitute the language studied by linguists; social words are the more broadly conceived subject that Bakhtin takes as his own." Katerina Clark and Michael Holquist, *Mikhail Bakhtin* (Cambridge: Belknap Press of Harvard University Press, 1984), 216.

28. Frolova et al., "Neskol'ko monologov," 92.

29. Gaiser-Shnitman, *Venedikt Erofeev*, 22. There is a mistake in Erofeev's letter: Beaumarchais' name is not Jerome, but Pierre-Augustin Caron de Beaumarchais (the author of an eighteenth-century French comedy which was the basis for Rossini's *Barber of Seville*).

30. Efim Etkind, "Sovetskie tabu," *Sintaksis*, no. 9 (1981): 19.

31. Smirnova, "Venedikt Erofeev glazami gogoleveda," 58–66.

32. From Erofeev's personal diary. In 1993 Erofeev's widow, Galina Erofeeva, forwarded me this diary, which has never been published except for some excerpts.

33. "Во дни тягостных сомнений, во дни тягостных раздумий о судьбах моей родины — ты один мне поддержка и опора, о великий, могучий, правдивый, свободный русский язык! Не будь тебя — как не впасть в отчаяние при виде того, что свершается дома? Но нельзя не верить, чтобы такой язык не был дан великому народу!" [In days of burdensome doubts, in days of burdensome reflections about the fate of my motherland—only you are my encouragement and support, you—the great, powerful, truthful and free Russian language! If not for you, I would be hopeless at the sight of what is happening at home. But one cannot but believe that such a language was bestowed on a great people!] I. Turgenev, "Russkii iazyk," in *Polnoe sobraniie sochinenii v*

28 tomakh, vol. 13 (Moskva: Akademiia nauk, 1960–65), 198.

34. M. M. Bakhtin, *The Dialogic Imagination: Four Essays*, trans. by Caryl Emerson (Austin: University of Texas Press, 1981), 51.

35. Roland Barthes. *Mythologies*, trans. by Annette Lavers (New York: Noonday, 1972), 142–43.

36. Andrew Baruch Wachtel, *The Battle for Childhood. Creation of a Russian Myth* (Stanford: Stanford University Press, 1990), 201.

37. О люди! все похожи вы
    На прародительницу Еву:
    Что вам дано, то не влечет,
    Вас непрестанно змий зовет
    К себе, к таинственному древу;
    Запретный плод вам подавай,
    А без того вам рай не рай.
    [We all resemble more or less
    our Mother Eve: we're never falling
    for what's been given us to take;
    to his mysterious tree the snake
    is calling us, forever calling—
    and once forbidden fruit is seen,
    no paradise can stay serene.]
    Pushkin, *Evgenii Onegin*, 152.

38. N. S. Ashukin, M. G. Ashukina, *Krylatye slova* (Moskva: Pravda, 1986), 444.

39. In *Anna Karenina*, "Все смешалось в доме Облонских" [Everything was in confusion at the Oblonskii household]. Tolstoi, *Anna Karenina*, 3.

Erofeev and Evtushenko

Guy Houk

In a television interview filmed shortly before his death,[1] Venedikt Erofeev, in obvious ill health, speaks through an electronic voice box pressed to his throat. Erofeev responds to a variety of questions; near the end, he is asked to rate contemporary Russian authors on a liquid scale (i.e., by how many grams of vodka he would offer them if they were guests in his home). Erofeev replies that he would, for example, give Valentin Rasputin 150 grams, Vasil Bykov a full glass, and so on. Asked what he would give to Evgenii Evtushenko, Erofeev chortles in reply, "a glass of fortified wine" (*bormotukha*).

While clever, Erofeev's answer is not startling. Something in that vein was clearly anticipated by the interviewer, and surely by most readers of *Moscow—Petushki*, in which Evtushenko, only slightly disguised in the character of *traktorist* Evtiushkin, is so scathingly parodied. Erofeev's reference here is unmistakable, but I would submit that his reworking of Evtushenko's public image is an important subtext in numerous other passages in the novel, where the technique is more subtly employed. In this paper I intend to show the ubiquitous presence and thematic function of this device, to show its crucial role in shaping the work's structural coherence, and finally to consider how Erofeev's parody of Evtushenko's image renders problematic certain of Erofeev's stratagems for the construction and presentation of his own public "self."

Mark Al'tshuller has identified three categories of cultural reference which inform *Moscow—Petushki*. These are: "1) the phenomena of western European culture; 2) those of Russian culture; and 3) the culture (or anti-culture) of [then] contemporary Soviet society, including the events of the October revolution, party slogans, utterances of the leaders and so on."[2] Perhaps unfairly, Erofeev's novel situates the life and work of Evgenii Evtushenko squarely within the third of these categories, which is repeatedly portrayed as the degenerate bastard offspring of the second. It is thus not surprising that the story of *traktorist* Evtiushkin, told by the woman in the beret to explain the loss of her teeth, mocks Evtushenko in several ways.

Most obviously, the combination of the names "Evtushenko" and "Pushkin" into the hybrid "Evtiushkin" invites the reader to compare the artistic genius of the two poets, a comparison hardly likely to favor Evtushenko. The association is reinforced by the woman's repeated assertion that she lost her teeth "for Pushkin," and her recitation of the *traktorist's* questions to her, "Мой чудный взгляд тебя томил?" [Has my wondrous gaze tormented thee?] and "В душе мой голос раздавался?" [Has my voice resounded in your soul?] (R76/E98). As Svetlana Gaiser-Shnitman has pointed out, these are direct quotations from Pushkin[3]:

> Ты в сновидениях мне явился,
> Незримый, ты мне был уж мил,
> Твой чудный взор меня томил,
> В душе твой голос раздавался.
> [You have appeared to me in dreams,
> Unseen, you were already dear to me,
> Your wondrous gaze has tormented me,
> Your voice has resounded in my soul.]

Of course, it is hardly devastating to say of any poet that he writes worse than Pushkin. The sharpness of Erofeev's irony here derives not from a simple comparison of talent, but rather from his derision of Evtushenko's astonishing audacity. The poet had only four years previously published *Bratskaia GES* [*The Bratsk Hydroelectric Station*], a work judged by many as an act of intellectual cowardice, the price which Evtushenko was willing to pay to maintain his privileged status. To add insult to injury, Evtushenko had begun his hymn of praise to socialist construction with an invocation to his predecessors, the *molitva pered poemoi* [prayer before the poem], in which he had beseeched Mayakovsky, Blok, Esenin and others to inspire his paean to Leninism. To Pushkin, Evtushenko had addressed the following plea:

Дай, Пушкин, мне свою певучесть,
Свою раскованную речь,
Свою пленнительную участь —
Как бы шаля, глаголом жечь.
[Pushkin, give me your gift of melody,
Your unfettered speech,
Your captivating destiny,
As though playing games, to burn with the word.][4]

It is this claim (that *The Bratsk Hydroelectric Station* has been infused with the genius of Russian poetry) which Erofeev so gleefully skewers in *Moscow—Petushki*. Erofeev's disdain for Evtushenko's hubris motivates the woman's continual torment of *traktorist* Evtiushkin with the odd question, "А кто за тебя детишек будет воспитывать? Пушкин, что ли?" [And who's going to educate your kids for you? Pushkin, is it?] (R77/E98). Future generations of Russians, and of Russian poets, will indeed by nurtured by Pushkin rather than Evtushenko.

Precisely this painful (for Evtushenko) truth renders the woman's question agonizing for Evtiushkin, so much so that eventually he becomes enraged and assaults his lover, fracturing her skull and, in a subsequent encounter, knocking out her teeth. These events may also reflect a widely-rumored (although difficult to substantiate) incident from Evtushenko's life—his alleged violent assault upon his then-wife, Bella Akhmadulina, in the presence of

Andrei Voznesenskii and Robert Rozhdestvenskii alongside the highway from Moscow to Peredelkino.

There are still other subtle references to Evtushenko in the woman's very brief account of her affair with Evtiushkin. She reports that, after fracturing her skull, the *traktorist* departs for Vladimir-on-the-Kliazma; having returned long enough to knock her teeth out, he sets out for Rostov-on-the-Don. Asked where he is now, she replies that if he has not died, then he is in Central Asia, but if he is dead, then he is in Siberia (R78/E100). This werewolf-like ability to be in many widely-scattered places simultaneously reflects Evtushenko's own account of his travels in his *Avtobiografiia* [*Autobiography*]:

> ...На Алтае я разговаривал по ночам у костров с трактористами, поднимавшими целину, о любви и политике. На Волге я спорил о Сталине с рыбаками. На Дальнем Востоке я размышлял вместе с охотниками на тигров, что сделать, для того, чтобы в мире не было больше войны. На Камчатке я дискутировал с краболовами о том, что такое счастье. В Грузии я говорил с виноградарями о поэзии.
>
> [...In the Altai I chatted at night by campfires about love and politics with the drivers of tractors who were plowing up virgin soil (hence the epithet *traktorist* Evtiushkin in *Moscow—Petushki* - G. H.) On the Volga I argued with fishermen about Stalin. In the Far East the hunters of tigers and I discussed what could be done so that there would be no more war in the world. In Kamchatka I discussed with crabbers the definition of happiness. In Georgia I talked about poetry with viticulturalists.][5]

The "Evtiushkin" character disappears at this point in the novel, to return only very near the end. However, the abrupt shift to the theme of travel, and particularly travel abroad, marks not a disjuncture, but a continuation of Evtushenko's public image as subtext. Here it is a different hypostasis of the poet—the self-styled sophisticated observer of life in the West—that Erofeev parodies. On the thematic level, the transition from the Evtiushkin-*traktorist* tale to Venichka's travel narrative does not mark a radical shift, but rather shows a logical metonymic progression, in which different aspects of the Evtushenko persona are pilloried.

In the "travel narrative," the reader again encounters an extraordinarily dense system of allusions in a very compact space. Marina Balina has shown that travel memoirs formed an important genre in official Soviet literature of the 1960s,⁶ but there can be no doubt that the best-known Soviet traveller of the time was Evgenii Evtushenko. While Iosif Brodskii was enduring imprisonment for the "crime" of poetry, Evtushenko was granted almost unbelievable privileges for the same activity. The difference, of course, was that Evtushenko was generally willing to respond with his art to what party leaders defined as the "demands of society," as in "Stikhi o zagranitse" ["Verses of Foreign Lands"], Part I of his 1962 collection *Vzmakh ruki* [*A Stroke of the Hand*]. In *Moscow—Petushki*, Venichka's assurance to his listeners that there are no blacks in America, and that, "свобода так и остается призраком на этом континенте скорби" [freedom thus remains a phantom on that continent of sorrow] (R79/E101), along with his puzzlement over the Americans' inexplicable sense of self-satisfaction, serve as ironic counterpoint to Evtushenko's travel poem "Serditye" ["The Angry Ones"], in which he writes:

По Европе мрачно бродят парни.
Мрачно бродят парни по Америке.
[Young men gloomily wander about Europe.
Young men gloomily wander about America.]⁷

In addition, old Mitrich's pathetic lament, "весь рис увозим в Китай, весь сахар увозим на Кубу...а сами что будем кушать?" [all our rice goes to China, all the sugar to Cuba...so what will we eat?] (R79/E102) reminds the reader of Evtushenko's status as special correspondent in Cuba for *Pravda* [*Truth*], a role which he played intermittently from 1960 to 1963. While on the island, Evtushenko regularly produced wildly enthusiastic poems about Castro and his revolution, such as "Internatsional" ["The Internationale"],

"Revoliutsiia i pachanga" ["The Revolution and the Pachanga"], "Koroleva krasoty" ["The Beauty Queen"] and the panegyric "Stikhi o Fidele" ["A Poem about Fidel"].

There are further significant references to Evtushenko among Venichka's travel notes. One of these is the ease with which Venichka crosses international boundaries, apparently walking from Italy to Paris to London (!) without hindrance. When questioned, he explains,

— Да что же тут поразительного! И какие еще границы?! Граница нужна для того, чтобы не перепутать нации. У нас, например, стоит пограничник и твердо знает, что граница эта — не фикция и не эмблема, и потому что по одну сторону границы говорят на русском и больше пьют, а по другую — меньше пьют и говорят на нерусском...

А там? Какие там могут быть границы, если все одинаково пьют и говорят не по-русски!... Так что там на этот счет совершенно свободно... Хочешь ты, например, остановиться в Эболи — пожалуйста, останавливайся в Эболи. Хочешь идти в Каноссу — никто тебе не мешает, иди в Каноссу. Хочешь перейти Рубикон — переходи.

[So what's so astonishing about it? And what boundaries, anyway? A boundary is necessary in order not to get nations confused. With us, for example, a border guard stands there and he knows absolutely that the boundary isn't a fiction or an emblem, because on one side of it people speak Russian and drink more and on the other they speak non-Russian and drink less.

But over there what kind of boundaries could exist, if they all drink and speak non-Russian in the same way?...In this sense, things are completely free. If you want, for example, to stay in Eboli, please, stay in Eboli. If you want to go to Canosa, nobody'll interfere with you, go to Canosa. If you want to cross the Rubicon, go ahead.]
(R83/E107–8)

Erofeev is obviously parodying Evtushenko's poem:

Границы мне мешают...

Мне не ловко

не знать Буэнос-Айреса,
                    Нью-Йорка.
Хочу шататься,
            сколько надо Лондоном,
со всеми говорить,
                хотя б на ломаном,
мальчишкой,
            на автобусе повисшим,
хочу проехать утренним Парижем!
[Borders bother me
I find it awkward
not to know Buenos Aires
Or New York.
I so much want to go swaying
Like a boy
On a raised (double-decker) bus
Around London
To talk to everyone
Albeit in broken (English)
I want to ride through Paris in the morning!][8]

While the interplay between this poem and Venichka's parodic reworking is straightforward enough, the other reference to Evtushenko in this section is more problematic, and echoes an earlier passage. When Venichka attempts to matriculate at the Sorbonne, his eligibility is to be determined by his response to the question, "А что тебе как феномену присуще?" [What kind of inherent phenomenon do you have in you?] (R80/E104). The poor Russian is in despair; he has an obvious handicap. He asks, "Ну что мне как феномену может быть присуще? Я ведь сирота. 'Из Сибири?' — спрашивают. Говорю: 'Из Сибири'" [What could be inherent in me as a phenomenon? I'm an orphan. "From Siberia?" they ask. I say, "From Siberia"] (R80/E104). For the second time in the novel, Venichka claims as his heritage not the expected sobriquet "Kazanskaia sirota" [orphan from Kazan], but rather the startling "orphan from Siberia." Nor does this statement conform to Erofeev's own biography, since he lived his entire life prior to enrolling at Moscow State University on the Kol'skii Peninsula. In order to grasp the full significance of this phrase, with its obvious link to Evtushenko (who actually was, in a sense, an "orphan from Siberia"), it is necessary to examine the circumstances of its first appearance in *Moscow—Petushki*.

Early in the morning of the fateful thirteenth Friday on which Venichka's journey takes place, the angels lure him into the restaurant of the Kursk Station with the false offer of sherry. As is invariably true of the promises made by the angels, this one proves to be a lie; there is no sherry, and Venichka's request brings him only pain and humiliation from the restaurant workers, who pitilessly cast him out. In his attempt to appeal to them, Venichka states for the first time, "— Я ведь... из Сибири, я сирота... А просто чтобы не так тошнило... хереса хочу" [I'm from Siberia, I'm an orphan...Just so I won't feel so nauseated...I'd like some sherry] (R22/E21). The motivation for Venichka's self-definition as "Siberian orphan" follows logically from the text of the preceeding passage, in which he meditates on the nature of greatness:

> О, если бы весь мир, если бы каждый в мире был бы, как я сейчас, тих и боязлив и был бы так же ни в чем не уверен: ни в себе, ни в серьезности своего места под небом — как хорошо бы! Никаких энтузиастов, никаких подвигов, никакой одержимости! — всеобщее малодушие. Я согласился бы жить на земле целую вечность, если бы прежде мне показали уголок, где не всегда есть место подвигам.
> [Oh, if only the whole world, if everyone were like I am now, placid and timorous and never sure about anything, not sure of himself nor of the seriousness of his position under the heavens—oh, how good it could be. No enthusiasts, no feats of valor, nothing obsessive! Just universal chicken-heartedness. I'd agree to live on the earth for an eternity if they'd show me first a corner where there's not always room for valor.] (R21/E20–21)

Here Erofeev rebels against the ideological pressure from all facets of official Soviet life. It would be possible to cite innumerable examples of literary texts, both well-known and obscure, which could serve as objects for Venichka's disgust; his target is multiple.

Among Evtushenko's works, Venichka may be attacking the collection *Shosse entuziastov* [*Highway of Enthusiasts*] as well as Part II of *A Stroke of the Hand*, entitled "Budem velikimi" ["We Shall Be Great"]. In the latter book, Evtushenko contrasts the despair and injustice of Western life, shown in the travel poems of Part I, with the magnificent future of the Soviet state, whose greatness is described in Part II. There is, however, an even more prominent Evtushenkan subtext for Venichka's almost psychopathological revulsion against deeds of great heroism. That is *The Bratsk Hydroelectric Station*:

In the "Introduction" to his epic Evtushenko writes:

> Может быть, некоторым читателям покажется странным обилие исторических глав в поэме с таким современным названием. Но на Братской ГЭС я думал не только о героическом труде ее строителей, а обо всех сыновьях и дочерях России, отдавших жизнь в борьбе за осушествление величайших идеалов человечества.
>
> Труд строителей Братской ГЭС по праву называют великим подвигом. Но этот подвиг был подготовлен всеми подвигами нашего народа за всю его многовековую историю...
>
> Через трудные судьбы мне хотелось показать наиболее убедительный пример несгибаемой веры, которая является главной, побеждающей темой поэмы.
>
> [Perhaps the abundance of historical chapters in an epic poem with such a contemporary title will seem strange to some readers. But at the Bratsk Hydroelectric Station I thought not only about the heroic labor of its builders, but also about all of the sons and daughters of Russia who had given their lives in the struggle for the fulfillment of the highest ideals of humanity.
>
> The work of the builders of the Bratsk Hydroelectric Station is properly called a great exploit. But this exploit was prepared by all of the exploits of our people in all of its centuries-long history...
>
> I wanted to use these difficult life stories to show a most convincing example of unshakable faith, which is the major, triumphant theme of this epic.][9]

Venichka's loathing for daring exploits, his expressed desire that everyone on earth be "certain of nothing," the abundance of historical references in the novel, the *traktorist* Evtiushkin character (and perhaps in part the novel's subtitle, *поэма*)—these motifs, considered as a whole, justify the hypothesis that *Moscow—Petushki* is, in large measure, Erofeev's derisive comment upon what he saw as Evtushenko's betrayal of truth and art in the sixties. Precisely *this* reading explains the "Siberian orphan" label which Venichka attaches to himself at the Sorbonne and the Kursk Station restaurant. In both scenes, that phrase is contiguous with passages dealing directly with the Evtushenko theme, and therefore is, in both places, metonymically motivated.

The contention that Evtushenko's image serves as a significant subtext in the novel is further supported by the appearance of *traktorist* Evtiushkin on Venichka's train at the moment when it "arrives in Petushki." The second evocation of the Evtiushkin character is consistent with Erofeev's device of "double appearance" by cultural figures, first noted by Paperno and Gasparov.[10] The second incarnation of Evtiushkin is, however, unique in several ways. First, he had previously served only as a character in a story told by a passenger; Evtiushkin had not hitherto been "physically" present on the train (whatever that means in this hallucinatory narrative; indeed, how would Venichka recognize him, having never seen him?). Second, his arrival is simultaneous with that of the train at its destination (Petushki/Moscow), which is accompanied by a series of apocalyptic images:

Пламенел закат, и лошади вздрагивали, и где то счастье, о котором пишут в газетах? Я бежал и бежал, сквозь вихорь и мрак, срывая двери с петель, я знал, что поезд "Москва — Петушки" летит под откос. Вздымались вагоны — и снова проваливались, как одержимые орудью...

А кимвалы продолжали бряцать, и бубны гремели. И звезды падали на крыльцо сельсовета. И хохотала Суламифь.

[The sun was ablaze in the west and the horses shied, and where is that happiness which they write about in the newspapers? I ran and ran through the whirlwind and gloom, ripping doors off their hinges. I realized that the Moscow—Petushki train was flying off over the embankment. The cars heaved upward, then fell back again, as if overcome by stupor...

They went on clanging their cymbals and clattering their tambourines. And stars fell on the porch of the Agro-Soviet. And the maid of Shulam roared with laughter.] (R112–13/E150–151)

In this crucial passage, Evtiushkin at first flees in terror from the Erinyes, and compassionate Venichka attempts to intercede on his behalf. He exhorts the Furies to stop, crying out, "В мире нет виноватых!" [No one in the world is to blame!] (R112/E149–50). Venichka even manages to seize one of the Furies as she passes, to which she responds in an extraordinary way: like Dostoevsky's Christ in "Legenda velikogo inkvizitora" ["The Legend of the Grand Inquisitor"], she unexpectedly takes her captor's head in her hands and kisses him on the forehead. This symbol of divine forgiveness throws Venichka into utter confusion. He releases the Fury, only to see, a moment later as the account of the apocalyptic train wreck reaches its crescendo, a reversal of the original chase. In the end, it is the Erinyes who race in panic, pursued by the enraged Evtiushkin.

The reversal from victim to persecutor parallels the transformation of Evtushenko's image among the Russian intelligentsia in the 1960s. At least twice in the early part of that decade, Russians voluntarily, without foreknowledge on the part of the poet, gathered around him to protect him from what they perceived as threats to his physical safety. This occured first after the publication of "Babii Iar"[11] and again after Khrushchev's infamous speech of March 8, 1963, which included his grotesque denunciation of modern art. When an anti-Evtushenko campaign followed in the press, Russians arrived in hordes at his apartment building, many coming from other cities, to prevent his arrest. The stairway was packed from the first to the sixth floor; when rumors began circulating that the poet had committed suicide, the police asked him to show himself frequently on his balcony to pacify the enormous crowds which had gathered in the street below.[12] At that time, like the *traktorist* Evtiushkin pursued by the Erinyes, Evtushenko was perceived as an innocent victim, whose plight provoked sympathy and the desire to intervene. In later years, when Evtushenko's public image had been reinterpreted by many Russian intellectuals to conform to a perceived change in the code of his conduct, he was largely redefined as an ally of the oppressors. This metamorphosis in the Evtushenko persona is symbolized in the novel by the turnabout of the chase through the train, with Evtiushkin ultimately occupying the place of vengeful power. It is no coincidence that precisely this figure and no other is present at the violent end of the train ride. Evtushenko/Evtiushkin personifies Venichka's assertion:

Я остаюсь внизу, и снизу плюю на всю вашу общественную лестницу. Да. На каждую ступеньку лестницы — по плевку. Чтобы по ней подниматься, надо быть жидовской мордою без страха и упрека, надо быть пидорасом, выкованным из чистой стали с головы до пят. А я — не такой.

[I'm staying below, and from below I spit on your whole social ladder. Yes, on every rung of your ladder I'll leave a gob of spit. In order to climb it, you have to have a kike's ugly face which displays neither fear nor reproach; you have to be a pederast forged from pure steel from head to toe. And I'm not like that.] (R36/E41)

It is clearly Erofeev's contention that Evtushenko had climbed the ladder of status precisely because he was "like that" (*takoi*), and that therefore the poet deserved to be the target of scathing satire. Erofeev mocks Evtushenko's personal life, his art, and his beliefs, but saves his most vicious attacks for what he perceives to be Evtushenko's most profound act of betrayal—the prostitution of his talent in exchange for the privileged life of the obedient lapdog.

Evtushenko, naturally, evaluates his own past differently. In numerous conversations, he has complained of the inexplicable "ingratitude" of those victims of Soviet oppression whom he altruistically and consistently aided, and there is little doubt that he is sincere.[13] Nor does he recognize the factors that motivate his condemnation by Russian intellectuals; Evtushenko sees no inherent contradiction in authoring both "Nasledniki Stalina" ["The Heirs of Stalin"] and *The Bratsk Hydroelectric Station* (indeed, both are included in his *Collected Poems*, published in 1991).[14] Alone among Russian literary figures, Evtushenko was capable both of joining the presidium of the Writers' Union, and of sending telegrams to protest the invasion of Czechoslovakia and the persecution of Solzhenitsyn. In this, Evtushenko's conduct bears a striking similarity to that of Tsar Aleksandr I, as described by Iurii Lotman,[15] and like Aleksandr, Evtushenko alienated most Russian intellectuals precisely as a result of his failure to maintain a consistent (from their point of view) ideological stance.

It is perhaps this demand for consistency that explains why Erofeev, while deconstructing the official Soviet version of Evtushenko's public image of 1970, simultaneously took such great care in the creation of his own. This is a process that began within the text of *Moscow—Petushki* and continued even after the death of its creator.

As many scholars have noted, there is a strong correspondence between the character "Venichka Erofeev" and certain aspects of the life of Christ. For example, at several key moments Venichka reenacts Christ's martyrdom.[16] The novel's hero is purported to conform to other saintly models as well: in an article in *Znamia* [*The Banner*], Mark Lipovetsky explores the theme of Venichka as holy fool.[17] Critics often accept the book's implicit message that Soviet alcoholics were victims of the system, martyrs persecuted by an overpowering evil who took comfort where they could find it.[18] Under such conditions, both Venichka's way of life and, more importantly, Erofeev's writing of the novel, can be evaluated as heroic acts of protest in defense of truth and humanist values. Many sources could be cited to demonstrate the widespread popularity of this approach to Erofeev's life and work; E. A. Smirnova, for example, wrote that

> The forcibly displaced aspiration "to genuinely laugh" was primarily turned upon those objects which one was expected to

revere. Erofeev did this with unsurpassed panache and with the recklessness of a man for whom the truth is not only dearer than some Plato, but also dearer than membership in the Writers' Union. This writer subjected all of the pompous falsity which was then flourishing in society to the utmost degree of laughter, and for this purpose employed the weapon which our literature inherited from Gogol—the well-chosen Russian word.[19]

The common interpretation of *Moscow—Petushki*—as courageous, subversive counterattack in defense of truth and humanity—thrust its author into a role which is time-honored in Russian cultural tradition: the writer as prophet, as political opposition, as voice of conscience. If Evtushenko was despised for refusing to don this mask consistently, Erofeev was determined to make it fit.

Evtushenko's non-compliance with the demands of his institutionalized role resulted in his ostracism by a large segement of Russian intellectual society (one is reminded of Brodskii's statement to Sergei Dovlatov that "if [Evtushenko] is against collectivization... then I am in favor").[20] On the other hand, the pressure to conform to the role of "author of *Moscow—Petushki*" presented Erofeev with a different dilemma. The desire to transform his biography into a kind of Quixotic *zhitie*, a canonical account of service to the causes of truth and art, apparently led Erofeev to attempt myth-creation through the process of rewriting his own history. One is led to conclude that Erofeev was operating within a cultural tradition dominated by the romantic *Weltanschauung*, in which (again citing Lotman), "...in the process of becoming theatrical the world as a whole is reconstructed according to the laws of theatrical space in which things become the signs of things" and "Life selects art as a model and strives to 'imitate' it."[21] It was almost certainly the perceived necessity to transform his life into romantic text, where "things become the signs of things," that induced Erofeev to invent and circulate a series of fables about his own youth. As a result, the modern scholar is faced with the choice of several unreliable versions, given by Erofeev himself, of the facts of his life. Describing, for example, his expulsion from Moscow State University in 1957, Karen Ryan-Hayes has written that Erofeev was dismissed "...either because of his participation in a student play which met with the disapproval of university authorities, or because of his failure to attend military preparation classes."[22] Wisely, she notes that "Most likely, his expulsion was the result of a combination of these (and perhaps other) factors, for his contemporaries recall his behavior in this period as consistently unconventional, bordering on the scandalous." Again, she explains his removal from the Vladimir Pedagogical Institute as "...either for writing satirical poems or because he was found in the possession of a Bible."[23] The one consistent element in all of these tales is that each redounds to the credit of Venichka Erofeev, courageously unwilling to be bound by the strictures of a corrupt society. The fact that Erofeev could not seem to get the story straight, however, casts doubt upon each of these variants, and lends credence to the assertion by his college roommate that they are all lies.[24] According to this source, Erofeev was expelled for the disappointingly prosaic reason that he simply stopped attending class and taking examinations, despite earnest pleas from his professors to continue his studies.

There are numerous further events in Erofeev's autobiographical accounts which strike this observer as contradictory and extremely dubious: for example, mysteriously vanishing manuscripts of literary masterpieces that never appeared (the number of works the Erofeev claimed to have written is approximately twice as large as the number extant). While much of this period of Erofeev's life remains currently shrouded in fog, one thing at least is beyond dispute. Erofeev's assault on official Soviet culture in general, and on Evtushenko in particular, was a double-edged sword. Having assumed the role of "Venicka the martyr" in life, Erofeev felt compelled to reinvent himself so that his chosen mask would seem credible, consistent and impenetrable. Such a burden, in its own way, must have been at least as heavy as Evtushenko's. Erofeev's inconsistency in playing his role bears witness to the difficulty of doing so, but his performance may well have been necessary in order to achieve the status of "classic" which has now been bestowed upon him by the Russian intelligentsia.[25] Perhaps the message here is that less condemnation and more compassion are in order for all human beings. Perhaps consistency is overrated. Perhaps ultimately, "No one in the world is guilty."

Endnotes

1. Venedikt Erofeev, "Venia — poslednee interv'iu," *Kino ne dlia vsekh*, NTV, Moscow, 14 July 1994.

2. Al'tshuller, "*Moskva — Petushki* Venedikta Erofeeva," 79.

3. Gaiser-Shnitman, *Venedikt Erofeev*, 177.

4. Evgenii Evtushenko, *Bratskaia GES, Iunost'*, no. 4 (1965): 27.

5. Evgenii Evtushenko, *Avtobiografiia* (London: Flegon, 1964), 127.

6. Marina Balina, "A Prescribed Journey: Russian Travel Literature from the 1960's to the 1980's," *Slavic and East European Journal* 38 (1994): 261–70.

7. Evgenii Evstushenko, *Vzmakh ruki* (Moscow: Molodaia gvardiia, 1962), 42.

8. Evtushenko, *Avtobiografiia*, 129.

9. Evtushenko, *Bratskaia GES*, 26.

10. Paperno and Gasparov, "'Vstan' i idi'," 397–99.

11. Evtushenko, *Avtobiografiia*, 137.

12. Andrei Mal'gin, "Byt' znamenitym nekrasivo," *Stolitsa*, no. 29 (1992): 45.

13. These discussions between the author and Mr. Yevtushenko took place in the United States and in Peredelkino from 1991 to 1993.

14. Evgenii Evtushenko, *The Collected Poems, 1952-1990* (New York: Henry Holt, 1991).

15. Lotman writes, "Alexander's 'play-acting' went beyond the style of the epoch; Romanticism demanded a consistent mask which would as it were become part of the individual's personality and form a model for his behavior...Alexander's 'Proteanism' was perceived by contemporaries as 'craftiness,' an absence of sincerity. The verb 'to dupe' occurs frequently in assessments of the Tsar, even by his inner circle. Changing his masks so as to 'captivate everyone,' Alexander alienated everyone. One of the most talented actors of the age, he was its least successful." Yuri Lotman, "The Theater and Theatricality as Components of Early Nineteenth-Century Culture," trans. G. S. Smith, in *The Semiotics of Russian Culture* (Ann Arbor: University of Michigan Press, 1984), 159.

16. Paperno and Gasparov, "'Vstan' i idi'," 388.

17. Lipovetskii, "Apofeoz chastits," 215–17.

18. See, for example, Muravnik, "Ispoved' rossiianina," 101.

19. Smirnova, "Venedikt Erofeev glazami gogoleveda," 63.

20. Mal'gin, "Byt' znamenitym nekrasivo," 43.

21. Lotman, "The Theater and Theatricality," 141–42. Peter Berger and Thomas Luckmann describe the function of social roles as follows: "...not only are the standards of role X generally known, but it is known that these standards are known. Consequently every putative actor of role X can be held responsible for abiding by the standards, which can be taught as part of the institutional tradition and used to verify the credentials of all performers and, by the same token, serve as controls... *All* institutionalized conduct involves roles. Thus roles share in the controlling character of institutionalization. As soon as actors are typified as role performers, their conduct is *ipso facto* susceptible to enforcement. Compliance and non-compliance with socially defined role standards ceases to be optional, though, of course, the severity of sanctions may vary from case to case." Peter Berger and Thomas Luckmann, *The Social Construction of Reality: A Treatise in the Sociology of Knowledge* (Garden City: Doubleday, 1966), 69–70.

22. Ryan-Hayes, *Contemporary Russian Satire*, 62.

23. Ibid.

24. Sedakova, "Gadkikh utiat liubil," 62.

25. Lipovetskii, "Apofeoz chastits," 214.

Заграница глазами эксцентрика: к анализу "заграничных" глав

Эдуард Власов

> ... *И сладок нам лишь узнаванья миг.*
> *Осип Мандельштам*

Постановка проблемы

Чтение и анализ поэмы Венедикта Ерофеева *Москва — Петушки* всякий раз превращается в своеобразный поединок двух интеллектов — автора и читателя. Многослойность подтекстовой структуры поэмы, в которой центральное место принадлежит огромному цитатному пространству требует расшифровки и определения места каждого из цитатных полей в единой семиосфере произведения. Строение реминисцентных полей у Ерофеева стандартно для мифологической поэтики: после вскрытия верхнего пласта такого поля, т.е. после установления прямого источника цитаты/аллюзии, неизбежно обнаруживаешь под ним новые, скрытые от поверхностного взгляда ассоциативные поля. Анализ поэмы предполагает одновременное исследование не только горизонтальных — на уровне источника — диахронических связей *Москвы — Петушков* с предшествующими текстами, но и вертикальных синхронических связей, определяющих функции цитаты/аллюзии в поэтике поэмы. На вертикальном уровне цитата/аллюзия функционирует уже, скорее, как "авторское изобретение," нежели банальное заимствование.

"Присвоение" цитаты/аллюзии, безусловно, не есть достижение постмодернизма, к российской классике которого причисляется *Москва — Петушки*. Подобным образом структурируется, например, *Божественная комедия*, герой которой тоже ведет повествование от первого лица и тоже, как ерофеевский Веничка, проводит все сюжетное время в путешествии по направлению к раю. В обеих поэмах содержится множество имен известных людей, с которыми центральные персонажи встречаются на синхроническом уровне, вопреки объективной диахронической разведенности во времени и пространстве. Прямой текстуальной связи между *Божественной комедией* и *Москвой — Петушками* нет, за исключением одного только пассажа, в котором некоторые исследователи отмечают связь ерофеевской поэмы с текстом Данте.[1] В начале поэмы Веничка, выходя утром из неизвестного подъезда, признается: "...все знают, какую тяжесть в сердце пронес я по этим сорока ступеням чужого подъезда и какую тяжесть вынес на воздух" (17), что сопоставимо с известными строками Данте:

Ты будешь знать, как горестен устам
Чужой ломоть, как трудно на чужбине
Сходить и восходить по ступеням. (Рай, XVII: 58–60)

Параллели между поэмами более очевидны на структурном уровне, где интертекстуальность становится центральным поэтическим механизмом, при помощи использованного вторично материала порождающего новые смыслы. Иными словами, проблему можно определить как *возникновение своего из чужого*. В этом *иностранном* контексте логичный интерес могут вызвать так называемые "заграничные" главы *Москвы — Петушков* — "Назарьево — Дрезна" и "Дрезна — 85-й километр," где описывается турне Венички по Западной Европе, в том числе и по родине Данте.

Путешествие с Эренбургом

В одном из самых обстоятельных на сегодняшний день исследований *Москвы — Петушков* И. Паперно и Б. Гаспаров справедливо отмечают аллюзию на книгу новелл Ильи Эренбурга *Тринадцать трубок* (1922).[2] Замечание исследователей можно оспаривать в связи с определением ими жанра книги Эренбурга как "путевые заметки," тогда как мне *Тринадцать трубок* представляются, скорее, циклом нравоописательных новелл. Однако, в целом, реминисцентная связь между циклом Эренбурга и фразами Венички "Выкурил я двенадцать трубок" (82) и "Я выкурил на антресолях еще двенадцать трубок" (82), произносимых на парижском фоне, очевидна, как очевидно и то, что "эренбурговское" пространство в *Москве — Петушках* только трубками не ограничивается.

Формирование миросозерцания Ерофеева — личности и художника — приходится на период хрущевской "оттепели," само метафорическое определение которой вошло в обиход благодаря Эренбургу. Заслуга Эренбурга — одной из культовых фигур в неофициальной советской идеологии рубежа 1950-х – 1960-х гг. — открытие для советского читателя западного мира. Роль произведений Эренбурга — главным образом, его мемуаров *Люди, годы, жизнь* — в формировании интеллектуального мира "невыездного" гражданина СССР была достаточно значительна, и *Москва — Петушки* являются лишним тому подтверждением.

Трубки, мансарды и суета

Тринадцать трубок состоят из новелл, объединенных оригинальной ключевой деталью — курительными трубками (из коллекции рассказчика), и сами новеллы посвящены людям, которые эти трубки когда-то курили. Владелец первой трубки — господин Невашеин, секретарь именитого дипломата Доминантова.

> Привыкнув к трубке, он курил ее часто;...вечером у себя, на пролежанном турецком диване, гадая, пойти ли в пивную, где скверный портер, но зато дипломатическая слава, или послать своего слугу Афанасия в лавку за четвертью милой белоголовки и распить ее безо всяких стеснений, вздыхая...о воздушном бюсте Елены Прекрасной, то есть жены Штукина....Поздно вечером Невашеин послал Афанасия за спиртом — водки давно не было.[3]

Подобное времяпровождение пародируется Ерофеевым в описании парижской жизни Венички (80–82), причем далее в *Москве — Петушках* следует схожая с процитированной выше сцена:

Вошел слуга...мой камердинер по имени Петр....

— Видишь ли, Петр, я никак не могу разрешить одну мысль. Так велика эта мысль.

— Какая же это мысль?

— А вот какая: выпить у меня чего-нибудь осталось?...

— И выпить тоже нет ничего, — подсказал Петр.... (109–10)

Сочетание иронии (трубка, по мнению героев и Эренбурга, и Ерофеева, — источник вдохновения и символ отрешенности от бренного мира) и мотива заграницы, наложенное на "алкогольный" фон, формирует в поэтиках писателей сопоставимые поля. Речь при этом идет именно об идентичном художественно-идеологическом механизме, а не о примитивном заимствовании второго у первого. "Заграничные" главы *Москвы — Петушков* не есть простой перифраз прозы Эренбурга — наложение на каждую сцену поэмы массы обертонов не-эренбурговского происхождения не позволяет свести ерофеевскую технику к элементарному одноплоскостному пародированию, тем более, что само творчество Эренбурга отнюдь не оригинально в смысле пародийного использования чужой речи. Тонкая насмешка Эренбурга является своеобразной прелюдией к абсурдистской иронии Ерофеева. Разница здесь только в регистрах эксплуатации чужой речи.

И в поэме, и в *Трубках* встречается достаточно экзотическое для русского уха слово "мансарда," данное в "парижском" контексте. У Эренбурга оно функционирует как нейтральное, лишенное иронических обертонов: "...ему [герою новеллы Ру] исполнилось двадцать пять лет и он переехал из одной мансарды улицы Черной вдовы в другую..."[4] Здесь парижская мансарда — реально освоенное пространство, пережитый топос как персонажа, так и самого писателя, и потому не располагающий к высокомерной насмешке. У Ерофеева же, для которого как Париж, так и заграница вообще оставались вещью чисто умозрительной, экзотическая лексика вызывает на остраненное ерничество: "Я пошел на Нотр-Дам и снял там мансарду. Мансарда, мезонин, флигель, антресоли, чердак — я все это путаю и разницы никакой не вижу" (81–82). Замечу, что Веничка выкуривает свои трубки именно в мансарде (или на антресолях —

какая для него разница?): "...я снял то, на чем можно лежать, писать и трубку курить. Выкурил я двенадцать трубок — и отослал в 'Ревю де Пари' свое эссе" (82); "Я выкурил на антресолях еще двенадцать трубок — и создал новое эссе" (82).

Как и для Ерофеева, для раннего Эренбурга характерны постоянные апелляции к тексту Священного Писания. Так, в "Третьей трубке" цитируется неоднократно поминаемый и в *Москве — Петушках* Экклезиаст: "Суета сует, все суета и томление духа,"[5] а рядом проскальзывает упоминание об икоте (которая столь важна для героя ерофеевской поэмы), причем опять же в "алкогольном" контексте:

Закончив танцы, я [бен Элия, герой новеллы] изучил щебет греков, плач турок, любовные вздохи арабов и даже странные звуки, напоминавшие икоту приезжих австрийцев. Постигнув все тайны веселья, я продал свои последние штаны, купил на них бутылку вина и, выпив ее до дна, принялся веселиться.[6]

Параллели текстов Эренбурга и Ерофеева на уровне деталей и мотивов — Экклезиаст, икота, вино,[7] купленное на последние деньги, постижение чужого опыта — здесь очевидны.

В "Десятой трубке" характеристика семейного положения главной героини — Эммы — дается в сходном с ерофеевским ключе: "После пятидесяти лет бесплодных ожиданий, в течение которых не только на руку, но даже на безусловную невинность Эммы никто не покушался, найти такого жениха было воистину чудом"[8] и "Неслыханная! Это — женщина, у которой до сегодняшнего дня грудь стискивали только предчувствия. Это женщина, у которой никто до меня даже пульса не щупал" (45). Здесь совпадают речевые фигуры. А что касается отношения к любви в целом, то герои *Трубок* и *Москвы — Петушков* выбирают в качестве авторитета в этом вопросе одного и того же русского классика. Герой "Седьмой трубки" вспоминает:

Перебрав все литературные воспоминания, я остановился на Тургеневе, я избрал его своим наставником и поводырем....следуя заветам Тургенева, я продолжал ходить в поле, декламировать стихи и выразительно вздыхать....Только однажды, в горячий июльский полдень, увидев [свою возлюбленную] Вильгельмину, плавно проносившую через двор облака своей божественной плоти, я не выдержал и, пренебрегая всеми литературными уроками, прилип губами к ее белой руке.[9]

Заветы Тургенева и их методичное несоблюдение определяют нравственный облик некоторых персонажей *Москвы — Петушков*: "... есть такая заповеданность стыда, со времен Ивана Тургенева" (30); "У нас тут прямо как у Тургенева: все сидят и спорят про любовь....Давайте, как у Тургенева!" (72); "'Ты читал Ивана Тургенева?' 'Ну, коли читал, так и расскажи!'...'у Ивана Тургенева все это немножко не так, у него все собираются к камину, в цилиндрах, и держат жабо на отлете'" (73). Тургеневский пласт у Эренбурга и Ерофеева структурируется идентично: сначала персонажами осваивается *чужая* территория (Тургенев как "наставник и поводырь," знание текстов Тургепева — "коли читал, так и расскажи"), затем предпринимается попытка следовать заветам классика (декламация стихов в поле, "все сидят и спорят про любовь") и, наконец, следует признание неспособности выполнять эти заветы (пренебрежение литературными уроками, "у Ивана Тургенева все это немножко не так"). Собственно, весь чужой материал эксплуатируется Ерофеевым именно таким образом: освоение (знание изначального текста) — использование (цитирование) — преодоление (пародирование, десакрализация, наделение новым смыслом).

Уроки Хуренито

Еще богаче материал для сопоставления поэмы Ерофеева и творчества Эренбурга дает роман последнего *Хулио Хуренито* (1922). Его структура сообразна с евангельскими текстами: роман представляет собой описание жизни, учения и смерти Великого Учителя Хулио Хуренито, выполненное "евангелистом" Эренбургом. Регулярные новозаветные коннотации связывают роман с поэмой — с той лишь разницей, что Хулио Хуренито представлен, скорее, не как Христос (с которым постоянно сравнивается ерофеевский Веничка), а как Антихрист, но для формальной стороны дела этот сугубо идеологический факт принципиального значения не имеет, тем более что Веня-Мессия также отнюдь не идеален.

Сходство романа и поэмы определяется, прежде всего, набором деталей, наложенных на евангельскую структуру. Так, в 1-й главе, действие которой происходит во Франции, евангелист Эренбург

> ...детально разрабатывал приглашение в Париж трех тысяч инквизиторов для публичного сожжения на площадях всех потребляющих аперитивы. Потом выпивал стакан абсента и, охмелев, декламировал стихи святой Терезы,...а в полночь тщетно стучался в чугунные ворота церкви Сен-Жермен-де-Пре. Дни мои заканчивались обыкновенно у любовницы, француженки, с приличным стажем, но доброй католички, от которой я требовал в самые неподоходящие минуты объяснения, чем разнятся семь "смертных" грехов от семи "основных." Так проходило мало-помалу время.[10]

Веничка, находясь в Париже, также демонстрирует свой непревзойденный интеллект, когда ощущает в себе "самовозрастающий Логос" (81) и пишет бессмертные эссе (82). Он также пытается преодолеть схоластические рамки словаря: "Мансарда, мезонин, флигель, антресоли, чердак — я все это путаю и разницы никакой не вижу" (82). Кроме этого, упоминается в поэме и святая Тереза — в связи с ее стигматами (26).

Парижская тема связана с мотивом *легкости преодоления государственных границ*, весьма существенным для "заграничных" глав поэмы: "Я, например, был в Италии...Махнул я рукой и подался во Францию....пошел через Тироль в сторону Сорбонны....Что ж мне оставалось делать, как не идти в Париж? Прихожу....через Верден попер к Ламаншу...А в окрестностях Лондона..." (80–83). Эренбург с его *Хуренито* (о мемуарах *Люди, годы, жизнь* см. ниже) является, несомненно, одним из главных источников для веничкиного "галопа по Европам": "...я еду в дорогой, любимый, возвращенный мне Париж!...Я пробыл неделю в гостеприимном Копенгагене...в Лондоне я ходил по улицам, как в храме, — на цыпочках и сняв шляпу...я наконец увидел дорогой Монпарнас и 'Ротонду'....Я отправился в радушную Бельгию."[11] Единственную разницу между Эренбургом и Ерофеевым как историческими личностями составляет тот факт, что первый в действительности с легкостью пересекал государственные границы, т. е. передвижения по Европе его персонажей отражают реальный авторский опыт. У Ерофеева же путешествие Венички по загранице построено исключительно на *чужом* опыте, заимствованным из предшествующих текстов.

В 4-й главе *Хуренито* рассказчик упоминает о "трансцендентальном мире"[12] (ср. знаменитое "Транс-цен-ден-тально!" [27]), а ниже помещает следующие откровения:

> Чаще гляди на детей. Я люблю в них не только воспоминание о легких днях человечества, нет, в них я вижу прообраз грядущего мира. Я люблю младенца, который еще ни о чем не ведает, который царственным жестом тянется сорвать — что? — брошку на груди матери? яблоко в саду? звезду с неба? Потом его научат, как надевать лифчик, как целовать руку отца, как шалить и как молиться. Пока он дик, пуст и прекрасен.[13]

У Ерофеева образ прекрасного младенца — один из ключевых в поэме, определяющий идеологическую ориентацию центрального персонажа, оправдывающий его жизнь и движение "за Петушки," туда, "где сливается небо и земля, и волчица воет на звезды" (38).

В 5-й главе появляется Алексей Спиридонович Тишин, человек благородного происхождения и нелегкой судьбы, который как-то из Версаля "сбежал в Париж и мертвецки напился," а после очередного бытового катаклизма в том же Париже "переселился на мансарду, и вместо 'Кафе де Монако' посещал различные притоны в районе рынков и вокзалов."[14] Помимо мансарды и алкогольной тематики, здесь возникает еще и завуалированный мотив загнивающего капиталистического общества, гипертрофированный у Ерофеева: у него в Париже "Все снуют — из бардака в клинику, из клиники опять в бардак. И кругом столько трипперу, что дышать трудно...что ноги передвигаешь с трудом" (81). На этом грязном парижском фоне Тишин пытается не загрязнить свои идеалы: "Разве можно читать Ницше или Шопенгауэра, когда рядом пищит младенец?,"[15] и потому он заводит специальный альбом для выписывания цитат из классиков: "Так, в отделе 'человек' значилось: 'Человек создан для счастья, как птица для полета' — В. Короленко, 'Человек — это звучит гордо' — М. Горький."[16] Ницше и сентенции Горького на мотивном и цитатном уровнях играют у Ерофеева существенную роль (ср., упоминание о сверхчеловеке [19] и постоянные апелляции к Горькому [35, 70, 71 и др.]).

Что касается знаменитых имен вообще, то круг совпадений между Эренбургом и Ерофеевым здесь достаточно широк. В *Хуренито* упоминается ветхозаветная Суламифь.[17] Действует она и в поэме: как прямо ("И хохотала Суламифь" [113]), так и опосредованно ("пастись между лилиями" [41, 44]). Фигурирует у Эренбурга Диоген Синопский[18] — есть он и у Ерофеева: "...и Диоген погасит свой фонарь" (87). Упоминает Эренбург Канта и Гегеля: "Изрубленные наподобие котлеток, во время периодических дуэлей, бурши...постигали великолепное построение вселенной в пафосе Канта или в остроте Гегеля, готовясь к честной карьере дрессировщиков крестьянских детей или чиновников государственного акцизма."[19] Аллюзии на Канта у Ерофеева регулярны (27, 53, 60 и др.), имя Гегеля и его "учение" также встречается в тексте поэмы (110). Кроме этого, есть в лексиконе Вени и редкий для русского речевого обихода "бурш" (67).

В общее для Эренбурга и Ерофеева цитатно-культурологическое поле входит ветхозаветное изречение из Даниила (5:25–28) "Мене, Текел, Упарсин," причем любопытно отметить, что при апеллировании к нему оба автора выбирают среднее слово: "Было ясно, что дело пахнет Навуходоносором, но вместо 'текел' и прочих нормальных слов появлялся бред,"[20] и "Мене, текел, фарес, то есть 'ты взвешен на весах и найден легковесным,' то есть 'текел'" (117). Помимо этого, герой романа мечтает о новом святом Граале[21] — реминисценция и мотив ею порожденный существенны и для *Москвы — Петушков*, где они даются опосредованно, через вагнеровского *Лоэнгрина* (20, 74), как мотив чаши, на мифологическом уровне связанный с Христом и средневековым европейским эпосом, а на бытовом — с выпивкой.

Пародируя пролетарскую революцию, оба автора заставляют своих героев издавать декреты, причем и Хуренито, и Веничка делают это не в столицах, а в русской провинции:

> ...в соседней комнате задорно трещали машинки — это Хуренито диктовал декреты. Начал он с равенства....Хуренито, не

отчаиваясь, приступил к подготовке всемирной организации и к истреблению растлевающего, по его словам, призрака личной свободы. Он опубликовал в один и тот же день — 12 апреля — три небольших декрета, относящихся к различным областям жизни.[22]

А я, сидя в своем президиуме, слушал эти прения и мыслил так: прения совершенно необходимы, но гораздо необходимее декреты. Почему мы забываем то, чем должна увенчиваться всякая революция, то есть "декреты"?...если ты хороший канцлер, садись и пиши декреты. Выпей еще немножко, садись и пиши....Надо вначале декрет написать, хоть один, хоть самый какой-нибудь гнусный. (93–94)

Упомянутый у Эренбурга "призрак личной свободы" соотносится и с обыгрыванием пропагандистских штампов у Ерофеева: "— Значит, вы были в Штатах....скажите: ...свобода так и остается призраком на этом континенте скроби?...— Да,...свобода так и остается призраком на этом континенте скорби" (78–79).

27-я глава *Хуренито* посвящена встрече главного героя с Лениным в послереволюционной Москве. При этом портрет Ленина, с которым сам Эренбург был знаком лично еще по его (Ленина) европейской эмиграции, далек от официальных штампов, определявшихся тогда ВЧК. Тональность главы по иронии и сарказму сходна с ерофеевским описанием Петушкинской районной революции. Оба писателя строят свой иронический дискурс на фактах ленинской биографии и чертах его характера, зафиксированных в официальных советских изданиях, т. е. оба выбирают объектом насмешек и пародирования "виртуального" Ленина:

— Я отрабатываю тезисы. Все давно готово к выступлениям, кроме тезисов. А вот теперь и тезисы готовы...
— Значит, ты считаешь, что ситуация назрела?...
— А кто ее знает!... я, как выпью немножко, мне кажется, что хоть сегодня выступай, что и вчера было не рано выступать. А как начинает проходить — нет, думаю, и вчера было рано, и послезавтра не поздно....Чтобы восстановить хозяйство, разрушенное войной, надо сначала его разрушить, а для этого нужна гражданская или хоть какая-нибудь война, нужно как минимум двенадцать фронтов... (90–91)

Здесь пародируются апокрифическая история о решении Лениным "мучительного" вопроса о сроках осуществления Октябрьского восстания в Петербурге и ленинские характеристики политического и экономического положения "молодой Советской России."[23]

Нетрадиционное обращение с такой культовой фигурой, как Ленин, откровенное высмеивание канонических реалий и фактов, с этим именем связанных, на структурном уровне поэмы может рассматриваться как реализация главного принципа обращения Ерофеева с цитатой, с чужим именем и чужим материалом. Не разделяя на идеологически *свои* (евангелисты, Кант, Достоевский и т. п.) и *чужие* (разночинцы, Ленин, Горький и т. п.) источники заимствований, Ерофеев игнорирует идеологические приоритеты и действует по принципу *ничего святого*. Центр тяжести в данном случае переносится на формальную оболочку цитаты или аллюзии, устанавливается идеологическое равенство, при котором высмеиваются и пародируются уже сами речевые формулы, а не лежащие в их основе идеологемы. В этом смысле установление связей Ерофеева с Эренбургом может выполнять и показательную функцию: с точки зрения идеологической, Эренбург — конформист, принявший коммунистический режим и работавший на него; как идеологема он чужд внутреннему диссиденту Ерофееву, который на компромиссы с режимом не шел; однако как художник Эренбург обнаруживает массу сходств с диссидентской поэтикой и заслуживает не отрицания, но внимания и почитания. Тем более, что сам Эренбург трезво мог оценить именно формальную, на речевом уровне, ситуацию, которая складывалась параллельно с утверждением нового политического строя: в *Хуренито* главный герой пророчествует: "Придет денек, и главки, гвозди, прочая дрянь претворятся в изумительную мифологию, в необычные эпопеи."[24]

Прозорливость Хуренито-Эренбурга очевидна на примере текста *Москвы — Петушков*. Реалии и детали нового, освященного бредовой идеей всеобщего благополучия и единомыслия мира в поэме работают уже не как носители конкретных предметно-понятийных смыслов, но как мифологические единицы, порождающие иные, абстрагированные смыслы. Производственные графики, настенные цитаты из Максима

Горького и Николая Островского, перемещенные в контексты библейских цитат и аллюзий, реминсценций пантеизма и немецкого классического идеализма, превращаются в поэме в архетипические компоненты, структурирующие определенный тип сознания. В этом типе советские реалии и детали не являются инородными, их идеологическая несовместимость с другими компонентами полностью игнорируется; они остаются здесь чужими только по происхождению — точно так же, как и все остальные, — но в плане функционирования действуют исключительно как свои, что, собственно, и обеспечивает "мирное сосуществование" в поэме дезинсекталя для уничтожения мелких насекомых как составляющей изысканного коктейля и текстов евангелистов как источников вдохновения иного рода, соцобязательств, которые не вызывают в опальном бригадире антисоветской истерии, а рассматриваются им исключительно как продукт натурального обмена на месячное жалованье, и постоянных апелляций к Богу и ангелам, поддерживающих Веничку на должной идеалистической высоте.

Поэтика поэмы фиксирует очевидный социо-культурологический парадокс: аллюзия (как прямая или косвенная цитата типа "В жизни всегда должно быть место подвигу") в силу своего постоянного и не зависимого от воли ее получателя присутствия в речевом обиходе, механически становится реалией ментального быта, и, наоборот, бытовая, предметная реалия благодаря своей магической абсурдности (производственные графики, отсутствие в ресторане Курского вокзала хереса) отрешается от конкретного предметно-понятийного значения и становится самостоятельной образо- или сюжетоструктурирующей единицей. Не последнюю роль здесь играют и масштабы, в которых данные встречные процессы происходили. Например, пародируемое Ерофеевым, образное высказывание Ленина о преемственности в русском революционно-освободительном движении из статьи "Памяти Герцена" — "Декабристы разбудили Герцена" — стало элементом речевого сознания советского человека через обязательное заучивание наизусть по программе средней школы — причем заучивание двойное, по двум предметам (истории СССР и русской литературы). И реминисцентные обертоны фразы декабриста-

"коверкота" относительно невменяемости его соседа по "купе" ("— Как же! Разбудишь его, вашего Герцена!...Ему еще в Храпунове надо было выходить, этому Герцену, а он все едет, собака!.." [65]) выявляют не насмешку над ленинской фразой (по сути, ничего смешного в ней нет), т. е. не устанавливают идеологическую оппозиционность, но активизируют известный компонент речевого сознания читателя, апеллируют к его интеллектуальной способности опознать чужую речь и соотнести пьяного "собаку-Герцена," проспавшего Храпуново, с одним из авторов знаменитой клятвы на Воробьевых горах.

Тот же процесс происходит и на уровне "называния имен." Амбивалентность процесса перехода мифологемы в реалию и реалии в мифологему обеспечивает беспрепятственное превращение чужих, абстрактных с точки зрения частной биографии героя имен Мусоргского, Гаршина, Чехова в своих, в действующих лиц этой биографии (ср., "Эх, Максим Горький, Максим же ты Горький, сдуру или спьяну ты сморозил такое на своем Капри? Тебе хорошо — ты там будешь жрать свои агавы, а мне чего жрать?.." [71]), тогда как реальные лица из биографии Венички (здесь самого Ерофеева), подобные "старой шпале" Алексею Блиндяеву, отославшему спьяну в Москву, в управление знаменитые веничкины графики, попадая в соседство с Кантом, Блоком и Моше Даяном, сами превращаются в мифологические фигуры.

Воспоминания. О будущем?

Помимо *Тринадцати трубок* и *Хулио Хуренито*, другим фундаментальным источником "заграничных" глав *Москвы — Петушков* являются мемуары Эренбурга *Люди, годы, жизнь* (1956–67),[25] ставшие в свое время интеллектуальной бомбой. Мир Запада впервые предстал перед советским читателем не как априорная абстракция, но как реальный живой мир, наполненный конкретным бытом и конкретными именами. Именно имена — первое, что бросается в глаза при чтении мемуаров: "Познакомился я с Модильяни," "Редко я беседовал с Модильяни, чтобы он не прочитал мне несколько терцин из 'Божественной комедии'," "Несколько раз я слышал Ленина на собраниях," "Я познакомился с Леже задолго до начала войны," "В начале 1914 года кто-то из художников позвал меня к столику в темном углу 'Ротонды': я тебя познакомлю с Аполинером," "Познакомившись с Пикассо, я сразу понял, нет, вернее, почувствовал, что передо мной большой человек," "В очень холодный день я встретил на Тверской С. А. Есенина, он предложил мне пойти пить настоящий кофе," "Вскоре после моего приезда в Москву я встретил Б. Л. Пастернака, который повел меня к себе," "Меня представили Андре Жиду," "Ужин Пен-клуба я вспоминаю с благодарностью — там я познакомился с Джойсом," "Марине Цветаевой, когда я с ней познакомился, было двадцать пять лет."[26] Среди обилия имен отечественных и западных знаменитостей у Эренбурга, есть и персонажи "заграничных" глав *Москвы — Петушков*: "Народу пришло много, почти всех я знал: Арагон, Эльза Триоле," "В объяснение хочу сказать о некоторых свойствах Сартра — подружившись с ним и с Симоной де Бовуар, я многое понял." При этом в общении с этими двумя французскими парами Эренбург демонстрирует свободу, близость и даже фамильярность: "В сентябре Арагон сказал мне, что Матисс хочет, чтобы я ему позировал," "Я предупредил Сартра.... Я ...упрекнул Сартра."[27]

Эмоциональная тональность мемуаров, создающая ощущение невероятной легкости встреч и общения со всеми современными Эренбургу (и Ерофееву) западными классиками, а также неизбежность встречи с ними в Париже, пародируется в поэме:

Я как-то выпил и пошел по Елисейским полям....Вижу: двое знакомых...оба жуют каштаны и оба старцы. Где я их видел? в газетах? не помню, короче, узнал: это Луи Арагон и Эльза Триоле. "Интересно, — прошмыгнула мысль у меня, — откуда они идут: из клиники в бардак или из бардака в клинику?" (81)

При этом пародируется и сам факт встречи, и его фамильярная, à la Эренбург атмосфера: "— а она [Триоле], как старая блядь, потрепала меня по щеке, взяла под ручку своего Арагона и дальше пошла..." (81). Комизм ситуации усиливается контрастом между искренним, частным интересом Венички к западной жизни ("откуда они идут: из клиники в бардак или из бардака в клинику?") и его общественным долгом гражданина СССР получить у признанных авторитетов ответы на "социальные вопросы, самые мучительные социальные вопросы" (81). То, что является реалией у Эренбурга (Арагон, Триоле, Сартр и де Бовуар суть его действительные, не абстрактные знакомые), абсурдируется у Ерофеева до степени комической абстракции: "Потом я, конечно, узнал из печати, что это были совсем не те люди, это были, оказывается, Жан-Поль Сартр и Симона де Бовуар, ну да какая мне теперь разница?" (81). Имя реального исторического лица освоено Веничкой, размещено в соответствующей системе координат (Париж, Елисейские поля, каштаны), но функционирует уже как абстрактное: для менталитета главного героя поэмы нет разницы между писателем-коммунистом и философом-экзистенциалистом, поскольку их имена работают не как носители энциклопедической информации, а как генераторы субъективного смысла данного фрагмента поэмы.

Как и в *Хуренито*, в *Людях, годах, жизни* рассказчик постоянно путешествует: "Я вернулся в Париж," "Летом 1910 года мы поехали...в Брюгге," "В молодости мне удалось дважды побывать в Италии," "Я полюбовался пиниями Рима," "В 1951 году в Стокгольме я пошел на большую выставку мексиканского искусства," "Я колесил по Европе, изъездил Францию, Германию, Англию, Чехословакию, Польшу, Швецию, Норвегию, Данию, побывал в Австрии, Швейцарии, Бельгии."[28] Эхом этим строкам звучат рассказы насмешника Венички: "я...сворачивал с Манхеттена на 5-ю авеню," "Я шел в Гарлем" (79), "Я, например, был в Италии....я был в Венеции, в день святого Марка....Прихожу в Помпею....Махнул я рукой и подался во Францию...пошел через Тироль в сторону Сорбонны. Прихожу в Сорбонну" (80), "Иду в сторону Нотр-Дама, иду и удивляюсь: кругом одни бардаки. Стоит только Эйфелева башня" (81).

Последний, парижский, фрагмент, высмеивающий советские пропагандистские штампы относительно характеристик безнадежно загнивающего Запада, без труда выводится из того же Эренбурга:

Часто я приходил Мафтар, по ней сновали огромные жирные крысы. Эйфелева башня порождала споры — еще жили современники и единомышленники Мопассана, считавшие, что она изуродовала город....Никогда раньше я не видел столько старых домов, пепельных, морщинистых, пятнистых!...Я входил в темную улицу, как в джунгли.[29]

Однако, несмотря на тяжелые условия жизни в капиталистическом городе, и Эренбург, и Веничка находят в себе силы заниматься в Париже творчеством: первый "сидел в 'Клозери де Лиля' и переводил французских поэтов,"[30] второй курил трубки и писал эссе (82). Мансарда и антресоль, которые в сознании Венички постоянно путаются с чердаком и мезонином, возможно, заимствованы из того же Эренбурга: "Я остановился в гостинице на левом берегу Сены, около бульвара Сен-Жермен; мне отвели мансардную комнату с балконом, откуда был виден Париж....Арагон и Эльза Юрьевна [Триоле] позвали Симонова и меня на 'Чердак' — так называлось помещение Комитета писателей."[31]

Эксплуатация в *Москве — Петушках* чужой речи, в данном случае иностранной лексики и реалий, позволяет, во-первых, отметить определенный, весьма высокий интеллектуальный уровень рассказчика и других персонажей (ср., "стигматы" [26], "Транс-цен-ден-тально" [27], "ноуменально" и "антиномично" [31]), во-вторых, служат материалом для бесконечных каламбуров ("какие агавы, какие хорошие капри" [71], "Так он там и питался почти полгода: акынами и саксаулом" [78]), и, в-третьих, дают возможность автору зафиксировать свою, остраненную позицию по отношению к объективному миру и исторической действительности. Если Эренбург как мемуарист демонстрирует *объективную* память, то в случае с Ерофеевым мы имеем дело с памятью *субъективной*, сохраняющей имена, детали и факты, однако каталогизирующей их не согласно закрепленности за определенным событием, а исходя из демонстративной незаинтересованности в объективности и верности факту: ср., "Читая о Франции 1793 года, мы видим Конвент, неподкупного Робеспьера, гильотину на площади Революции, клубы, где витийствовали санкюлоты, памфлеты, заговоры, битвы"[32] и "Все выступавшие были в лоскут пьяны, все мололи одно и то же: Максимилиан Робеспьер, Оливер Кромвель, Соня Перовская, Вера Засулич, карательные отряды из Петушков, война с Норвегией" (91).

На уровне отдельных деталей и эксплуатации одних и тех же реминсценций между мемуарами и поэмой также много сходства.

Так, в третьей книге воспоминаний Эренбург читает Паскаля, причем именно его известный пассаж о мыслящем тростнике[33]; в *Москве — Петушках* тот же классический образ эксплуатируется (возможно, через посредничество Тютчева) в сцене с пьяным ревизором Семенычем (88). Рассказывает Эренбург и о своем знакомстве с Карлом Леви, упоминая его книгу *Христос остановился в Эболи*,[34] название который обыгрывается у Ерофеева в "заграничных" главах включением в цитатно-идиоматический контекст: "Хочешь ты, например, остановиться в Эболи — пожалуйста, останавливайся в Эболи. Хочешь идти в Каноссу — никто тебе не мешает, иди в Каноссу. Хочешь перейти Рубикон — переходи..." (83).

К Эренбургу восходит и история с отказом Веничке в ангажировании Британским музеем[35] и в обучении на бакалавра в Сорбонне и соответственном изгнании его как из музея, так и из Сорбонны (81, 83–84): в 6-й книге мемуаров есть рассказ о том, как Эренбурга — советского гражданина и носителя "коммунистической заразы" — изгоняли из Англии и Франции. Более того, эти сюжеты проецируются на признание Эренбурга: "Когда я впервые пришел в Лувр, я был дикарем."[36] Таким образом, изгнание Венички с его самоопределением как "сибирского сироты" (80) из центров западно-европейской науки находит себе параллели в объективной, исторической действительности. Однако, если на дальнейшей судьбе Эренбурга факты временного неприятия его Западом никак не сказались и он оставался одним из лидеров советского "выездного" истеблишмента, то для ерофеевского Венички изгнание из Сорбонны стало очередным звеном в бесконечной цепи отторжений его от общества — теперь уже не только советского, но и заграничного.

Вечные спутники

Разрушение Ерофеевым диахронических связей с предшествующими текстами и установление синхронного сосуществования своего и чужого позволяет при прочтении поэмы расширять рамки восприятия текста и устанавливать на ассоциативном уровне диалогические контакты с самыми разноплановыми источниками чужой речи. В связи с Эренбургом следует назвать по крайней мере еще два имени.

Образ центрального персонажа поэмы Ерофеева как изгоя, отторженного обществом, живущего "на дне," но обладающего тонким интеллектом и чувствительной, поэтической душой, с его проекциями на "парижскую" ситуацию (в частности — на попытки учиться в Сорбонне на бакалавра) ассоциируется с фигурой Франсуа Вийона. У Эренбурга, который перевел в 1910-х и 1950-х–1960-х гг. на русский язык практически всего известного Вийона (его издание переводов Вийона 1963 г. — совместно с Ф. Мендельсоном — вышло всего за 6 лет до написания Москвы — Петушков), в стихотворении, посвященном поэту-парии, контаминируются детали, которые могут быть условно определены как перифраз трагического финала Москвы — Петушков:

> Пошел — монастырский двор,
> И двери раскрыты к вечерне.
> Маленький черт
> Шилом [!] колет соперника.
> Все равно!
> Пил тяжелое туренское вино. ("Над книгой Вийона," 1915)

Поэзия же самого Вийона (в переводах Эренбурга) также порождает ряд ассоциаций — уже вертикальных, на уровне идеологического единства. Особенно близки ерофеевскому Веничке лирические герои "Спора между Вийоном и его душой" (внутренний диалог 30-летнего поэта), "Большое завещание" (одиночество и непонятость, взывания к ангелам, трогательная забота о своем мнимом имуществе [ср., веничкин чемоданчик]), "Баллада примет" (энциклопедические познания и незнание самого себя), "Баллада заключительная" (любовная страсть, вино, смерть). Вийоново "Я знаю книги, истины и слухи" ("Баллада примет") звучат краткой характеристикой поэтики Ерофеева, не признающей никаких формальных, установленных ранее законов — реминисцентный слой в поэме зиждется равно на книгах и на слухах, ибо за границей — на чужой территории — никто не признает никаких ограничений: "А там? Какие там могут

быть границы, если все одинаково пьют и все говорят не по-
русски!...Так что там на этот счет совершенно свободно....Так что
ничего удивительного..." (83). Иными словами, декларируется
специфическое освоение чужой территории, где — благо она
чужая — можно быть до конца свободным, не зависящим от *своих*
собственных убеждений, от которых Веничка страдает на
протяжении всей поэмы — вспомнить хотя бы "безгранично
расшир[енную] сферу интимного," которая исковеркала Венички
всю жизнь (28).

Принятие правил ерофеевской поэтики позволяет множить
реминисцентно-ассоциативные поля *Москвы — Петушков*
подобно волнам, расходящимся кругами от брошенного в воду
камня — будь то камень Сизифа или Тютчева. Или —
Мандельштама. Такие поля покрывают иные, прямо не связанные
с текстом поэмы зоны и устанавливают новые синхронные
магистрали, выводящие к иным семиологическим массивам. Так,
в треугольнике Ерофеев — Эренбург — Вийон среднее звено — по
ассоциациям — может быть заменено другим именем. Когда
Веничка, изгнанный из ресторана Курского вокзала, восклицает:
"О, пустопорожность! О, звериный оскал бытия!" (22), начинает
работать еще одна из смежных поэме структур. Помимо
библейских коннотаций (Псалтырь 21: 12–14; Иеремия 2:16, 3:46),
здесь возникают ассоциации с Осипом Мандельштамом, с его "За
гремучую доблесть грядущих веков," (1931). В этом же
стихотворении присутствует и отмеченный уже в поэме мотив
чаши ("Я лишился и чаши на пире отцов"). Ситуация в поэме
дублирует положения стихотворения: именно в ресторане
Курского вокзала Веничка лишается чаши ("Вымя есть, а хересу
нет!" [20]), а заодно — при помощи вышибал — "веселья и чести."
Есть в *Москве — Петушках* и прямая цитата из Мандельштама: в
главе "85-й километр – Орехово-Зуево" пьяный контролер
Семеныч, "как гитана, заломил свои руки" (87) — ср., у
Мандельштама: "И в исступленьи, как гитана, / Она заламывает
руки" ("Кинематограф," 1913).

Замена в ассоциативном ряду Эренбурга Мандельштамом
вряд ли покажется искусственной — достаточно взглянуть на их
судьбы и творчество. Ровесники, они были знакомы друг с другом.
Мандельштам рецензировал ранние поэтические опыты

Эренбурга, а тот в свою очередь отвел Мандельштаму страницы своих мемуаров и сыграл далеко не последнюю роль в реабилитации его имени и стихов. Как и Эренбург, Мандельштам писал о Вийоне, вносил вийоновские мотивы в свои стихи. И хотя Вийон отнюдь не главная личность, под чьим влиянием поэт формировался как художник и мыслитель, его интерес к французскому поэту стабилен и окаймляет все его творчество, от очерка "Франсуа Виллон" (1910) до стихотворения "Чтоб, приятель и ветра и капель" (1937), где Вийон получает показательную характеристику: "любимец мой кровный, утешительно-грешный певец." Во "Франсуа Виллоне" Мандельштам высказывает мысль о существовании во Франции XV века "двух самостоятельных, враждебных измерений" — поэзии и жизни, и обвиняет далекий XV век, превративший "многих порядочных людей...в Иовов, ропщущих на дне своих смрадных темниц и обвиняющих Бога в несправедливости."[37] Здесь у Мандельштама не только слышно пророчество относительно своей собственной судьбы, но и закладывается универсальная формула, определяющая функционирование так называемой "литературы нравственного сопротивления" (выражение Гр. Свирского), к которой причисляется обычно и поэма Ерофеева.

Греховность лирического героя стихов Вийона и Веничкина страсть к алкоголю (в обоих случаях — черты для авторов сугубо автобиографические) одновременно задают координаты физического существования центральных персонажей (воровская шайка на парижском дне и компания опустившихся попутчиков-выпивох в пригородной электричке) и обеспечивают читательский шок — потрясение при восприятии текстов Вийона и Ерофеева вызванное контрастом между социальным положением героев, средой обитания, и их богатыми духовными мирами и поэтическими натурами — или, по Мандельштаму, между жизнью и поэзией. Существование в недостойной самого себя обстановке либо вызывает в человеке стремление вырваться из нее (ср., отказ тайного советника Гете пить [66–68] или принятие Эренбургом, имевшим перед глазами живой пример Мандельштама, условий игры в социалистический реализм), либо утверждение веры в уникальность своего положения, в котором низкая действительность игнорируется (именно потому, что она низкая), а собственно существование переносится в высокие сферы, конструируемые из собственных произведений и чужих цитат. Здесь низкие топосы играют роль родной, отечественной территории, а высокие сферы превращаются в заграницу — место для временного пребывания, откуда необходимо время от времени возвращаться на родину. Соотношения социально-политической окружающей среды и "поэтических" существований Вийона, Мандельштама и Ерофеева, их судеб и творчества, несмотря на формальное различие индивидуальных хронотопов, обнаруживают генетическое родство всех трех авторов. Каждый из них своим творчеством конструировал иную, отличную от окружающей, — *заграничную* — действительность, которая оказывалась вне досягаемости законов действительности отечественной. При этом "более убедительная действительность"[38] конструировалась по законам органики, дабы усилить ее естественность и, следовательно, реальность. Упоминание об органике вызывает в памяти мандельштамовскую микротеорию аллюзии и цитаты, изложенную в "Разговоре о Данте," который может использоваться не только, как теоретический автокомментарий к собственным стихам, но и к любому другому произведению, где цитатно реминисцентные конструкции не виньеточные украшения текста, а один из важнейших структурных элементов индивидуальной поэтики, будь то *Москва — Петушки* или та же *Божественная комедия*.

Обрушив на читателя уже в самом начале *Божественной комедии* лавину великих имен (Сократ, Сенека, Электра, Орфей и т. д.), Данте спешит признаться:

Я всех назвать не в силах поименно:
   Мне нужно быстро молвить обо всем,
   И часто речь моя несовершенна.

Синклит шести распался, мы вдвоем;
   Из тихой сени в воздух потрясенный
   Уже иным мы движемся путем,

И я — во тьме, ничем не озаренной. ("Ад," IV:145–51)

Сочетание рифмованных заявлений "мне нужно быстро молвить обо всем" и "уже иным мы движемся путем" метафорически кратко характеризует принципы формирования текста, в котором завоевание чужих территорий имеет исключительно созидательный характер, а отказ от традиции есть утверждение собственного начала, но никак не нигилистическое отрицание "святого." Что касается местонахождения дантовского рассказчика — "во тьме, ничем не озаренной," — то оно совпадает с обстановкой, в которой оказывается читатель текстов Данте, Мандельштама, Ерофеева. Поиски ключей к пониманию их всегда напоминают блуждание в темноте ("Durch Leiden—Licht" [54]) — вопрос только в том, сколько света прольет читателю сам автор и сколько света в самом читателе, чтобы он мог осветить им путь к истине.

Примечания

1. Смирнова, "Венедикт Ерофеев глазами гоголеведа," 64.
2. Паперно и Гаспаров, "'Встань и иди'," 387.
3. Илья Эренбург, *Собрание сочинений в 8-ми тт.*, т. 1 (Москва: Художественная литература, 1990), 458.
4. Там же, 473.
5. Там же, 484.
6. Там же, 485–86.
7. Ср., частушка, которую поют в "Одиннадцатой трубке": "Девочки-бутончики / Пьют одеколончики, / А я, малец, сдуру / Крою политуру." (Илья Эренбург, *Собрание сочинений в 9-ти тт.*, т. 1 [Москва: Художественная литература, 1962], 492.)
8. Эренбург, *Собрание сочинений в 8-ми тт.*, т. 1, 502.
9. Эренбург, *Собрание сочинений в 9-ти тт.*, т. 1, 448.
10. Эренбург, *Собрание сочинений в 8-ми тт.*, т. 1. 221–22.
11. Там же, 445–47.
12. Там же, 238.
13. Там же, 248.
14. Там же, 254, 255.
15. Там же, 253.
16. Там же, 252–53.
17. Там же, 268.
18. Там же, 278.

19. Там же, 291.

20. Там же, 379.

21. Там же, 400.

22. Там же, 388, 399.

23. Эренбурговский Ленин, скорее, ближе ерофеевскому не как объект насмешки и ерничества в *Москве — Петушках*, но как центральный персонаж *Моей маленькой ленинианы*, достаточно выслушать его монолог о непонимании искусства и непреложном насилии над "непонимающими коммунизм" (Там же, 403–405).

24. Там же, 407.

25. В сходной с *Хулио Хуренито* поэтике написан другой ранний роман Эренбурга — *Бурная жизнь Лазика Ройтшванеца* (1927), в которой также можно обнаружить множество сходных с ерофеевскими технических приемов.

26. Эренбург, *Собрание сочинений в 9-ти тт.*, т. 8, 145, 143, 63, 166, 141, 212, 361, 517, 517, 518, 230.

27. Эренбург, *Собрание сочинений в 9-ти тт.*, т. 9, 497, 654, 544, 655.

28. Эренбург, *Собрание сочинений в 9-ти тт.*, т. 8, 176, 75, 99, 473, 186, 545.

29. Там же, 87–88.

30. Там же, 107.

31. Эренбург, *Собрание сочинений в 9-ти тт.*, т. 9, 536. Безусловно, тексты Эренбурга не единственный источник для заимствования ситуации "русский литератор в парижской мансарде." Ср., у Вяч. Иванова: "В мансарде взор стремил мой к небесам" ("Париж," 2; 1915), или у Ходасевича: "Да, меня не пантера прыжками / На парижский чердак загнала" ("Перед зеркалом," 1924).

32. Эренбург, *Собрание сочинений в 9-ти тт.*, т. 8, 223.

33. Там же, 473.

34. Эренбург, *Собрание сочинений в 9-ти тт.*, т. 9, 610.

35. Британский музей как конечный пункт заграничного турне встречается у Владимира Соловьева:

    Не света центр, Париж, не край испанский,

    Но яркий блеск восточной пестроты, —

    Моей мечтою был Музей Британский,

    И он не обманул моей мечты. ("Три свидания," 1898)

36. Эренбург, *Собрание сочинений в 9-ти тт.*, т. 8, 100.

37. Осип Мандельштам, *Сочинения в 2-х тт.*, т. 2 (Москва: Художественная литература, 1990), 137.

220

38. Там же, 141.

Note on Contributors

Laura Beraha is Assistant Professor of Russian at McGill University, where she received her Ph.D. in 1990. Her doctoral dissertation examines structural issues in the work of Fazil' Iskander. Her publications include studies of *skaz* in Iskander, and picaresque elements in Sasha Sokolov's *Palisandriia* and Voinovich's *Chonkin* novels.

Valentina Baslyk is Assistant Professor of Russian at Mary Washington College. She received her Ph.D. from the University of Toronto in 1995; her doctoral dissertation is entitled "Venedikt Erofeev's *Moskva — Petushki*: The Subversive Samizdat Text." She has published a number of translations, including "A Schoolgirl's Memoirs" and "The Autobiography of Sokhanskaya," in the collection *Russia Through Women's Eyes: Women's Memoirs from Tzarist Russia*.

Mark Lipovetsky is a *dotsent* at Ural State Pedagogical University in Ekaterinburg and Visiting Assistant Professor of Russian at Illinois Wesleyan University. He has also taught at the University of Pittsburgh. He received his Doctor of Sciences degree at Ural State Pedagogical University in 1996 and has published extensively on contemporary Russian prose and Russian postmodernism. His most recent book is entitled *Dialog s khaosom. Russkii postmodernizm: Poetika prozy*.

Karen Ryan-Hayes is Associate Professor of Russian at the University of Virginia. She received her doctorate at the University of Michigan in 1986 and has taught at Williams College and Iowa State University. Her previous publications include *Contemporary Russian Satire. A Genre Study* and *Russian Publicistic Satire Under Glasnost: The Journalistic Feuilleton*.

Konstantin V. Kustanovich is Associate Professor of Slavic Languages at Vanderbilt University. He received his Ph.D. from Columbia University and has also taught at Brooklyn College, Hunter College and Lafayette College. His book *The Artist and the Tyrant: Vassily Aksenov's Prose in the Brezhnev Era* was published in 1992. He has also published articles on contemporary prose, Pasternak, Trifonov and Solzhenitsyn.

Marie Martin currently teaches at the University of Chicago. She received her *diplom* from the Institute of Foreign Languages (now the Moscow Linguistics University) in 1978. She received her doctorate at the University of Chicago in 1995. Her dissertation is entitled "From *byt* to *bytie*: The Game of Parody in the Poetics of Venedikt Erofeev."

Guy Houk is Assistant Professor in the Russian Studies Program at Stetson University in DeLand, Florida. He received his doctorate at Stanford University in 1987 and has also taught at Portland State University. His publications include "Soviet Culture and Society under Gorbachev" and "Prevrashchaias' v Don Kikhota: *Podvig* Vladimira Nabokova i *Spisok blagodeianii* Iuriia Oleshi."

Eduard Vlasov is a doctoral candidate in the Department of Modern Languages and Comparative Studies at the University of Alberta. He holds a degree from Moscow State University (Faculty of Philology) and has taught Russian Studies at Sapporo University in Japan. His publications include articles on Russian literature (Dostoevsky, Gogol, Tynianov, Bakhtin and others) and film (Eisenstein, Tarkovskii and Mikhalkov).

Bibliography

Works by Erofeev

Artistic Works

Erofeev, Venedikt. "Blagovestvovanie." *Russkaia viza*, no. 1 (1993): 23–24.

___ "Dissidenty, ili Fanni Kaplan." *Kontinent*, no. 67 (1991): 285–314.

___ *Fanni Kaplan. Tragediia v piati aktakh. Moskovskii nabliudatel'*, no. 2 (1991): 58–64.

___ *Glazami ekstsentrika*. New York: Serebrianyi vek, 1982.

___ "Moia malen'kaia leniniana." *Kontinent*, no. 55 (1988): 187–202.

___ *Moskva — Petushki. Ami* 3 (1973).

___ *Moskva — Petushki*. Moskva: Interbuk, 1990.

___ *Moskva — Petushki i pr*. Moskva: Prometei, 1989, 1990.

___ *Moskva — Petushki*. Paris: YMCA-Press, 1977, 1981.

___ *Moskva — Petushki*. Riga: Rakstneks, 1991.

___ "Moskva — Petushki." *Trezvost' i kul'tura*, no. 12 (1988); nos. 1–3 (1989).

___ "Moskva — Petushki." In *Vest'*, edited by L. Gutman et al., 418–506. Moskva: Knizhnaia palata, 1989.

___ *Ostav'te moiu dushu v pokoe*. Moskva: Kh.G.S., 1995.

___ "Val'purgieva noch', ili Shagi komandora." *Kontinent*, no. 45 (1985): 96–185.

___ "Val'purgieva noch', ili Shagi komandora." *Teatr*, no. 4 (1989): 2–32.

___ "Val'purgieva noch', ili Shagi komandora." In *Vosem'*

nekhoroshikh p'es, edited by Z. K. Abdullaeva and A. D. Mikhaleva, 5–74. Moskva: Soiuzteatr, 1990.

___ "Vasilii Rozanov glazami ekstsentrika." In *Zerkalo,* edited by M. K. Kholmogorov, 32–45. Moskva: Moskovskii rabochii, 1988.

Other Works

___ "I ia ostaius' v zhivykh: pis'ma k sestre." *Stolitsa,* no. 32 (1992): 58–63.

___ "'...Ia debelogvardeets.' Iz zapisnykh knizhek." Introduction by Irina Tosunian. *Literaturnaia gazeta,* 17 September 1993, 6.

___ "Iz zapisnykh knizhek." *Teatral'nia zhizn',* no. 20 (October 1991): 16–18.

___ "Iz zapisnykh knizhek." *Znamia,* no. 8 (1995): 166–77.

___ "Iz zapisnykh knizhek raznykh let." *Konets veka* 4 (1992): 237–92.

___ "Pis'ma k sestre." *Teatr,* no. 9 (1992): 122–44.

___ "Sasha Chernyi i dr." *Kontinent,* no. 67 (1991): 316–17.

___ "Zapisnaia knizhka pisatelia ot 22/XI — 73 g. (Fragmenty)." *Teatr,* no. 9 (1991): 117–18.

Translations

Jerofejew, Venedikt. *Die Reise nach Petuschki.* Translated by Natascha Spitz. Munich: Piper, 1978.

Eroféiev, Vénédict. *Moscou-sur-vodka (Moscou—Pétouchki).* Translated by Anne Abatier and Antoine Pingaud. Paris: Michel, 1976.

Erofeev, Benedict. *Moscow Circles.* Translated by J. R. Dorrell. London: Writers and Readers Publishing Cooperative, 1981.

Erofeev, Venedikt. *Moscow to the End of the Line.* Translated by H. William Tjalsma. New York: Taplinger, 1980; Evanston: Northwestern University Press, 1992.

___ "Through the Eyes of an Eccentric." Translated by Stephen Mulrine. In *The Penguin Book of New Russian Writing. Russia's Fleurs du Mal,* edited by Victor Erofeyev and Andrew Reynolds, 126–45. London: Penguin, 1995.

Jerofiejew, Wieniedikt. *Moskwa — Pietuszki. Poemat.* Translated by Nina Karsov and Szymon Szechter. London: Kontra, 1976, 1986.

Interviews

Erofeev, Venedikt. "Nechto vrode besedy s Venediktom Erofeevym." By V. Lomazov. *Teatr*, no. 4 (1989): 33–34.

___ "Ot Moskvy do samykh Petushkov." By Irina Tosunian. *Literaturnaia gazeta*, 3 January 1990, 5.

___ "Venedikt Erofeev: 'Umru, no nikogda ne poimu...'" By Igor' Bolychev. *Moskovskie novosti*, 10 December 1989, 13.

___ "Zhit' v Rossii s umom i talantom: Beseda s V. Erofeevym 7 marta 1989 g." By L. Prudovskii. *Aprel'*, no. 4 (1991): 236–50.

Works about Erofeev

Books

Gaiser-Shnitman, Svetlana. *Venedikt Erofeev. "Moskva — Petushki" ili "The rest is silence"*. Bern: Peter Lang, 1989.

Levin, Iu. *Kommentarii k poeme "Moskva — Petushki" V. Erofeeva*. Grats: Grazer Gesellschaft zur Forderung slawischer Kulturstudien, 1996.

Component Parts of Larger Works

Aikhenval'd, Iurii. "Strasti po Venediktu Erofeevu." In *Vosem' nekhoroshikh p'es*, edited by Z. K. Abdullaev and A. D. Mikhalev, 74–78. Moskva: Soiuzteatr, 1990.

Akhmadulina, Bella et al. Afterword to *Moskva — Petushki i pr.*, by Venedikt Erofeev. Moskva: Prometei, 1989.

Chuprinin, S. "Bezboiaznennost' iskrennosti." *Trezvost' i kul'tura*, no. 12 (1988): 26–27.

Dunham, Vera. Introduction to *Moscow to the End of the Line*, by Venedikt Erofeev. Translated by H. William Tjalsma. New York: Taplinger, 1980.

Epshtein, Mikhail. "Posle karnavala, ili vechnyi Venichka." In *Ostav'te moiu dushu v pokoe*, by Venedikt Erofeev, 3–30. Moskva: Kh.G.S., 1995.

226

Heller, M. "Voyage vers le bonheur dont parlent les journaux." In *Moscou-sur-vodka.* (*Moscou—Pétouchki*), by Vénédict Eroféiev, 193–204. Translated by Anne Abatier and Antoine Pingaud. Paris: Michel, 1976.

Mikhaleva, Alla. Foreword to *Fanni Kaplan. Tragediia v piati aktakh*, by Venedikt Erofeev. *Moskovskii nabliudatel'*, no. 2 (1991): 58.

Murav'ev, V. S. Foreword to *Moskva — Petushki*, by Venedikt Erofeev. Moskva: Interbuk, 1990.

___ Foreword to *Moskva — Petushki i pr.*, by Venedikt Erofeev. Moskva: Prometei, 1989.

Porter, Robert. "Venedikt Erofeev—A Short Journey to Eternity." In *Russia's Alternative Prose*, 72–87. Oxford: Berg, 1994.

Ryan-Hayes, Karen. "Beyond Picaresque: Erofeev's *Moscow—Petushki.*" In *Contemporary Russian Satire. A Genre Study*, 58–100. Cambridge: Cambridge University Press, 1995.

Simmons, Cynthia. "*Moscow—Petushki*: A Transcendental Commute." In *Their Father's Voice: Vassily Aksyonov, Venedikt Erofeev, Eduard Limonov and Sasha Sokolov*, 57–90. New York: Peter Lang, 1993.

Vail', Petr and Aleksandr Genis. "Strasti po Erofeevu." In *Sovremennaia russkaia proza*, 41–50. Ann Arbor: Hermitage, 1982.

Velichanskii, A. "Fenomen Erofeeva." Foreword to *Moskva — Petushki i pr.*, by Venedikt Erofeev. Moskva: Prometei, 1990.

Zveteremich, Pietro. "Il poema dell'emarginazione: Mosca sulla vodka." In *Fantastico grottesco assurdo e satira nella narrativa russa d'oggi (1956–1980)*, 47–51. Messina: Peloritana Editrice, 1980.

Journal Articles

Al'tshuller, M. "*Moskva — Petushki* Venedikta Erofeeva i traditsii klassicheskoi poemy." *Novyi zhurnal*, no. 146 (1982): 75–85.

Colucci, Michele. "Il diavolo e l'acquavite: Quel viaggio Moskvà—Petuski." *Belfagor*, 31 May 1983, 265–80.

Epshtein, Mikhail. "Posle karnavala, ili vechnyi Venichka." *Zolotoi vek*, no. 4 (1993): 84–92.

Fast, L. V. "Osobennosti rechevogo standarta v iazyke sovremennoi dramaturgii." *Russkii iazyk za rubezhom*, nos. 5–6 (1992): 73–76.

Geller, Mikhail. "Puteshestvie k 'schast'iu, o kotorom pishut v gazetakh'." *Vestnik PKhD*, no. 121 (1977): 107–12.

Kavadeev, Andrei. "Sokrovennyi Venedikt. Rasskaz-polet v trekh empireiakh." *Solo*, no. 8 (1991): 85–88.

Kuritsyn, Viacheslav. "My poedem s toboiu na 'a' i na 'iu'." *Novoe literaturnoe obozrenie*, no. 1 (1992): 296–304.

Levin, Iu. "Klassicheskie traditsii v drugoi literature: Venedikt Erofeev i Fedor Dostoevskii." *Literaturnoe obozrenie*, no. 2 (1992): 45–50.

Lipovetskii, Mark. "Apofeoz chastits, ili dialog s khaosom: Zametki o klassike, Venedikte Erofeeve, poeme 'Moskva — Petushki' i russkom postmodernizme." *Znamia*, no. 8 (1989): 214–24.

Muravnik, Maiia. "Ispoved' rossiianina tret'ei chetverti XX veka." *Tret'ia volna*, no. 6 (1979): 99–105.

Novikov, Vladimir. "Tri stakana tertsovki. Vydumannyi pisatel' (O Venedikte Erofeeve)." *Stolitsa*, no. 31 (1994): 55–57.

Paperno, I. A. and B. M. Gasparov. "'Vstan' i idi'." *Slavica Hierosolymitana*, nos. 5–6 (1981): 387–400.

Rudenko, Mariia. "Palata No. 3, ili v chuzhom piru." *Strelets*, no. 1 (1992): 159–76.

Simmons, Cynthia. "An Alcoholic Narrative as 'Time Out' and the Double in *Moskva — Petushki*." *Canadian - American Slavic Studies* 24 (summer 1990): 155–68.

Sluzhevskaia, Irina. "Poslednii iurodivyi." *Slovo/Word*, nos. 10–11 (n.d.): 88–92.

Smirnova, E. A. "Mifologema stradaiushchego boga i strasti Venichki Erofeeva." *Sintaksis*, no. 33 (1992): 96–107.

___ "Venedikt Erofeev glazami gogoleveda." *Russkaia literatura*, no. 3 (1990): 58–66.

Vail', Petr and Aleksandr Genis. "Strasti po Erofeevu." *Ekho*, no. 4 (1978): 109–17.

___ "Strasti po Erofeevu." *Knizhnoe obozrenie*, no. 7 (14 February 1992): 8–9.

___ "Vo chreve machekhi. Vozvrashchaias' k Erofeevu." *Moskovskii nabliudatel'*, no. 2 (1992): 22–25.

Verkhovtseva-Drubchek, Natasha. "*Moskva — Petushki* kak parodia sacra." *Solo*, no. 8 (1991): 88–95.

Zhivolupova, N. V. "Palomnichestvo v Petushki, ili problema metafizicheskogo bunta v ispovedi Venichki Erofeeva." *Chelovek*, no. 1 (1992): 78–91.

Zorin, Andrei. "Venichka: opoznavatel'nyi znak." *Stolitsa*, no. 30 (1991): 58–63.

___ "Opoznavatel'nyi znak." *Teatr*, no. 9 (1991): 119–22.

Newspaper Articles

Dravich, Andrei. "Bilet ot Petushkov v odnu storonu." *Russkaia mysl'*, 19 April 1984, 8–9.

Kunin, Lev. "Erofeev prodolzhaetsia." *Novoe russkoe slovo*, 6 March 1983, 4.

Posunian, Irina. "Ot Moskvy do samykh Petushkov." *Literaturnaia gazeta*, 3 January 1990, 5.

Vail', Petr. "Zhabo iz lyka. Tsitiruia Venedikta Erofeeva." *Moskovskie novosti*, 9–16 January 1994, 5.

Reviews

Glusman, John. "Under the Soviet Volcano." Review of *Moscow Circles*, by Benedict Erofeev. *New Leader*, 26 January 1981, 15.

Hardwick, Elizabeth. "Through Vodka Darkly." Review of *Moscow to the End of the Line*, by Venedikt Erofeev. *New Republic*, 17 October 1983, 30–33.

Hosking, Geoffrey. "Drinking Mystically, Travelling Sentimentally." Review of *Moscow Circles*, by Benedict Erofeev. *Times Literary Supplement*, 15 January 1982, 63.

Kunin, Lev. Review of *Moskva — Petushki*, by Venedikt Erofeev. *Novoe russkoe slovo*, 6 March 1983, 4.

Kuznetsov, Pavel. "*Vest'* i drugie." Review of *Moskva — Petushki*, by Venedikt Erofeev. *Russkaia mysl'*, 6 April 1990, 14.

Lakshin, V. "Bezzakonnyi meteor." Review of *Moskva — Petushki*, by Venedikt Erofeev. *Znamia*, no. 7 (1990): 225–27.

Minart, Cella. Review of *Moscou-sur-vodka*, by Vénédict Eroféiev. *Cahiers de l'est*, no. 6 (1976): 112–14.

Monas, Sidney. Review of *Moscow to the End of the Line*, by Venedikt Erofeev. *Slavic Review* 40 (fall 1981): 509.

Review of *Moscow Circles*, by Benedict Erofeev. *Observer*, 8 November 1981, 29.

Review of *Moscow Circles*, by Benedict Erofeev. *Publishers Weekly*, 8 October 1982, 55.

Review of *Moscow to the End of the Line*, by Venedikt Erofeev. *Kirkus Review*, 15 June 1980, 793.

Review of *Moscow to the End of the Line*, by Venedikt Erofeev. *Russian Literature Triquarterly* 17 (1980): 266–67.

Review of *Moskva — Petushki*, by Venedikt Erofeev. *Kontinent*, no. 14 (1977): 369–71.

Symons, Julian. "Bottoms Up." Review of *Moscow to the End of the Line*, by Venedikt Erofeev. *New York Times Magazine*, 3 December 1981, 32–33.

Updike, John. "How the Other Half Lives." Review of *Moscow Circles*, by Benedict Erofeev. *New Yorker*, 21 February 1983, 126–32.

Zorin, Andrei. "Prigorodnyi poezd dal'nego sledovaniia." Review of *Moskva — Petushki*, by Venedikt Erofeev. *Novyi mir*, no. 5 (1989): 256–58.

Dissertations

Baslyk, Valentina. "Venedikt Erofeev's *Moskva — Petushki*: The Subversive Samizdat Text." Ph.D. diss., University of Toronto, 1995.

Martin, Marie R. "From *byt* to *bytie*: The Game of Parody in the Poetics of Venedikt Erofeev." Ph.D. diss., University of Chicago, 1995.

Reminiscences

Erofeeva, Galina. "I priroda cheshet v zatylke." *Stolitsa*, no. 30 (1991): 62–63.

Frolova, Nina et al. "Neskol'ko monologov o Venedikte Erofeeve."

Teatr, no. 9 (1991): 74–122.

Ignatova, Elena. "Venedikt." *Dom*, no. 1 (1993): 66–95.

___ "Venedikt." *Panorama*, 3–9 February 1993, 22–23.

Liubchikova, Lidiia. "Krasiv, beden i schastliv v liubvi." *Stolitsa*, no. 30 (1991): 63.

Maryniak, I. "A Hero of Our Time: Filming Venedikt Erofeev." *Index on Censorship* 20, no. 2 (1991): 8–9.

Murav'ev, Vladimir. "My zhili veselo." *Stolitsa*, no. 30 (1991): 62.

Sedakova, Ol'ga. "Gadkikh utiat liubil, ot lebedei — toshnilo." *Stolitsa*, no. 30 (1991): 62.

___ "Neskazannaia rech' na vechere Venedikta Erofeeva." *Druzhba narodov*, no. 12 (1991): 264–65.

Shmel'kova, Natal'ia. "'Vremeni net...'" *Literaturnoe obozrenie*, no. 2 (1992): 39–45.

Obituaries

Akhmadulina, Bella. "Pamiati Venedikta Erofeeva." *Literaturnaia gazeta*, 23 May 1990, 5.

Avdiev, I. "Nekrolog, 'Sotkannyi iz pylkikh i blestiashchikh natiazhek'." *Kontinent*, no. 67 (1991): 318–23.

Obituary. *Russkaia mysl'*, 18 May 1990, 19.

Popov, Evgeny. *Moscow News Weekly*, 3–10 June 1990, 10.

Other

Bethea, David M. *The Shape of Apocalypse in Modern Russian Fiction*. Princeton: Princeton University Press, 1989.

Brown, Deming. *The Last Years of Soviet Russian Literature: Prose Fiction 1975-1991*. Cambridge: Cambridge University Press, 1993.

Brown, Edward J. *Russian Literature Since the Revolution*. Cambridge: Harvard University Press, 1982.

Chudakova, Marietta. "Put' k sebe: literaturnaia situatsiia — 89." *Literaturnoe obozrenie*, no. 1 (1990): 33–38.

Clowes, Edith. *Russian Experimental Fiction. Resisting Ideology after Utopia*. Princeton: Princeton University Press, 1993.

Dark, Oleg. "Mif o proze." *Druzhba narodov*, nos. 5–6 (1992):

219–34.

___ "Mir mozhet byt' liuboi: Razmyshleniia o 'novoi proze'." *Druzhba narodov*, no. 6 (1990): 223–35.

Kaganskaia, Maiia. "Shutovskoi khorovod." *Sintaksis*, no. 13 (1984): 139–90.

Kasack, Wolfgang. *Dictionary of Russian Literature Since 1917*. Translated by Maria Carlson and Jane T. Hedges. New York: Columbia University Press, 1988.

Lipovetskii, Mark. "Svobody chernaia rabota: ob 'artisticheskoi proze' novogo pokoleniia." *Voprosy literatury*, no. 9 (1989): 3–44.

___ "Zakon krutizny." *Voprosy literatury*, nos. 11–12 (1991): 3–36.

McMillin, Arnold. "Russian Prose in the 1970s: From Erofeev to Edichka." *Journal of Russian Studies* 45 (1983): 25–33.

Mal'tsev, Iurii. *Vol'naia russkaia literatura: 1955-1975*. Frankfurt: Possev-Verlag, 1976.

Malukhin, V. "Post bez modernizma." *Izvestiia*, 8 May 1991, 4.

Pomerants, Grigorii. "Sny zemli." *Poiski*, nos. 7–8 (1984).

___ "Ten' Venichki Erofeeva." *Literaturnaia gazeta*, 22 February 1995, 5.

Pomerants, Grigorii and Boris Khazanov. "Pod sen'iu Venichki Erofeeva." *Literaturnaia gazeta*, 9 August 1995, 5.

Svirski, Grigori. *A History of Post-War Soviet Writing: The Literature of Moral Opposition*. Translated and edited by Robert Dessaix and Michael Ulman. Ann Arbor: Ardis, 1981.

Terrras, Victor, ed. *Handbook of Russian Literature*. New Haven: Yale University Press, 1985.

Terts, Abram. "Anekdot v anekdote." *Sintaksis*, no. 1 (1978): 77–95.

Tolstaia, Tat'iana. "Chto prochitali?" *Knizhnoe obozrenie*, 8 September 1989, 5.

Vail', Petr and Aleksandr Genis. "Literaturnye mechtaniia. Ocherk russkoi prozy s kartinkami." *Chast' rechi* , no. 1 (1980): 204–32.

___ "Novaia proza: ta zhe ili 'drugaia'?" *Novyi mir*, no. 10 (1989): 247–50.

Woll, Josephine. *Soviet Dissident Literature: A Critical Guide*. Boston: G.K. Hall, 1983.